DR. NOGUCHI'S JOURNEY

DR. NOGUCHI'S JOURNEY

A Life of Medical Search and Discovery

Atsushi Kita

Translated by Peter Durfee

KODANSHA INTERNATIONAL
Tokyo · New York · London

NOTE: Apart from a few historical figures, Japanese personal names in this translation are given in the Western way, with the surname last.

Photographs were reproduced with the cooperation of the Hideyo Noguchi Memorial Hall, Aizu-Wakamatsu City Public Library, and Minoru Tan.

Originally published in Japanese as *Shoden Noguchi Hideyo* by Mainichi Shimbunsha.

Distributed in the United States by Kodansha America, Inc., and in the United Kingdom and continental Europe by Kodansha Europe Ltd.

Published by Kodansha International Ltd., 17–14 Otowa 1-chome, Bunkyo-ku, Tokyo 112–8652, and Kodansha America, Inc.

ISBN-13: 978-4-7700-2355-1
ISBN-10: 4-7700-2355-3

First edition, 2005
10 09 08 07 06 05   10 9 8 7 6 5 4 3 2 1

Library of Congress Catalogue-in-Publication Data available

www.kodansha-intl.com

CONTENTS

PREFACE

In all ages humans must face fears of the unknown and the invisible. The threats to their lives and well-being can take many forms—from the terrorist acts that fill our news reports today to the bacteria and viruses that have always threatened our health.

Terrorist threats are a relatively easy concept to grasp, and the world's nations are on the move against them, devising policies to suppress this menace. But such a clear, coordinated effort is not seen—and perhaps not possible—in the case of the microscopic threats to our bodies. Each year brings still more reports of deadly epidemics, and we can never know when we may find ourselves sick in bed, our immune systems under attack from these tiny enemies. This has always been a terrifying experience, and it is only in the modern era that we have begun effectively to fight back against it.

Hideyo Noguchi was one man who led this fight nearly a century ago. His name is well known in Japan, but perhaps not in other countries around the globe. It is a name that deserves recognition, though, and I wrote my book to help spread the word of his actions and his dedication to the cause of defending humanity from the threat of illness.

At the beginning of the twentieth century Noguchi made his way from his native Japan to New York, where he took up a position at the world-famous Rockefeller Institute. From this base he traveled the world, carrying out his research across the United States, as well as in Europe, Central and South America, and Africa. The results he achieved in this work electrified the medical community and made him a hero in the eyes of the people among whom he worked; many in Africa ranked him alongside Albert Schweitzer, calling him a "savior" for the cures he brought them.

His life was no series of constant triumphs, though. Born to a desperately poor farming family in Fukushima Prefecture in 1876, his educational opportunities were few; it is miraculous that he managed to learn as much as he did. Poverty was compounded with physical hardship when as a toddler he fell into his home's fireplace, charring his left hand to a stump. This handicap would be an obstacle to his work throughout his life and a source of psychological anguish in an unusually proud man.

He regained some use of his fingers thanks to an operation carried out by a doctor who had trained in America. This ignited two fires in Noguchi. He found himself deeply attracted to the field of medicine, which promised miracles like the one that had given him back his hand again, and to America, the nation where his healer had learned his craft. A journey to the United States, where talent counted for everything, became even more essential in his mind as he learned the limits that Japan—with its emphasis on schooling (expensive education in Germany in particular) and seniority—would place on him. In the end he overcame his devastating injury and his poverty; hardship polished his rough stone into a gleaming jewel.

So brilliant was his career as a scientist that many people are content to gaze at it alone with awe. But when a person shines so very brightly, surely the shadows he creates will be equally as dark. His powers of concentration were legendary, and they served him well in his studies. But they proved a detriment when they blinded him to the results his single-mindedness had on himself and others around him. His finances were constantly in a shambles, and his failures were often spectacular enough to drag his close companions down with him. These negative facets add to the complexity of the picture we have of the man, though, and we are left in the end with a more human, more approachable figure.

The story of his life is filled with admirable supporting characters. He would have accomplished nothing without the steady stream of people who saw promise in him and made great sacrifices to ensure that his weaknesses would not bring him crashing down. Morinosuke Chiwaki, the Tokyo dentist who stood by Hideyo and financed his extravagances for years, is an especially impressive figure—the kind of utterly dedicated friend we see few of in any age.

Part of the attraction of Noguchi's irresponsible temperament was his obliviousness to social status. The heights of success he reached never went to his head. He never sought to conform to the rules of an upper echelon that would admit him for his achievements, at times earning disdain for "unbecoming" behavior as a result. This purity of outlook was intimately linked to the focus that brought his groundbreaking discoveries within reach.

He ended his life as he lived it, in a manner that moves all who hear of it years later. The inscription on his grave in New York's Woodlawn Cemetery sums up his remarkable existence:

THROUGH DEVOTION TO SCIENCE
HE LIVED AND DIED FOR HUMANITY

Humanity today lives in an age when nations once self-determined must now share with one another, culturally and otherwise, to improve the lot of the world as a whole. We look back at Hideyo Noguchi as a pioneer in this effort, an early contributor to the good of the global community. He has been celebrated on postal stamps in his native country and in many other places around the world; in late 2004 Japan again honored him by putting his portrait on the thousand-yen note. Foreign visitors to this country may see this man staring out at them and wonder who he was. Coming from a family of doctors, and a native of the same Fukushima soil on which he was born, I am proud to be able to present the traces of his life to a broad international readership.

In closing, I would like to thank those who made this book a possibility: the editorial staff at Kodansha International and translator Peter Durfee. Through their hard work I hope to see the story of Hideyo Noguchi reach new generations of people around the world.

Atsushi Kita

A FUKUSHIMA FAMILY

Tokyo is more or less in the middle of the long Japanese archipelago. Travelers head west from Tokyo to go to the cities of Osaka and Kyoto and the other islands of Kyushu and Shikoku. There is no traveling to the east, though; the island of Honshu extends to the north from the capital, and travelers heading in that direction find themselves in the Tohoku region of northern Japan.

In the southern part of this region lies the area known as Aizu. Aizu is buried in deep snow in the winter months; in the summer it sees crowds of tourists who come to visit the high mountains and picturesque lakes of the national parks and other protected areas nearby. This natural splendor was the backdrop for a dramatic episode in Japan's modern history. It is also the backdrop for the beginning of the story of Hideyo Noguchi.

The middle of the nineteenth century saw the collapse of the Tokugawa shogunate, which had ruled the country for two and a half centuries, and the birth of the modern Japanese state. In 1868 the Boshin War broke out between the forces of the new imperial government, whose leaders hailed mainly from Kyushu in the southwest, and the remaining supporters of the old regime, concentrated in Tohoku. Aizu was the battlefield for this war, which—like the American Civil War—was a painful part of the birth pangs of a modern nation.

But just as this pain opened the way for the creation of a new Japan, it opened doors for a generation of talented young Japanese who sought to play a role in this creation. Without the battles that dragged Tohoku into the modern era, Hideyo Noguchi—a son of that wild region—would never have brought his talents to the national stage, much less to the entire world.

And the history of modern medicine would have been that much poorer for it.

■ ■ ■

Noguchi was born in 1876 in what is today the town of Inawashiro in Fukushima Prefecture. His birthplace was then known as Sanjogata, an impoverished hamlet of perhaps thirty households in the village district of Okinajima. The volcanic cone of Mt. Bandai overlooked the village from the north, and the broad expanse of Lake Inawashiro lay just a kilometer or so distant. The rich volcanic soil near Bandai made for abundant crops, but the altitude of this village ensured harsh winters and shortened the growing season. It was a beautiful place to live in, but life there was far from easy. All these factors combined to deeply affect Noguchi during the impressionable childhood years he spent there.

Sanjogata was located on a major lakeside route to Aizu Wakamatsu, the largest city in the region. Despite its small size this quarter of the village district was its central community, with three inns, a general store, restaurants, a police station, an elementary school, and even a village office.

The Noguchi family had been in the village for a long time. Family members were mentioned in the registers maintained by the local headman as early as 1797, when Seitaro Noguchi—five generations removed from Hideyo—was listed as the recipient of land producing twelve bushels of rice a year. The average family's paddies produced only nine bushels, so he was one of the wealthier farmers at that time. Seitaro was said to have earned respect as a hard worker, and he had a relatively spacious home and even a horse to till his land.

The family remained intact for some generations thereafter, but its fortunes gradually went downhill. The upkeep of a horse was expensive, and the family sold its animal and rented one instead during the spring planting season. Various calamities struck until eventually the Noguchis were reduced to borrowing rice from the village headman's storehouse. No longer able to make a living from farming alone, the younger family members began leaving the home to learn new skills. Iwakichi and Zennosuke, Seitaro's grandson and great-grandson respectively, both went to serve in the house of a local warlord.

Once a person became accustomed to life in a town it was hard to go back to the toil of farming, and people clever enough to be hired on at the house of a samurai were hardly likely to be content with the life of a rice farmer. (Hideyo's own early life would be deeply molded by these themes—the hard life of an Aizu farmer and the strong desire to leave that life behind.) But as more people left to make their fortunes elsewhere, the family itself rapidly came down in the world, and the house grew more and more dilapidated. By the time Shika, Hideyo's mother, was four years old, things had hit rock bottom.

Shika's father had gone off to work for a samurai just like Iwakichi had before him. Now Shika's mother, too, was gone, leaving her with just her grandmother Mitsu for company. And even Mitsu—despite suffering from a bent back at the age of just forty-eight—spent what time she could outside the home, earning money at one of the teahouses in the village. All things considered, Shika seemed reasonably content during the time she spent at home alone, but the sight of other children with their parents must have reminded her of her own loneliness.

In the evenings, in the house whose very walls were crumbling, the girl would ask sadly: "When is Mother coming home?"

Mitsu always had the same reply. "She'll be back any day now. You just wait and see. Any day now." Shika would nod and accept this, but at night she used to take out her mother's old kimono and curl up under it to sleep, breathing in the comforting scent that still clung to the cloth.

■ ■ ■

Shika's difficult childhood would be a huge factor in the life of her son in later years. She was shaped by her harsh experiences, and the stoicism she learned in the face of them defined her throughout her life. She was a person who could endure great hardship while she worked toward a goal. She was also unselfish, suppressing her own desires and doing what she could for others first. Her intelligence and inner strength were evident in her face—not an attractive one, but expressive of the person underneath. No consideration of the sacrifices Shika would make as a mother to Hideyo should come without a look at the youth she spent learning that hard-working spirit of sacrifice.

At the age of six Shika decided to help the family finances by taking on some work herself, and she went out to watch over the village children while their parents worked. This resulted sometimes in a kind parent giving her some sweet treat to eat, but she always took it back to her grandmother rather than eat it herself. It was during this time that she learned from village gossip where her father was and set out to find him. He was serving then in the house of the official charged with looking after Inawashiro Castle. This was no easy trip for a girl of seven who hardly knew which way to go, but she pressed on with her journey, and before long was standing in front of the house gates. Word of this came to the mistress of the house, who gave Zennosuke some time off from work, and it was a happy child who returned home with her father that day.

This happiness did not last long, though. Hard work and bitter cold soon overcame the child's grandmother, who became bedridden with what appeared to be rheumatism. At this Zennosuke—who had been adopted into the family he worked for, and who perhaps saw their house as his own by now—left the girl and her grandmother once again. Shika would go out and watch over the village children during the day, then return to care for Mitsu. There was not enough money for a doctor, but Shika took what little money she earned and bought medicine. She helped her grandmother to survive two winters in this fashion, but eventually Mitsu closed her eyes for the last time and her hard life came to an end. Shika lay down beside her lifeless body and wept aloud.

Once again, Zennosuke returned home, and soon her mother also came back after a nine-year absence. At last, at the age of twelve, Shika had a complete family again. But it was not a happy one. Her grandfather was infirm by now and needed care. Her mother, too weak to work very much, argued constantly with her father about money. And before long he had left this house to serve once more in the samurai residence.

The welfare of the Noguchi household now rode on Shika's young shoulders. For generations it was up to the women in the Noguchi family to keep the household running, while the less reliable men spent little time at home. Now Shika had to find proper work to support her mother, so she went into service under a local landowner. This man's wife, who directed the laborers in their duties, was a harsh taskmaster—people said that it was hard to stay working under her for more than ten days. Shika was expected to do the same work as an adult, and when the grown men and women took their breaks she kept on working to catch up with them. Her labors were endless: in addition to this fieldwork she was still performing her child-care chores and weaving straw into baskets and sandals at night. The winters were especially hard. Shika's fingers froze to the point where she could no longer straighten them out. The boss used to yell at her for slacking as she stared at her useless hands, and she would strike her fingers against a nearby post until the blood began flowing painfully through them again. Then it was back to work.

Luckily, Shika was an extraordinarily tough girl. Being the kind of person who hated giving in to anyone else, she would press forward with the most difficult of tasks. But she also had a keen interest in self-improvement. Okinajima was home to a Buddhist priest named Unoura, who had begun teaching the village girls to read and write. It was rare for rural children to attend school in this era, and those who did get some learning generally got it from religious men like this. Shika desperately wanted to join the group learning under Unoura, but her labors left no time for this.

She did not give up on this ambition, though; she told herself she would learn at least the *hiragana* syllabary if she couldn't study Chinese characters with the other students. She went to Unoura and asked him to write a *hiragana* primer for her. With this book in hand, she went happily off to her child-watching job. When she had a little time there she would take out the book and study the characters, etching them into memory. On moonlit nights she would wait until everyone else had retired and take a tray from the kitchen, sprinkle some ash on it, and practice writing the characters on the tray with her finger. In an age when literate women were not so numerous in rural Japan, self-taught ones were a true rarity.

Some time later, Shika put herself in great danger when Unoura's entire family fell sick with dysentery. Nobody would enter this infected household to care for them, but the girl saw her chance to repay the priest's kindness. Ignoring the risk to herself, she went into the house and cared for Unoura and his family and saw them all return to health.

It was around this time that Shika developed a deep faith in Kannon, the Buddhist deity of compassion. Okinajima was the site of a Zen temple much grander than one would expect to find in such a small village. The head priest, Genzui Hatano, was surprised one day when Shika approached him on the temple grounds:

"Please, sir," she said, "take this as an offering to Kannon, and pray for the happiness of the Noguchi family." She had a considerable sum in her hands.

The priest was impressed by the girl's gesture, but wondered how a child like her could get this much money to offer.

"For years now," she told him, "I've been saving it up, bit by bit, from my pay. Please, sir, I haven't done anything wrong to come by it!"

Shika's faith began at an early age, and it would stay with her for the next fifty years and more, helping her get through all manner of difficulties in her life. Anecdotes such as this one give a clear indication of the qualities she would later pass on to her son—her drive to improve herself and her self-sacrifice paramount among them.

■ ■ ■

Life remained hard for Shika. Heavy snows crushed the horse shed one year, and the main house was in bad shape too, with its walls crumbling here and there. These dilapidated walls let in bitter drafts in the winter and melting snow in spring, chilling the occupants inside. Shika took it upon herself to repair them, using a handful of thin bamboo stalks to brush fresh daub onto the bare spots. Every moment she could spare from her work was spent patching up the house. After months of this, she became the talk of the other villagers for completing these repairs with no help whatsoever.

Her perseverance and frugality did lead at times to small victories like this. Some years later the season rolled around for the village shrine festival. On this day the village's young women all wore their finest kimono and white *tabi* socks to take part in the festival dance. Nobody expected a poor girl like Shika to have this sort of thing to wear, though, and it would have been the height of embarrassment for a young person to show up without the proper garb. They were all surprised, therefore, to see Shika on the day of the festival wearing a cotton kimono and white *tabi*! Everyone wondered where she had obtained the expensive footwear. Closer examination showed that the industrious young woman had made herself a pair of socks out of white paper.

This little holiday was over quickly; tomorrow was another day of toil. Shika had to focus on nothing but her work to keep the Noguchi family afloat. Other girls were getting married at sixteen or seventeen, but Shika was already twenty years old and still without a husband. A helpful person who shared her workplace began to ask around, looking for prospective husbands who might want to be adopted into the Noguchi family. Soon a candidate came up: Sayosuke Kobiyama, the eldest son of a farmer in the nearby village of Kohiragata. He was twenty-two.

Some four kilometers distant from Sanjogata, Kohiragata was the site of a Tenmangu shrine, one of many around the nation honoring the god of learning. This hamlet had produced Inawashiro Kensai (1452–1510), one of Japan's greatest masters of *renga* linked verse. The Kobiyamas counted Kensai among their ancestors.

The eldest son was expected to succeed his father in his own house, not to seek adoption into another house through marriage. But Sayosuke's father, Sohei, had drunk away the family's fortune, and it would not have been easy to find a woman willing to become a Kobiyama. Here was Shika, though— the hardest-working woman in Sanjogata. With such a reliable wife, Sayosuke must have thought he would be able to live a relatively easy life. Shika, too, couldn't have expected to make a better match than this. She was beyond her most marriageable years, and her family was destitute; also, one of her eyes was a bit crooked. She was prepared to make a go of it with any man willing to enter her run-down home and join her in her work. Perhaps the two of them together would be strong enough to bring the Noguchi name back to respectability. In the spring of 1872 Shika told her boss she would no longer be going to work and married Sayosuke.

On their wedding day Shika witnessed a disturbing sign of things to come. The traditional Japanese ceremony involves a ritual exchange of cups of sake— three cupfuls for each partner, to be drunk in three sips each. Sayosuke, however, followed these formal nine sips with another large cup for himself. This was neither expected nor welcome behavior at a wedding, but it turned out to be par for the course for Shika's new husband. Ordinarily quiet and well behaved, once he had a bit of liquor inside him he was a different man entirely.

Shika had heard rumors about this side of Sayosuke, but she was disappointed just the same. In all other respects he was an ideal man to marry. Short, sturdy, and dark-skinned, he had a reputation as a pleasant man, if shy in front of others. He was a person of simple tastes who rarely showed any trace of ambition. When he put his talented hands to work he revealed real skill at delicate tasks like the weaving of straw sandals. An ordinary person might complete one pair in the morning before having breakfast, but Sayosuke could turn out three pairs of considerable quality. He was also a bird-catcher, and an expert fisherman who put his creativity to work finding ways to catch fish without a float on the line, for instance. He had many talents like this that remained hidden most of the time. But unfortunately he was also the kind of person who only put these talents to use when he felt like it, and not necessarily when it would benefit him or his family.

Sayosuke eventually found a job as one of the first postmen in the area, working out of what is now the Tsukinowa Post Office in the town of Inawashiro. His route was the forty kilometers from Motomiya to Sekito, and from there another twenty-eight kilometers to Wakamatsu. This was a brutal job. The postman was on foot, the mail in a satchel slung over his shoulder, and he had to average some eight kilometers an hour to finish his route on time. The post offices along the way had a supply of cloudy, unrefined sake on hand to fortify the delivery man; Sayosuke used to say he could never have done this job without those drinks. He proved a reliable worker, though, and no matter how much alcohol he consumed, he could be counted on to deliver the mail to its proper recipients without fail.

But the drinking that was part of this job meshed all too well with the love for sake that he shared with his father before him, and soon the liquor was ruling his life. He couldn't stand to be without a drink at any time of day—morning, noon, and night were all the same to him. If he had no food to go with it he would drink his sake on its own out of a large bowl, and he took to finishing off his nights of drinking with stronger brews like the *shochu* distilled from grain or yams. As soon as he got a paycheck he was off to a local tavern, where he would sing and cheerfully wave his arms about as he drank the money away.

His drinking led to other unsavory habits. During the Boshin War he had been drafted into the imperial forces and had transported goods to the front lines of the fighting. The images of battle had shocked him, and he took to alcohol and gambling in order to drive them from his mind. The more he drank, the bigger his bets would be. Even now he stayed in touch with his gambling partners from those days, and he looked with envy at a few of them who managed to make a living off the dice. When he tried to follow their lead, though, he ended up in the hole; and unable to turn his back on the games, he was soon searching the house for the money Shika brought home from her odd jobs.

For the poor farmers in the snow country of northern Japan, there is little besides alcohol to take their minds off their hard existence. It is an easy thing for the weaker-willed among them to take the habit too far. Sayosuke may have been especially susceptible to this—he was at heart an optimistic man with a sunny outlook, married to an eternally serious woman in a family he could not really call his own. His inability to come to grips with this reality sent him spinning into alcoholism.

Shika had suffered throughout her childhood due to an unreliable father. Now she was seeing her dreams of a stable married life melt away as well. Soon their first child was born—a daughter—but this didn't make her husband change his ways at all. Almost all the tales of Hideyo Noguchi's parents that have come down to us focus on Sayosuke's shortcomings. It may well be that he was a comfort to his wife in some ways—certainly his easygoing attitude that made him a popular fellow locally must have brightened their home from time to time—yet in the end his inability to improve himself and Shika's own stubborn streak proved irreconcilable. The two would not remain living together for long.

ROUGH BEGINNINGS

It was into this troubled home that Seisaku Noguchi was born on November 9, 1876. Despite the advanced stage of her pregnancy, Shika had been out working. The first labor pains sent her rushing home, where she soon gave birth to her first son. He gave a great, healthy cry to mark the occasion. Shika was twenty-four and her husband twenty-six.

The neighbors crowded in to see the baby, bringing gifts of dried bonito and red beans to build Shika's strength back up. "Ah, a boy this time, is it?" they exclaimed, and Shika accepted their congratulations with joy. Some said the infant looked just like the mother, and others said no, his chin came from the father. Everyone agreed that it was a fortunate addition to the family. Shika's mother and grandmother had had only girls, and the men who married into the family showed little dedication to it. Since Sayosuke could not be counted on to restore the Noguchi name to respectability, it would be up to this dark-skinned child with twinkling eyes and a healthy set of lungs to do so. Shika gave him the name Seisaku—which he would answer to until he received the name Hideyo as a young adult—selecting the characters *sei* from old Seitaro's name and *saku* from the word *kosaku*, or "tillage," in the hope that he would grow up to be a diligent farmer. He was born at the high tide, a time believed to herald strength in a child; and he would grow up in a household run by a hard-working mother, another guarantee of vigorous health.

The close of the Tokugawa era in the 1860s had brought with it an end to the traditional caste system dividing Japan into samurai, peasants, artisans, and merchants. All were equal in Meiji Japan. The nation looked outward for the first time in centuries, and the Japanese began traveling abroad and learning and importing all they could from the powerful nations of the West. It was at last an age when even a boy born into the poverty of small-time farming could, with drive and talent, move far ahead in life.

The waves of change had been particularly powerful in Aizu. The domain had been on the losing side in the Boshin War, and just ten days after the castle fell to imperial forces tens of thousands of farmers had rampaged through the region attacking members of the upper classes in retribution for the years of oppressive rule under which they had suffered. Mobs smashed these rulers' homes into rubble and demanded an end to the feudal system of the past. As these movements spread across the land many of the ruling samurai families found themselves forced from their homes and hounded all the way to the northernmost tip of Honshu. The peasants next set their sights on the village headmen. Japan's poor battled furiously against whatever agents of government power they could. Others formed groups to move to the United States and look for better opportunities there. It was a time of great upheaval.

Times were no less eventful in the Noguchi household. There were five mouths to feed, with Shika's mother—now a grandmother—living with her daughter. Misa had never shown much willingness to work, and her eyesight was not what it once had been and her body was weak. Sayosuke rarely lifted a hand to help with the family farming chores. Any free time he had was spent out duck-hunting or fishing on the lake. Inawashiro was filled with carp, crucian, chub, catfish, and even freshwater shrimp, but Sayosuke brought only part of this bounty home to feed his hungry children; he sold most of it for money that went straight to the tavern. Once again it was up to Shika to support the family.

The Noguchis had lost their land over the years, and Shika was now sharecropping a small plot. Fully half of the crops vanished in the form of fees to the landlord. She could not feed her family on the remainder alone, and this busy mother did her farm chores as quickly as possible, making time to do other work. She helped other families with their farming. She gathered whatever seasonal foods she could—from persimmons and sweet potatoes to *inago*, the edible crickets that are a delicacy in rural Japan—and hauled them off to the town of Inawashiro and even as far as Wakamatsu to sell for a bit of extra money. On other days she rose before dawn to head to the lake shore, where she caught shrimp, cleaned them in the dark, and took them to town to sell at daybreak. Her days were spent in the fields and her nights in the light of a lamp, where she spun hemp into twine, wove reeds into baskets and sandals, and mended kimono for the villagers. During the long winter months there was no fieldwork, and Shika trudged through the deep snow selling *tsukegi*; matches were a precious commodity, and people used these thin sticks dipped in sulfur as kindling for their hearths.

Shika had been a tireless worker since her childhood. She bore this toil day in and day out without complaining. Her trips to town were particularly grueling but they brought in badly needed cash. On the way back from selling her wares Shika would buy things the family needed—sometimes a length of cloth for the children's clothes. This woman's pleasure came from making things for them and, most of all, from taking short breaks from her labor to nurse the baby.

■ ■ ■

These brief moments of happiness would not last long, though. In May 1878 the Noguchi family would confront a still harsher experience—one that would decide the course of Seisaku's life and alter the very history of medicine.

The baby Seisaku was just eighteen months old. He lay in the main room of the house while Shika, back from the day's farm work, bustled around the yard picking some vegetables for the evening meal. The village was already quiet; not many people worked as late as Shika, and not many homes ate as late as the Noguchis.

It happened as she headed back to the kitchen with an armful of vegetables. A shriek of pain erupted from the house. Her baby! She flung the food aside and dashed in to see what was happening to Seisaku, whose wails went on and on.

Shika's fear mounted as she entered to find a sickening smell filling the home. There—in the hearth—her son lay face down, thrashing wildly about and flinging clouds of ash into the air. For an instant Shika thought the child was done for, taken from her by the orange flames that now leapt in the darkened room. In a rush of fear she snatched him out of the fire and held him close. In her panic she couldn't think what else to do.

It was Shika's mother whose job it was to look after the children while Shika went out to work for the day, but she was not much of a babysitter, with her eyesight and hearing both going downhill. On that fateful day

Seisaku was in a small straw basket, with his sister, Inu, keeping an eye on him. But she was young herself and easily distracted, and now—feeling hungry, perhaps—she had gone to see what her mother was doing about dinner. Misa, meanwhile, had seen Shika return home and retired to the back room. Seisaku was left on his own. Babies his age do not sit still for long, though: he had crawled out of his pen and headed for the hearth.

Perhaps he wanted to play with the pot and ladle his mother was always using. Maybe he just wanted to run his hands through the ash in the pit. But today the ash covered live embers that burst into flame as Seisaku's tiny arms exposed them to the air. His first surprised cries went unheeded by Misa, who may have mistaken them for the complaints of a hungry baby, if she heard them at all. And the more he struggled, the deeper he plunged into the fire.

Now he was out of the fire and in his mother's arms, but the situation was grim. When Shika came to herself enough to examine the child she found his face luckily untouched by the flames and his leg just slightly scorched. But his left hand was charred to the bone. Seisaku was shaking in pain and terror; over and over he exhausted himself crying, fell silent, and then dredged up the energy to cry again. Staring down at his ruined hand, Shika felt overwhelmed with self-reproach and despair.

Misa and the rest of the family gathered around the injured child, but there was little they could do for him. No doctor lived nearby, and even if one were available, there was no money to pay for treatment. Indeed, Shika thought bitterly, that kind of money could have paid for a nursemaid to watch over the children and prevent this tragedy in the first place. She did the only thing she could at this point—she ran to the priest Unoura and begged him to pray for her child's life. Prayer was all she had to depend on now. Shika began intoning the Kannon Sutra, and this she continued, almost without a break, for the next three weeks. She cared for Seisaku without sleeping as she murmured the sutra over and over again, dedicating her prayers to the Nakada Kannon—one of the three most magnificent statues of this deity in northern Honshu—that she had gone to visit as a child. The image of the bronze figure swam before her eyes, which grew redder and heavier until she resorted to propping up her eyelids with twigs to keep from sleeping.

She ground up some potatoes and wrapped the sticky pulp in bits of cloth, applying this poultice to the baby's burns. This cleared up the inflammation.

But when she took the bandages off some weeks later to uncover Seisaku's tiny hand she flinched unwittingly at the horrible scarring and disfiguration that remained. His thumb was bent back and fused to his wrist, and the middle finger was similarly stuck to the palm of his hand. The end of Seisaku's left arm looked like nothing so much as a knot on an old pine tree. The sight of the angry pink scars coating her baby's hand must have torn at the mother's heart.

Seisaku had survived. But now that the extent of his injuries was clear Shika's thoughts turned worriedly to the future he faced. No farmer could be successful with a claw like this. Once again she cursed her own lack of caution in leaving the boy in the house, and she made a heroic decision: she would care for Seisaku no matter what he required, for as long as she lived. This was a heavy addition to the tasks she already performed to support her family, but Shika never backed down from it.

From that day forward she never let the toddler out of her sight. She took him to the fields where she worked during the day, putting him in a basket that she hung from a tree branch. When the weather worsened she fashioned a roof for the basket out of reeds; when there were no reeds to build one she tied the child to her back, keeping him warm against her body. Her faith was a support to her throughout these years. Never the kind of person to blame the gods for ignoring her prayers and allowing her son to be burned, she thanked Kannon instead for saving him from death, and continued offering her daily prayers as she watched Seisaku grow.

■ ■ ■

During childhood Seisaku did not stand out among the children of the village. This was partly because he was always small for his age, but he developed a notably introverted personality over time, almost certainly because of his disfigured hand. He couldn't help comparing his situation with that of other people of his age. He may have been comfortable eating at home with his family, but when he was out of the house watching the other children eat their lunch, he would compare their effortless meals with the difficulty he had holding the rice bowl still with his injured hand as he ate with his right, or his need to slurp his soup from the bowl like an animal. When in the presence of others he became painfully aware of his disability. He seems to have been willing to show his hand to someone younger than him from time to time, but he went to great lengths to keep people his age and older from viewing his scars. By the time he was five or six, his sense of caution around others and his self-consciousness about his ugly hand won out, and he stopped exposing it completely.

History is not without examples of people who overcame some disability to achieve greatness. One can look back as far as ancient Greece to find the examples of Homer, whose blindness did not keep him from producing epics known to this day, and Demosthenes, who went from a stutterer who could barely get words out of his mouth to the greatest orator of the age, whose speeches to the Athenians inspired them to resist the Macedonian conquest of Greece. In recent history, Helen Keller inspired the world despite being both blind and deaf, and Franklin Roosevelt became America's longest-serving president from the wheelchair where his childhood polio placed him. Would Noguchi have joined these famous figures in history had he not suffered his accident as a baby? An uninjured Seisaku might have ended up as a bright man whose influence reached only his Fukushima surroundings. His burned hand may well have propelled him to greatness by pressing his sense of inferiority deep into him as a child so he had further to rebound when he attained adulthood.

When the boy played with other children, he invariably kept his left hand tucked safely inside his kimono sleeve or under his sash, or held behind his back when this was not possible. He truly seemed to hate the sight of his own twisted and scarred fingers. Pictures taken of him in later life, too, rarely capture his hand; he almost always managed to conceal it before the shutter clicked.

As an adult he was able to camouflage his injury when posing for pictures, but in his youth it wasn't so easy to hide it away from the other children. Many biographies of Noguchi report that he acquired the nickname Tenbo as a child, a word meaning "Hand like a stick." This was not the first name given to him by his playmates, though. The first was Sei-bokko, which came from his own name and from *bokko*, a word in the local dialect for the clumps of snow that stuck to wooden sandals. The boy's arm appeared to be capped with one of those *bokko* that made it so hard to walk in wintertime. Children are always quick to judge and brutally honest in their observations, and Seisaku's companions had no compunction about using this colorful phrase to describe him.

The boy was generally quiet and well behaved, but this name sent him into a rage. He would fly at whoever was using it with a ferocity that usually scared the teaser off. But the antagonist would then round up reinforcements, and they would soon be back, throwing stones at him . . . with Seisaku retaliating with whatever stick he could find nearby. After these battles he would slowly make his way home, often stopping to sit sulking by the shore of Lake Inawashiro.

In the spring of 1883 Seisaku entered Mitsuwa Primary School, right across from the Noguchi house. He was reluctant to go at first, but he was pressed into it by his mother and encouraged by the kindness of the villagers, who helped the impoverished family in whatever ways they could. The neighbors took it upon themselves to help him get an education, and the shopkeeper at a store called Matsushimaya put together a package of everything he would need as a student, from writing brushes to books. These gestures were a sign of the warm human relations not infrequently found in rural communities, and they were the first in a long series of helping hands that would be extended to Noguchi throughout his life.

■ ■ ■

The Mitsuwa school had been established in 1873, the year after a nationwide school system was put in place. Called Sanjogata Primary School initially, it occupied part of the village mayor's home until the student body outgrew these rooms and classes were moved to an unused public storehouse east of the temple Choshoji, with rough benches and long desks shared by pupils. Unoura, the parish priest, taught classes there until a teacher was appointed in 1879. In the year Seisaku entered the school there were fifty students in his class, forty-three of them boys, and the school as a whole taught 177 students, which made for a school attendance rate of about sixty percent in the community.

Now that Seisaku was attending school Shika needed even more money than before. She had been thinking up ways to increase her income for some time, and now she started working even harder. She did odd jobs for local merchants, carrying packages for them between Inawashiro and Wakamatsu. This work paid about twice as much as the chores she did for other farmers in the district, but it was at least twice as hard. Even for a tough fellow like Tsunesaburo Nihei—the only other person in the village willing to do this work—it was a tough job. The two of them lugged the heavy parcels over twenty hilly kilometers, a route that became truly brutal in the winter. Deep snow and fierce winds would stop them in their tracks, but it was no easier to go back than to continue forward. A number of times Shika came close to lying down in the drifts for good.

But the money she made was well spent, as Seisaku proved to be a quick learner and a fairly capable student. His hand, however, caused problems. It was impossible to keep it hidden during physical education hours, and when it came time to practice calligraphy, it took him so long to grind his ink cake that the other students all started writing their characters before he even had a supply of ink to write with. The boy began dreading these classes each day. Eventually his teacher allowed him to sit out the physical exercises, but this only called attention to himself; and when the students discovered why he was no longer joining them in PE they showed no mercy. "Pestle hand!" they shouted at him. "You've got a pestle for a hand!"

Seisaku enjoyed school less and less, and in his third year he began refusing to attend. He would leave the house each morning as if he were heading to class, but instead made his way to the foothills of Mt. Bandai. There he could lie in the grass, undisturbed by anyone. Usually, the prospect of school and the mockery he endured there made him angry and tearful, but here he was able to relax in the placid view of Bandai's summit and the clouds flowing around it. When the time came to head back home, he would wet his brushes in some water to make it look as if he'd been using them all day.

On other days the truant would go instead to a nearby stream. There he dammed up the flow and waited for the water to pool. Digging in the exposed streambed below the dam would reveal loaches. Even a pestle-handed boy could capture these wriggling fish! This was far more enjoyable than being cooped up in the schoolhouse all day. As he grew older he began exploring other ways to catch these fish, setting up traps in the small canals that brought water to the rice paddies. He wove these from thin strips of bamboo and put some crushed pond snails in them to attract the fish, sinking them into the water in the early evening before heading home. Early the next morning he would pull up his catch, which he used to sell in the town of Inawashiro for pocket money.

For a while, Shika was not aware of these goings-on. She left early in the morning and returned home, exhausted from her work, late at night; she had little time or energy left to concern herself with Seisaku's school attendance. In any case, a child missing school was not a cause for undue worry in those days. Farming families often used to keep their children at home to help with the planting and harvesting. Rural schools, for this reason, rarely made an effort to contact families and ask about their children, and Shika received no teacher's report about her son's truancy.

But she did eventually notice. In the spells of rest between bouts of work, she began to add things up. Seisaku had changed: he had become more helpful around the house, and announced that he would pay for his own brushes with money he'd made by selling fish. He no longer talked about his days at school, though, and his mind seemed no longer to be on learning. She questioned some of the other schoolchildren about this and learned of his extended absences from class.

This news surprised and confused the mother at first. But given more time to think about it, she recognized what lay behind her son's dislike of school. Now she proved herself to be a wise as well as hard-working mother. Of course she felt pity at the thought of Seisaku's distress, but she didn't wallow in it. She composed herself and spoke to him. First she praised his desire to help the family by making himself useful around the house and catching fish to sell in town. But, she explained, her greatest joy was to see her children learning new things, and if Seisaku did not attend school, then why should she bother to work so hard? Tearfully she apologized for not realizing that the other children were bullying him. But, she admonished, he had to be stronger than them. He had to do his best at school precisely because his hand would prevent him from succeeding in other fields. She asked him not to worry about the family chores and finances, but to work harder at his studies. This was what motivated every moment of her own working days; this was what she prayed to the Nakada Kannon to see happen.

How could the boy turn his back on this sort of devotion? Knowing what Shika had gone through to bring up the family, he swore to her with tears in his eyes that he would go to school and study. The crisis had passed. He was a changed student from that day forward.

■ ■ ■

The other students continued to rag him about his deformed hand. But the boy just met this teasing with angry glares and concentrated on his studies.

Perhaps surprisingly, he had not shown any real academic promise so far. He did get fairly good marks, and records show that he once took third prize in an academic contest run by the county government, but he was also described as having a vacant expression on his face much of the time. His mother scolded him for this—"Only fools sit around with their mouths hanging open all day long!"—but it was not an easy habit to change.

The boy was nowhere near the top of his class in the early years of his schooling. Biographers have given various reasons for this, most of which focus on some sort of inequality present in the system of the day. Some say that Japan's feudal past still colored the way people thought in the 1880s, and that the children of a village's more influential residents received more attention and higher marks than the sons of sharecroppers. Others noted that students entered school at different ages, so Seisaku was probably in the same class as older children with a greater capacity for learning.

But after a time all these arguments ceased to matter. From 1887, when the boy was eleven or so, he was consistently at the head of his class. This was the year that he made his promise to Shika. School textbooks were no longer enough to quench his thirst for new knowledge, and he went to the owner of the Matsushimaya store to borrow more advanced materials. The shopkeeper had primers teaching how to read and write a thousand Chinese characters in three styles—block printing, semicursive writing, and the running cursive style seen on old scrolls—and Seisaku learned them all. He went to an officer in the local police station and learned Japanese and Chinese composition from him. And together with Daikichi, a young man working at Matsushimaya, he went to the temple Choshoji, where the boys learned more advanced Chinese characters and even English. This was astounding progress for a primary school pupil in any age, and even more amazing for a poor farmer's child in the Meiji era.

Daikichi was no slouch himself, and he worked steadily through the first reader in the *National* series of English texts at the temple. But before he had finished the first one, Seisaku was already well into the second reader. A powerful urge to learn—and learn as quickly as possible—had awoken within the young boy. From his mother he had learned to work tirelessly toward a goal; when joined with his desire to overcome his physical handicap, it resulted in an aggressive drive to gain new knowledge. People who lose the use of one sense are said to develop their other senses to make up for that loss; in Seisaku's case, his inability to take part in physical activities may similarly have led to an increase in his mental abilities. It was hardly surprising that he leapt ahead of the other kids in class.

One year the school saw the arrival of a new instructor, Junjiro Matsumoto, who had graduated from one of the normal schools established in the early 1870s to train teachers. In this same year Seisaku was tapped to serve as the class prefect. A year later he moved up once again, getting the position of head boy. This provided a welcome boost to the family finances as well as a feather in his cap; in Meiji Japan there weren't enough trained teachers to staff all the schools in the nation, and talented students received a small stipend in exchange for helping to teach classes.

After more than a decade of worry and toil, Shika at last felt some of the weight lifting from her shoulders. For the first time she began to allow herself a bit of hope for her son's prospects. Afflicted with a devastating injury, Seisaku had outshone the children of wealthy villagers to become the school's head boy! Filled with pride, she scraped together more money than she could comfortably spare to buy him clothes appropriate for his new position. Until then only privileged children—sons of the innkeepers and the head of the post office—wore shirts and pants, but now Seisaku left his kimono behind to join their ranks.

The other children soon showed their dissatisfaction with this turn of events. It is a natural response among young people to rebel against one of their own who has been set above them, and it was especially hard for these students to accept the treatment this poor boy with a mangled hand now enjoyed. A group of them began actively resisting his control over the class, hiding his lectern, for example, in the graveyard behind the temple next door. Without this platform he could no longer look over the entire classroom. But they had reckoned without his mother's reaction to it, which was to take precious time off work to stand guard at Choshoji, preventing further mischief and ensuring that her son could do his job. Once again Shika had helped prop up her son's career.

If there was one blemish on Seisaku's school record during these years, it was his below-average marks in morals. He could boast the highest grades in every subject but this one. Moral education in the late nineteenth century focused less on book-learning and more on the students' day-to-day behavior, and evidently Seisaku's was such that not even Matsumoto could overlook it in favor of his stellar marks in all other subjects. Today teachers may keep tabs on their students' character and behavior, but at a time when this resulted in a grade on each student's academic record, this was a serious problem for Seisaku.

His biographers have approached the question of his moral character in a variety of ways. Some tend to let the positive side of things outweigh the negative, looking at his superior talent in the medical field as indicative of his quality in all areas of his life. Others, meanwhile, acknowledge his social shortcomings, claiming that they were necessary to propel him to the heights he reached later in life. Raised in adversity, he could not afford a tolerant, easygoing manner, and it was his blunt individuality that allowed him to maneuver around the obstacles in his path. Other Noguchi men—his grandfather and great-grandfather in particular—had shown streaks of extraordinarily selfish behavior even as they built reputations as well-meaning people. The lives of men like this show that "the highest mountains cast the longest shadows," as the old saying goes, and Seisaku illustrated this even more clearly.

■ ■ ■

On July 15, 1888, came an event that shook Seisaku—and, indeed, the whole region. Mt. Bandai erupted at around 8:30 that morning. There was no school that day, and the thirteen-year-old was looking after his younger brother, Seizo, who had been born the previous year. But he had more interesting things to watch than his baby brother: early that morning he had witnessed the bizarre sight of numerous rats running into the open as though fleeing from something.

He had just stepped down to the bank of a nearby river, with Seizo in his arms, when he heard the noise. It began as the far-off rushing of a great wind. This was soon punctuated by a series of massive booms, so loud he felt his eardrums might burst. These sounds still filled the sky when the ground began to shake beneath his feet, and a deep rumbling came up from the depths of the earth.

Seisaku threw himself down under a sheltering willow and held his brother to his chest. The scared thirteen-year-old had no idea what was going on, but he peered up toward the mountain to see a huge cloud of black smoke mounting and spreading over the whole sky. A pillar of white-hot smoke and flame erupted from the top of the peak to plunge into that blackness above. Bandai—the geographic centerpiece of the Aizu region—had exploded.

This mountain had been revered since prehistoric times, and the Iwahashi Shrine on its slopes was held to be the home of the spirits of the peak. Long before, it had erupted much more frequently—one of its early names had been "Troubled Mountain"—but it had not blown its top like this in over a thousand years. This eruption, even larger than the one that had taken place in 806, astounded researchers in the fledgling field of volcanology. In an instant the Kobandai peak just north of the main mountain lost a full third of its height. Rock, mud, and ash rained down from the sky for kilometers around the mountain, and magma and lahars flowed down its slopes, swallowing up five villages and eleven smaller hamlets in just a quarter of an hour. These flows dammed up numerous rivers, eventually forming more than two hundred ponds and lakes including Hibara, Akimoto, and Onogawa, today the jewels of Bandai-Asahi National Park. Nobody in the area then thought of the beauty that would one day rise from the destruction, though; this was a disaster on a massive scale. The eruption had smashed homes, killed livestock, and covered fields and rice paddies with a deep layer of ash. The mountain killed 462 people that day and injured more than seven thousand.

This was a terrifying but exhilarating experience for Seisaku. The ground continued to rock beneath him and the deep roar of the mountain and the cries of frightened villagers filled his ears. Working in the fields at the time, Shika had also been flung to the ground by the blast; as soon as she came to her senses she thought first of her children. Ever since almost losing Seisaku to the fire, she had worried constantly about the safety of her daughter and sons, and now she dashed madly through the falling ash and the roaring sounds to reach the house.

The children were all safe, she learned with great relief. But this relief turned again to concern as she thought next of her husband, who had been living in the hills northeast of Bandai and working at a copper mine there. Disturbing reports came to her through the village hall: the damage had been greatest to the north of the mountain. The village of Hibara was almost completely buried, and the few houses left standing had been washed away by rivers finding new courses. There was no telling how many were dead, injured, or missing.

The family lost all hope at this news. But three days later Sayosuke came through the door—pale and drained, but alive! His children listened eagerly to his tales of how he had witnessed the blast from the northeast side of Bandai and survived to come back to them.

What effect did the eruption of Mt. Bandai have on the young Noguchi? Writers have put forth various theories over the years about the psychological impact on the boy, explaining how the mountain changed him inside. There is no denying that events of this magnitude have a profound effect on all who live through them—particularly children at an impressionable age. But those seeking to draw some connection between the eruption and the improvement in Seisaku's studies somehow fail to notice that his studies took a turn for the better a year before the mountain exploded.

It is inviting, though, to consider the ties between humans and nature when we examine this stage of Noguchi's life. Coincidence though it may have been, the Bandai eruption is a handy metaphor for the life of the child who grew up below the mountain and watched it explode. Seisaku Noguchi would go on to live an explosive life himself—shaking the ground under the feet of the Japanese with his accomplishments, making his presence known to the rest of the world like a column of billowing smoke, and amazing everyone who witnessed his deeds.

This son of Aizu taking his cues from a mountain in Aizu is an attractive and poetic image. But as a young teenager he was not yet ready to erupt. At this stage his life was still filled with uncertainty. His family remained destitute, and his course after graduating from primary school was murky. He may have seethed with an inner fire, but at the age of thirteen it was far from certain that his fire would break through into the wider world.

BROADENING HORIZONS

Young Noguchi was approaching a turning point in his life. On his own he would not have known what to do, but luckily he came under the influence of just the right person around then. This was a young educator named Sakae Kobayashi.

People with extraordinary raw talent are not as rare as history suggests. What is truly rare is the natural genius fortunate enough to encounter a person capable of discerning that talent and helping to stimulate it. As an old Chinese saying has it, "There are many horses that can run a thousand *li*, but few men with the eye to pick them out of the herd." Chance encounters can change the course of a person's life. This is especially true for the young: they haven't yet reached the stage when they can strike out on their own, but a great many paths still remain open to them.

Seisaku had finished his primary school learning. He remained at school for an additional year of supplementary classes. Final examinations at the end of this year were administered by a proctor with advanced qualifications: Sakae Kobayashi, the school inspector for all of Yama County. He was also the head teacher at Inawashiro Higher Elementary School, the equivalent in terms of today's student ages to a middle school, but one of the more advanced institutions of secondary learning at that time.

Kobayashi and one other teacher tested the students in two stages. The first was a written exam covering arithmetic and writing. The second was an oral exam in which the students expounded on moral questions and showed their ability to read Chinese characters aloud. For this second stage the students entered a room one by one to face the proctors.

At last Seisaku's turn came around. He walked into the room and stood before the teachers, a small figure dressed in the rough clothes of a poor farm boy. He was polite and respectful, though, and he showed considerable composure in front of these visitors, unlike the other students. There was something different about Seisaku, and that difference was easy for talented teachers like these to spot. Sure enough, once they began their questioning they saw that he answered accurately and without hesitation.

Kobayashi noticed, however, that the boy kept one hand behind his back. He asked about this odd pose: "Have you injured your arm?"

Seisaku's whole body tensed at this casual question. "No sir, my hand is scarred. I burned it when I was a baby."

The observant examiner sensed the pain behind this unexpectedly direct statement. In calm, reassuring tones he asked Seisaku for the whole story, and his face grew graver as he listened.

He looked the boy in the eye. "What do you intend to do after graduating?"

"I'm not sure, sir. My family has always farmed, and that's probably what I'll end up doing, too."

"I see. Well, do you enjoy reading?"

At this the boy's eyes lit up. "Yes sir, very much. I would love to keep studying if I could."

Kobayashi was silent for a while, then said: "Listen, I want you to come to my place in two or three days' time. And bring your mother." He gave Seisaku the address and made a point of confirming that he'd be there.

Kobayashi lived in a house near the castle in Inawashiro. His father had been a warrior in the service of the lord of Aizu. After the fall of the domain, though, the rank of samurai meant nothing. A family adviser told the young Sakae that only two appropriate jobs remained for a swordless warrior in this new era: police officer and teacher. He chose the latter path, and entered a normal school.

Normal school graduates were rare and highly valued in those early years of the new education system. Degree in hand, Kobayashi had his pick of posts all over the nation. But he chose to return to his family home. There was just one higher elementary school in Inawashiro, and he was made its head teacher. When he came across Noguchi he was a thin, sharp-eyed teacher of just twenty-nine. Shika greeted his appearance in their lives as a gift from Kannon.

On the day of their private meeting with Kobayashi, Shika arose early as usual. She and Seisaku went to the lake and caught some shrimp, which they cleaned and wrapped in oak leaves as a gift for the teacher. When mother and child arrived at what they expected to be a mansion, they found a simple affair with just one story and a thatched roof. Kobayashi invited them in and they sat before him as he asked about Seisaku's plans for the future. Shika opened up to this earnest young educator, telling him everything—about the accident that had disfigured her son, about the family's hardships. Kobayashi listened quietly and then replied with news of Seisaku's outstanding scores on his final exams. He urged the boy to enter his school in Inawashiro.

This was no school for a child of desperately poor farmers. Its students were the sons and daughters of privileged families—mayors, wealthy merchants. But Kobayashi spoke with passion: "This is a new age for Japan. Learning comes first now, not social rank. There's no need to be subservient to others because you're poor! Whatever I can do to help you, I will."

Shika was moved to tears not only by this generous offer but by the thought that her son—this one-handed boy with no future in farming—now had a chance to make a life for himself. She made her decision then and there: to send him to the Inawashiro school. One year after the mountain had exploded, these two people, a decisive mother and a dedicated teacher, set a fourteen-year-old boy on a path that led away from physical toil toward the pursuit of knowledge.

■ ■ ■

The other villagers saw this as a bizarre choice. Was that woman mad to think her son belonged in a place like the higher elementary school? "Seisaku does a bit better than the others in school, and it goes straight to her head," they muttered. "No amount of schooling will change that hand of his. She's wasting her time! A kid with a quick mind like that, she should apprentice him to a traveling storyteller. That would bring in some cash much sooner." Seisaku was indeed at an age when most rural kids—even if they had stayed in the classroom through the end of primary school—returned to the fields or found other ways to earn money for their families.

This criticism was harsh, but it was not delivered in a mean spirit. Shika's neighbors were genuinely worried that she was making a bad choice, reaching for more for her child than was wise. The higher elementary school was far beyond the dreams of most people in the area. Its students came from nine municipalities including the town of Inawashiro, but even so just thirty-five new pupils in all had been admitted that year. Katsuzo Kaneda was the only other child from Mitsuwa Primary School who had made it in, and he was no farmer.

Inawashiro was at the time a town known for its educational institutions, among which was the Nisshinkan, a campus of the venerable Aizu domain school. Inawashiro Primary was nicknamed "the glass school"; visitors would come from several villages over to see the classrooms' glass-paned windows. The modern facility also boasted Western-style desks and chairs, rather than the long, low tables used in most schools, and employed first-rate teachers and the latest learning methods. The upper elementary school, which also occupied this facility, offered a four-year course of study covering material roughly equivalent to today's high-school curriculum.

Into this culturally advanced center of education came Seisaku Noguchi, determined that if his hand kept him from prosperity as a farmer he would achieve success through his mental abilities instead. He was old enough to know what a burden this would be on his mother, but she pushed him harder than anyone, telling him not to worry about working for the family, but to learn.

This was a far cry from his time at Mitsuwa Primary, though. In Inawashiro he was surrounded by the region's brightest children, and he would have to work much harder to stand out among them. In addition to this he had to walk the six kilometers to school each morning; and even after walking that distance home again later, he usually had to take care of various chores around the house, since his mother would still be out working. This left little time for his studies. With almost no money for lamp oil, the Noguchis lived in darkness when the sun went down. Seisaku soon found a way to read his books, however—he got a job stoking the fire for the bathwater at Matsushimaya. He kept the fire banked high, and the flames and the lamp nearby gave him the light he needed to prepare for the next day's lessons.

In any place and any era, the teenage years bring with them their own set of problems. Seisaku of course faced these too. He was prone to waves of self-conscious embarrassment. His clothes marked him as a poor farmer, unlike his well-to-do classmates. More than anything else his hand was a factor. Seisaku's school report cards showed a row of blank spaces where he was left ungraded in gymnastics. He limited himself to rice balls for lunch—these were eaten with one hand, unlike the *bento*, or boxed lunch, that he would have to hold in his clumsy left while he wielded chopsticks with his right. Before long he had stopped eating with the other students entirely. When lunchtime came he would slip off to the janitor's room to eat there quietly alone.

Seisaku showed his hand to no one. Amazingly, almost a year passed before another student caught a glimpse of it. He began to ask: "Hey, what happened to your . . ." But he got no farther. The generally docile farmer's son came at him—and flung him to the ground!

Even without this kind of outburst, there were reasons to be concerned about Seisaku's progress. Without two healthy hands he couldn't even keep his pencils properly sharpened. He was lucky to have Kobayashi teaching him in most subjects, but would this be enough to keep his marks as high as they could be?

The young student redoubled his efforts to ensure that he would continue to excel. Always a physical impediment, his hand once again proved to be an incentive for his academic drive. He considered himself to be in direct competition with his able-bodied classmates, and if his own desire to surpass them ever flagged he had only to think of the long hours his mother was putting in to pay his considerable tuition. Photographs of Shika taken around this time show the shadowed face of a woman on the edge of exhaustion. With this face to spur him on, it is no wonder that Seisaku pushed himself to the limit as well.

At times he appeared to go beyond that limit, however, and even his mother would caution him: "Take a rest now. Studying that hard will only make you sick." But how could he follow these instructions?

There was nothing easy about Noguchi's early life. Most accounts of it that remain today are so caught up in the hardships he faced that they focus on the powerful individuality that brought him through them. Both nature and nurture play a role in the formation of every young man, though, and it is worth examining both Seisaku's innate character and the experiences molding him from outside to gain an accurate picture of his formative years.

■ ■ ■

Seisaku was smaller than most students, and he lacked the stocky build one would expect in a farm child. Even as an adult he would be just 160 centimeters tall, and he never weighed more than sixty kilograms or so. But he was strong and compact, taking after his father in his well-proportioned build and his sturdy neck and head. Indeed, with the exception of his burned hand, he was a fine physical specimen.

He put this strength to use in the sport of sumo. Despite his injured arm—or perhaps due to his drive to prove himself on that account—he eagerly took part in sumo matches with the other students. His left hand served him well in this grappling. The thumb pointed toward his wrist and the fingers were fused together. Once he got a grip on his opponent's belt with this powerful claw it was rare for that opponent to shake free from the hold.

One time Daikichi, the son of the Matsushimaya shop owner, got into an argument with Seisaku. He was soon beaten in verbal debate and spat out: "You won't find it so easy to beat me at sumo, though!" Seisaku jumped up instantly to accept this challenge. It was no easy fight: Daikichi was older and considerably larger than Seisaku, who found himself being pushed steadily backward. But the smaller boy looked for his opening, and in a flash he plunged his left arm between Daikichi's torso and right arm. He ground his "pestle hand" into the larger boy's armpit—and when Daikichi proved to be ticklish, the match was soon over. The cleverness of this sneak attack was only to be expected from Seisaku.

This turned into a common pastime for the young boy. One of Seisaku's schoolmates would later recall: "Noguchi was tough; he was always fighting with one kid or another." This wasn't a simple case of the handicapped boy being picked on by those around him, though—he was quick to take offense at any perceived slight, and he would go after the offending party with surprising fierceness. This fighting spirit made Seisaku an aggressive young student, but it would serve him well in later years as he turned his energy to more beneficial uses.

He was excused from taking part in gymnastics class, but when winter came around he always managed to be included in the organized snowball fights that took place then. The upper primary school students divided into two teams, with Yasuhiko Urakami, the gymnastics teacher, directing them in the contest. Everyone was surprised when Urakami tapped Seisaku as one of the team captains. But their surprise soon vanished as this unobtrusive boy emerged as a daring leader in battle. One by one he called out the biggest students on the other team, taunting them and then blasting them with a barrage of snowballs when they came charging at him. He may not have been as tough as them physically, but his guts and vitality made him stand out on the snowy school grounds.

As fierce as he could be in a snowball fight, however, his outward appearance gave a different impression entirely. He was ordinarily unassuming and mild-mannered. Years of self-consciousness about his injured hand and his family's poverty had given him a surprisingly quiet demeanor—not the kind of personality one would expect after seeing the combative attitude he brought to his fights at school. His face, too, suggested the son of a wealthy home rather than a rough farmer's child, with its oval shape and slightly plump cheeks. Only his bright eyes gave a hint of the spark burning inside him. Perhaps the blood of his more successful ancestors ran in his veins, making this child of a poor home look pretty much like any other talented student.

What drove this student more than anything else was the determination he shared with his mother. He couldn't bear the thought of coming in second in any competition—as an individual or as a member of a team—and he prepared for whatever competitions came up in his life with an energy that didn't seem to match his outward manner. This competitiveness served him well each winter in another contest—the *torioi*. Here the village children split into an east team and a west one in a contest to see which group could wake up earlier on the fifteenth day of the first month of the year. The winning team would gather in the sacred grove of the local shrine near town and sing *torioi*, or "bird-chasing," songs meant to keep birds out of the crops for the year. It was an honor to win this contest, and every year Seisaku stayed up all through the night on the fourteenth, waking up his teammates before dawn and leading them to the grove to claim that honor. The east team won every year until he reached adulthood and stopped taking part in the festival.

■ ■ ■

Statements from people who knew him in those years paint an interesting picture of this passionate young man. They refer to his pugnacity: "He was an intense person, and that led him to do things that perhaps he shouldn't have done." They mention an almost snobbish attitude: "He seemed to have little time for ordinary, slow-and-steady people like us." Seisaku also didn't always come across as a faithful friend: "He could be pushy. There were lots of times when he did something that made you mistrust him." And he was known early on for his unreliability in money matters: "He'd borrow from friends, but he seemed to think that instead of paying them back he could just wait until he made a name for himself and let them ride his coattails."

There may be an element of jealousy in these comments from people who knew Noguchi when he was dirt-poor and unknown. But it is hard to discount them all. Even in his academic work, the one area where he excelled without question, he was likely to show this fiery side to his personality. Once, when studying world geography, he and a friend were quizzing each other on various place names. It was Seisaku's turn to answer, but he had no ready response when the friend asked: "Where is the Pechora River?"

"There's no such place."

"Yes there is," retorted the friend. "Now where is it?"

Seisaku was incensed. "There's no such river! You're making things up! What place would have a name like that?" Just as in the sumo ring, when he felt himself getting into a disadvantageous position he tried to attack from some unexpected direction. And there was nothing for his friend to do but bring out the map and show him the river on it.

Still another story tells of the time when he was standing looking at the rice paddy his family took care of. Water was failing to pool up in the paddy, and the rice stalks his mother had planted were in danger of drying up. Annoyingly, however, the field next to the family plot was well watered. So Seisaku opened up a trench between the two paddies to get some of the water into the Noguchi side. But this was the Matsushimaya paddy, and Daikichi, when he saw what had happened, crept up behind Seisaku and shoved him right into the mud.

Seisaku was not the kind of boy to give up after this, and he went on thinking about how to solve the problem. An examination of the waterway showed that it split into two channels just above the paddy, and most of the water flowed down the other course. All he had to do was to block off the other course to send water into the Noguchi paddy. This, however, would be an easy scheme to spot, so he went a bit further downstream to find a place to dam the flow. The water began to pool up. Soon enough, while the boy sat reading nearby, the water backed up to the point where the stream split into two, and again flowed down the proper channel. But it wasn't long before someone came and discovered his handiwork, and the dam was smashed.

Seisaku next looked further up the hill for a way to get the water he needed. With a long stick he opened several holes in the dike surrounding an uphill paddy belonging to a neighbor. He camouflaged these holes carefully with handfuls of dry leaves and straw. The owner of this upper field used a waterwheel to fill it, but once the water reached the level of these holes it would drain out and head down to the Noguchi plot. This neighbor never caught on, fortunately, and the boy obtained the water his family needed—although in a less than honest manner.

One year a new principal came to the Inawashiro school and began giving lectures in the Chinese classics. Four texts were needed for this class, and they were not cheap: they cost three yen, the equivalent of several tens of thousands of yen today. There was no way for the Noguchis to obtain these books. Seisaku approached a classmate, Yasuhei Yago, to see if he could help. Yasuhei was a kind-hearted boy with considerable respect for Noguchi's academic ability and sympathy for his poverty. Noguchi knew this about his friend, and he was not above exploiting it when he needed something, as he did now. Yasuhei first offered to give him his own books, but the offer was turned down, since Yasuhei was bound to run into trouble when he came to school without those texts. The Yago family ran a store and was relatively well off, but not so rich that Yasuhei could casually ask his father to get another set of books. After thinking long and hard about how to help Seisaku, he went to his father and explained the situation to him. Tomeshiro, who turned out to be as generous as his son, agreed to give the poor boy the three yen he needed for the Chinese books. Later, Seisaku went to the Yago home to thank them for their help, and even wrote them an IOU—a nice gesture, but in the end nothing more than a gesture. Evidently the unpaid IOU remains in the Yago house to this day.

On the way to school Seisaku often ran into Katsuzo Kaneda, the other Mitsuwa graduate going to Inawashiro Upper Elementary. "You're running late, Noguchi!" Kaneda would shout.

Seisaku's response was to hold his arm out to the east, lining up his thumb with the top of a nearby hill and placing his finger over the sun, so he could see roughly what time it was. "You're right, it is late!" he would reply.

From an early age Seisaku had thought up a number of ways to work out the time. One method involved drawing a circle on the ground and standing in its center, looking at his shadow in this human sundial to gauge the hour. His creativity reminded those around him of his father. At times, though, so did his approach to the day's schedule. He woke up quite early each morning, but he was never in a hurry to get to school—there was the paddy to water, or a book to read by the fireside. He was often late for class.

Seisaku cut a rough figure during his youth. He wore the simplest of kimono along with sandals, often the straw ones his mother made. A filthy *furoshiki*, or carrying cloth, contained his schoolbooks and his day's lunch; he tied this bundle around his waist or slung it across his back from one shoulder. During the summer he wore his robe loosely with a simple sash around his waist to hold it together; the colder months saw him in the baggy pants worn for farm work. Needless to say, he was the only one in his class to wear these farm clothes, and he stood out among the other pupils in their fine *hakama*, the skirts worn over kimono. Yoshiji Akiyama, a classmate who also lived some distance from town, felt sorry for him and offered him his old *hakama*, which the boy was happy to accept—they may have been second-hand to Akiyama, but they were the nicest clothes the young Noguchi had worn.

On rainy or snowy days the schoolyard filled with students wearing cloaks and carrying oiled-paper umbrellas. Seisaku once again stood out in his straw overcoat. But, not surprisingly for someone of his age, he preferred not to be too obviously unconventional, and as he came closer to Inawashiro he would shed this peasant's cape and dash to join a friend under his umbrella.

This does not mean that he was always taking from his classmates, always using them for his own means, without ever giving anything in return. Indeed, it is unlikely that they would have put up with him for long if he didn't have something to offer. In the depths of winter he proved his worth as a friend many times as he led groups of students to school through snow-storms. At these times, when the roads were smothered by drifts of snow and it was hard to keep one's eyes open in the stinging wind, they were glad to have him at their head. He never steered them in the wrong direction; nobody ever plunged into a river or got lost in a whiteout. One time a large, fierce dog came after the group of students as they were trudging through the snow. The others panicked and backed away; Seisaku, though, was quite an imposing presence despite his small size, and after groping in the snow for a stick he advanced on the snarling animal, yelling at it: "Get back, you! And never bark at us again!" This seemed to stop the animal in its tracks, and Seisaku remained staring at it as the other kids filed past, bringing up the rear of the line. This became a daily occurrence for the group for some time.

In this way other students came to look to Seisaku for help and guidance. In turn he grew more outgoing, and he took it upon himself to deal with various problems he spotted around him. There was a group of delinquent kids, for example, who went around town stealing sweets and other things from the local shops. When Seisaku learned of this gang and its activities he confronted them one by one and threatened them, calmly and coldly, telling them: "If you don't stop stealing I won't be answerable for what happens to you." And that was all it took; the shoplifting apparently stopped.

■ ■ ■

At school he began to take on a leadership role. Three or four times a year the entire student body would gather for a debate and speech contest. Kobayashi directed this event, but it was the person selected from among the students who served as master of ceremonies. The students generally chose Seisaku to handle these duties.

The respect he enjoyed among his schoolmates helped him to put an end to problems at school from time to time. Once, some small incident led to a fight in the hallway, and Hideichi Kobayashi, perhaps the biggest student in the school, started yelling and lashing out with his fists at anyone who came near him. One of the people who went to calm him down was Seisaku, and he, too, went flying across the hall. Surprisingly, though, the smaller boy didn't lose his temper; instead, he stood up, dusted himself off, gave a wry grin, and shouted in a shockingly loud voice: "Shut up!" To everyone's amazement, this jolted Hideichi out of his rage, and he calmed down at once.

Given Seisaku's tendency to brawl with anyone who so much as spoke about his left hand, this was an uncharacteristically subdued response for him. But it was a good example of his perseverance—a word that he made his motto in later life. He preferred not to waste his time in meaningless disagreements. Thanks to his tough childhood he had learned to soak up all manner of suffering, turning it into energy that he directed toward making progress.

This proved to be energy well spent. When he came to the end of his first year at Inawashiro Upper Elementary School and the grades for the year were announced, Seisaku was at the top of his class. He had overcome more than his fair share of problems to achieve this, and Kobayashi was gratified to see that his judgment of this young student had been spot-on. Shika, for her part, was ecstatic at the news. And once the news of Seisaku's achievement spread around Okinajima, the other villagers began to look at him—and at his mother's decision to send him to Inawashiro for more schooling—in a new light.

Other students wanted to know how he managed to get the grades he did. A group of the village kids got together and went to talk to him as well as one other student—Kaneyasu Nihei, who was a year younger than Seisaku and also a bright pupil at school. First they asked Kaneyasu the best way to improve one's grades at school. He replied: "Well, after you get home, you need to carefully review what you learned at school that day." But Seisaku smirked as he answered: "No, if you pay close attention to the teacher while he's explaining things in class, there's no real need to review anything at home." This was the confident response of a talented student, but it came across as boastful to these listeners. In fact, though, this style of learning was one he had learned from necessity. He couldn't count on having time to study at home, where household chores and a lack of lamp oil kept him from reading as much as he would have liked. Compared with other students who had the luxury of poring over their notes each night, he had to absorb information much more efficiently during school hours alone.

However, he was no slacker during the time spent away from the classroom, either. His notebooks, which one can still see today, are filled with neat, detailed explanations and explorations of the subjects that interested him. He was not taking these notes to prepare for his classes, but to teach himself far more advanced material—probably one reason he had such an easy time in the classes he took.

His accelerated independent study made him stand out in the examinations. One year's science test was observed by school inspectors who examined the students' answers to questions like "Why does water occupy more volume when it freezes into ice?" Most of the students wrote responses based faithfully on what Kobayashi, their science teacher that year, had taught them: water reaches its highest density at four degrees centigrade, and as the temperature goes below that point, the density is reduced and the volume thereby increased. Since water turns into ice at zero degrees, ice is less dense than water, and it floats to the top.

One test amazed them, though—Seisaku's paper. His answer differed from the others in its explanation of the molecular structure of water, which forms a lattice at very low temperatures as the substance begins to crystallize and turn into ice. In its solid form, water has more space between its molecules due to this latticing, and ice therefore occupies more volume than water. He had even attached a drawing illustrating this principle.

Despite his claim that he never needed to review material at home, Noguchi was in fact almost never without a book in his hand. He studied everywhere he could. Often this was at Matsushimaya, where he and Daikichi would read and review their lessons together. At these times—indeed, at virtually all times—Seisaku showed astonishing powers of concentration. When he read a book its pages were all he was conscious of. He was so eager to learn new things that he generally ended up reading while he tackled some other task. He also cut his hours of rest to a bare minimum, getting just a few hours of deep sleep each night. He learned this habit during his years at the upper elementary school and it stayed with him for the rest of his life—certainly no habit an ordinary person would choose to pick up, but one that would serve him well in his continuing pursuit of knowledge.

Seisaku worked out difficult math problems or pored over his English reader as he stoked the bath fire at Matsushimaya. During the winter this work kept him warm in addition to providing light for his studies. Sometimes he would be invited in for a bath, and he and Daikichi would each scrub the other's back in turn. But sure enough, books would find their way even into the bathhouse, and Seisaku only had one hand and one eye for his friend. This once led to a painful situation for Daikichi when Seisaku, engrossed in his reading, groped for the bar of soap and began rubbing his classmate's back. Daikichi's shrieks made him realize that he had picked up a pumice stone instead.

After their bath the two boys would head to Daikichi's room, where Seisaku would study for hours. Some small noise would wake up the other boy deep in the night, and he would find Seisaku still there at his desk.

"Sei, you're up studying this late?"

"Oh, sorry, did I wake you?"

"Instead of worrying about my sleep, why not think of your own? You're going to wreck yourself staying up all night like this all the time."

"Don't worry, I'll be okay. Did you know Napoleon slept just three hours a night all his life?"

To revive himself when he grew sleepy, he used to splash cold water on his face. But when this trick no longer worked he would crawl into Daikichi's bed—much more comfortable than his own back home. This was just one of many ways that Seisaku used the resources around him to make up for what his own family lacked. To read the *Nihon Gaishi*, an expensive multi-volume history of Japan, he snuck into the unlit village office after dark, where he was caught in the act by someone who noticed that the supply of candles in the storage closet had been dwindling; when they opened the door late one night there he was, reading by candlelight in the tiny space.

■ ■ ■

Seisaku's academic achievements drew admiration from most people. There were some, however, who saw them in a less than favorable light—people who disagreed with Shika's choice to keep her son in school. Some of these people were in a position to put an end to his schooling for good. These were Shika's creditors.

The boy was already sixteen or seventeen years old—a young man, really—and more than old enough to be earning money on his own as a farm worker by now. But he was off at school all the time, and the Noguchi family fields were not as well tended or productive as they should be. Shika made excuses to lenders about the low crop yields, pointing to her son's injury as the reason he couldn't be expected to help raise them, but they were having none of it. The boy was off filling his head with useless knowledge—not what a farmer's son should be doing at his age.

Now and again a creditor could be seen sitting on the Noguchis' porch, giving Shika a bad time: "Look, you've got money enough to pay for school tuition, so it's no use telling us that you don't have the cash to pay us back as well. You can't keep coming up with stories like this—'my son is too crippled to work, he needs to be in school'—and expect us to fall for them all."

The family was in bad financial shape. Shika had been borrowing money not just for Seisaku's schooling but for everyday living expenses, which were impossible to cover with her meager income. There were of course no scholarship programs in those days, and certainly nobody to turn to within the family. Sayosuke was not a totally uncaring husband, but he couldn't shake his drinking habit. From time to time he would show some remorse for his behavior and promise to bring some money home for the family, but the promise never held.

Shika thought of a new scheme to get the family out of these straits. She would find a husband for Inu, Seisaku's sister—someone willing to marry into the Noguchi family and support it through thick and thin. Shika tried to convince her daughter of the benefits of this idea, but Inu thought it unlikely that a man would be found willing to enter this household and take on its debts as his own. Nor was she particularly happy with the idea of her brother getting to study while she had to crawl in the mud of a rice paddy. She called Seisaku out and confronted him with this:

"Look, you're the eldest son, and it's you who should be taking over the family work one day."

"I don't see much future in becoming head of a family of farmers," he replied. "I've got talent, and I'm going to use it to make something of myself. I'll leave the family in your hands."

Their debate went nowhere. Neither was willing to take on the responsibility for this home. Inu could not escape the fact that she was of marriageable age, though; the longer she stayed under this roof the more likely it was that some man would be found to marry her and keep her here forever. Her mother's sudden proposal jolted her into action. She quietly left home that year and went to serve as a maid in the house of a former domain official from the pre-Meiji days. Shika despaired at this turn of events. Now there were not nearly enough working hands in the house, and the Noguchi family and Seisaku's future were in grave danger.

Shika was a clever woman, but here her cleverness led her into what can only be described as manipulative tricks. In the same village lived a distant relative named Sataro Nihei. His daughter Otome, a large, strong young woman of nineteen, was known in the village as a hard worker with a forthright personality. Shika approached him to see if this girl might come into the Noguchi family as Seisaku's wife. The Nihei family knew of Seisaku's intelligence and his future prospects, and Sataro jumped at the chance to place his daughter with Shika's son.

People married early in nineteenth-century Japan, particularly in rural areas. Plenty of men in and around Okinajima had wives by the time they were Seisaku's age. It was also common then to forego a formal wedding ceremony. The young woman would come to live with the man's family almost like an adoptee rather than a bride; and over time she and her partner would, with luck, grow into the roles of husband and wife. Shika now invited Otome to enter the Noguchi home. Seisaku was not at all happy with the idea of being anyone's husband, but his mother noted that with Inu gone they had little choice, and that was that.

Seisaku grudgingly put up with this relationship in form alone. He spoke to Otome as little as possible. Sleeping in the same room with her was out of the question. The kind-hearted girl made him his rice balls as he prepared for school in the mornings, but he seemed too immature even to put on the appearance of gratitude for this. He used to turn his back on her and stick his hand out behind him to receive the food.

Otome did not put up with this shabby treatment for long. She left the Noguchi house and returned home. Soon after that she married into a family on the other side of the mountain. Happily there were no hard feelings between her and Shika; she came to visit a number of times afterwards.

Eventually Inu would return home with a husband, Zengo, from a village north of Inawashiro, bringing some stability back to the Noguchi family. But this was some years in the future; right now Shika only knew that she was again the sole source of income for the household.

It upset Seisaku to see his mother in this situation. He couldn't tell her to stay at home and take it easy, but he could take on some of the work to lighten her load, so he began returning from school as early as possible, sacrificing his study time and heading straight for the fields. It seemed Shika was right about him, though: he would never make a decent living as a farmer. The cloth he wrapped around his left hand was always slipping off, exposing his twisted fingers to the hardness of the soil he was working in.

At times like these the boy cried out in pain as anyone would. But he also channeled his distress in productive ways. Cradling his aching limb, he lost himself in boys' magazines borrowed from friends, and with these tales rolling through his head he set his own brush to paper, writing page after page as he tried to forget his throbbing fingers. One generally thinks of Noguchi the doctor as a specialist in the natural sciences, but in his youth he developed a considerable interest in literature and in writing skills. He internalized his suffering and used it to help him branch out into other fields.

■ ■ ■

But despite the outlet these pages gave him, the pain and frustration he felt building up inside him reached a point where he couldn't hide them from other people any longer. Late in his fourth and last year at the upper elementary school these feelings came pouring out in an essay he turned in to Kobayashi.

Most of the other students wrote about their postgraduation plans in this assignment. But Seisaku had no idea what he wanted to do after leaving the Inawashiro school. In his paper he laid bare this uncertainty about his future, the pain of his hand, and the frustration he had lived with for years. A cry of rage and sorrow, the essay shocked Kobayashi even as it dazzled him with its brilliance as a composition.

"I can contain it no longer; here let me write it all." With this opening line Noguchi launched into his recollection of all the times the cold attitudes of other people had hurt him over the years. When he was among people he was consumed with nervous fear, but he went to great lengths—putting considerable pressure on himself—to avoid exposing this inner turmoil. Physically, each day was a long series of obstacles that his clumsy hand threw up before him. His fingers wouldn't serve him. His family knew only grinding poverty. His life seemed without hope. Great ambition seethed within him—surely even with one ruined hand a man could make something of himself in this world!—but all his efforts so far had achieved little. These dark thoughts overcame him at times. . . He did have friends, the essay continued, but even time spent with them reminded him of the physical difference between them. He wanted to grasp things freely. He wanted fingers. At times, he wrote, he came close to taking a knife and cutting his joined digits apart.

This essay was a cry for help from the student. He desperately wanted to know what he could do with his life. Now and again Kobayashi caught his breath or felt tears in his eyes at some passage in Seisaku's paper. He had to help him. He showed the essay to the principal and to his colleagues, exclaiming: "We can't let such a talented young man fall by the wayside."

"You're right," they told him. "If an operation can fix his hand, let's scrape together the money for it. We can't leave him in this situation without offering a helping hand."

Before long, talk of this plan had spread through the school. Kobayashi took Seisaku's essay and read it aloud to the other students. They were restless at first as they listened to this lecture, but the more they heard of the piece the quieter they became, until they were hanging on every word. They had always seen the intense Noguchi as a somewhat unapproachable classmate, or perhaps as a knowall, a showoff who wasn't worth their time. But listening to his essay opened their hearts to the pain he was willing to expose. Had his life been this miserable all along? "We've got to help Noguchi!" they decided, too.

Yasuhei Yago, Yoshiji Akiyama, and Genji Matsu, along with the head teacher, Kobayashi, led the students in their movement to help their friend. Every pupil in the class put ten sen into the pot; when the school's teachers all added their contributions the total came to over ten yen—an astounding sum, equivalent to hundreds of thousands of yen today. One writer has explained this outpouring of aid as something orchestrated by Noguchi himself, but his theory does not hold water—this was, after all, a young man without the ability to feign even simple gratitude for the lunches Otome had made for him. Here it was the force of his true feelings that sparked this emotional response in others. By daring to expose his pain to his teachers and classmates he earned their trust and friendship.

When they stopped and gave some thought to the matter, though, they realized that nobody knew whether an operation could ever succeed in giving Noguchi the full use of his hand. The more they considered things, the less likely it seemed that there would even be a surgeon in this rural area with the skill to repair his burned fingers. Surgery itself was still a rarity in this age when Western medicine was just beginning to play a larger role in Japan. But Kobayashi knew one man who could help. This was Kanae Watanabe, a doctor living in Wakamatsu who had trained in the United States.

Kobayashi called Noguchi in and told him: "Go and meet Dr. Watanabe, and have him take a look at your hand. He'll know right away whether surgery can help you or not."

The boy had already been to one doctor in town, who had taken one look at his hand and told him nothing could be done. Now he recalled the despair he had felt at that time. Could this new doctor really tell him anything different? With a trembling voice and a brightly blushing face he bowed deeply to Kobayashi, thanked the teacher, and went to Wakamatsu.

Dr. Watanabe's practice, the Kaiyo Clinic, lay in the center of the city of

Wakamatsu. The clinic occupied a sturdy, imposing, two-story structure that survives to this day. It had a high stone wall around it and boasted modern touches like glass-paned windows and Western-style swinging doors. Watanabe, too, was a modern kind of doctor. He had graduated from what would later become the University of Tokyo, and had gone on to study in California, where he earned his doctorate in medicine. He even practiced for a time in San Francisco, an astonishingly cosmopolitan move for a Japanese of the nineteenth century. Watanabe had returned to Japan following the death of his father, a practitioner of traditional Chinese medicine in western Aizu.

Seisaku saw the doctor as a larger-than-life figure, with his impressive sideburns, his Western suit and bow tie, and the gold pocketwatch in his waistcoat pocket. Most doctors in those days still dressed in kimono and wielded ink brushes, and probably seventy percent of all medicine consisted of Chinese herbal treatments. Watanabe stood out among this crowd, to say the least; his wife, too, looked as if she had just been to some elegant party in Paris.

Seisaku had never been as nervous as he was on the examination table that day. Was his case hopeless? What would this stern-faced doctor say? But Watanabe put down his left hand and smiled at the young man. "Your fingers have been fused together for more than ten years, and the bones haven't grown properly. I can't make your left hand look like your right. But I can give you the use of all your fingers again."

"Really?" Seisaku almost shouted at this news. "I'll really have five fingers again?" This gnarled stump of his . . . could he dare to believe that he would have a hand again?

When he went out to the waiting room and told his mother, Shika's face lit up, and right there in the Kaiyo Clinic she turned to face toward the Nakada Kannon and offered a prayer of thanks.

■ ■ ■

On the day of his operation Seisaku left his mother at home. His classmate Akiyama went along with him on behalf of his friends at school. Watanabe began the operation by injecting anesthetic to numb the entire hand. Local anesthesia was not as effective as it is today; Seisaku's feeling was deadened only in the outer layers of the skin. But as soon as it took effect the doctor began cutting. First he separated the thumb from the wrist in a relatively easy procedure. The fingers proved trickier, though. Seisaku's index and middle fingers had been fused to the palm of his hand long enough for new blood vessels to grow between them, and cutting these fingers free was a bloody process as a result. Watanabe worked steadily to tie off these vessels and stop the bleeding as he cut the fingers free. Now and again Seisaku moaned softly as the scalpel cut deeply. Watanabe injected more painkiller and continued working. Not even this additional anesthetic was enough, though: the boy's face was pale and he was sweating heavily.

After an hour of grimaces and gritted teeth, the operation was over. Watanabe had successfully separated the five digits of Noguchi's left hand. These were stubs of fingers, lacking the top two joints, but they moved independently. The palm of the hand was in bad shape. No skin remained there, and the underlying tissue was open to the air. Today it would be a simple matter to transplant skin from elsewhere on the patient's body, but this was not an option a century ago. Watanabe could do little more than slather unguent on the hand and wrap it in gauze. He also splinted the fingers to keep them from curling back toward the palm and wrist. The doctor was in fact making much of this up as he went along; his specialty was the digestive and other organs, not this kind of reconstructive surgery. All ended well, though, and Seisaku was taken off to a room in the clinic where he was put to bed with his hand heavily bandaged.

Akiyama could not contain his excitement at the operation's success. He ran the twenty-three kilometers of hilly road back to Okinajima to tell Shika the news. The sun set on him well before he reached the village, but he was young and buoyed up by the good news he was bringing. He ran on through the dark.

Seisaku's mother listened to his report, thanked him again and again, and made him wait while she disappeared into the house to emerge again with an armful of broiled fish on skewers to give to his family. With lantern in hand she accompanied him to his home, where she thanked his parents profusely for the friendship he had shown her boy. She was a poor woman, and she lived a hard life, but at times like this she shone just as brightly as the lantern that lit her way home to wait for her son.

The family's poverty had not ended, though, and medical treatment was not cheap. Seisaku's hospitalization fees amounted to one yen, twenty sen per day—no small amount in an era when the finest inns in Wakamatsu charged just twenty-five sen for a room. Add to this the costs of surgery and medicine, and the money that Seisaku's teachers and schoolmates collected would only last him around ten days at the Kaiyo Clinic, far less than the three weeks of hospital recuperation that Watanabe recommended. Even after the patient went home he had long weeks of outpatient treatment to look forward to, which would cost still more money as well as take time away from his schooling. In all he missed more than two months of classes, from mid-October to the end of December.

His treatment and recovery went well. At last the day came for his bandages to come off for good, and Seisaku took his first close look at his new hand. It was not a pretty sight. The severity of his burns and the long years his hand had remained untreated would always keep it from recovering fully. But he did have five separate fingers now, and—he discovered to his joy—he could spread them apart! Watanabe's explanations had led him to expect this but the actual sight of his own wiggling digits moved him to speechless happiness. He grabbed at objects in the clinic room, grasped them, lifted them up. . . The thumb had a greater range of motion than before, and his index and middle fingers were far more dexterous than he had hoped.

Nogichi found his new dexterity liberating. "They won't call me Tenbo again!" This was a miracle, a dream. For as long as he remembered, he had suffered, and now the marvels of medical science had put an end to that pain. Medicine! This word—the possibilities in this field of learning—now filled his mind.

■ ■ ■

"What if?" scenarios, while they may be entertaining, serve little purpose in the proper study of history. Too much depends on chance—the mysterious choices humans make, the unexpectedly harsh realities of life—to make any meaningful projections along alternate historical timelines. But it is tempting to think about the life an uninjured Noguchi would have lived. Without the pain of his charred hand to drive him in his studies, he would not have gone so far in his academic work; and Shika would not have sent a physically capable worker to the upper elementary school with the family in such a dire financial situation. Seisaku would have become the head of the Noguchi house, and then . . . what? Mayor of the village, perhaps. Had he followed his grandfather's lead and run off to the city to find work, his lack of learning would not have opened many doors. An uneducated man from a domain defeated in war would have no career in medicine—indeed, not much of a career at all.

Falling into the fire had been a key event in his life. By itself it would not have been enough to push Noguchi to greatness, though: it was not until Dr. Watanabe gave him five independent fingers that he truly opened his mind to the potential the world offered a young man of his talents. The world-renowned Dr. Noguchi would never have existed without these twin experiences—of his hand's destruction and its subsequent restoration.

SETTING OUT ON
THE ROAD TO MEDICINE

Noguchi had a new hand and a new life spread out before him. But soon after he came back from the city he received a shock: Sakae Kobayashi announced that he had been asked to leave Inawashiro Upper Elementary for another school located in between the town of Inawashiro and Okinajima. Chisato Elementary School was in the middle of nowhere—a district boasting little more than rice paddies—and Seisaku couldn't understand why his mentor was heading off there.

Seisaku shared his outrage with his classmates: "Are we supposed to stand for this? Can we let our school lose a teacher of Mr. Kobayashi's caliber? His kind doesn't come along every day. We've got to find a way to keep him in Inawashiro!"

"Noguchi is right," they responded. "There's no reason for our school to lose a teacher like Kobayashi to a place like Chisato."

Before long they had a movement on their hands. First they went to members of the Inawashiro town assembly; with their help they were soon filing petitions with the authorities to keep Kobayashi in their school. Under Noguchi's leadership the students made their demands firmly and passionately, but in an orderly, reasonable fashion.

Noguchi is often described as a silent man, due mainly to the complex he suffered as a result of his handicap. But he could be as passionate as any other young man at times like these. He didn't often choose to take a political stance on some issue, but when he did—as he did to keep Kobayashi at his school—he proved adept at the game, with a persuasive speaking style that benefited from the sheer energy with which it was delivered. He seemed to have something of a split personality, in fact: the talent he showed for coming up with schemes and expressing his feelings showed him to be quite the performer, not at all like his usual introverted self.

His performance had the desired effect. The student movement was successful: Kobayashi was told to stay at the Inawashiro school until Seisaku's class graduated. Luckily the students had not forced him to take a demotion; beginning the following September he was able to step into the position of principal and chief instructor at Chisato Elementary.

Seisaku's classmates had managed to keep this teacher at their side for the interim, but eventually the time came for them, too, to leave the school halls behind. Seisaku was ambivalent about his graduation—a diploma from the upper elementary would not get him a rewarding position. He had passed the prefectural examination that brought him a step closer to a job as a school instructor; becoming a full-fledged teacher, though, generally meant graduating from a normal school. This academic gap was not the only obstacle keeping Noguchi from a teaching career, either—his hand, as always, was a factor. Surgery had returned much of its use to him, but it remained a deformed thing he preferred not to expose to a room full of schoolboys.

One day his friend Akiyama stopped in to see him. He brought news of their classmates, telling him what everyone was doing after graduating. Akiyama himself, Noguchi learned, was preparing to continue his studies. Noguchi expressed his happiness at Akiyama's prospects, but inside he was seething: after earning higher marks than any of them throughout their years together in school, was he now going to fall behind them all? He saw four years of effort turning to nothing. This humiliation was hard to bear.

Again his thoughts turned to medicine. Becoming a doctor was his best option. Doctors relieved people of their suffering. A doctor had saved his own hand. The power to perform miracles like this was something worth pursuing for a lifetime. His desire to enter the field of medicine had awoken with the successful operation on his fingers; now that desire became firmer. Objectively speaking, this was a foolish ambition for him to cling to—his family's circumstances made it an unlikely one to realize—but he was willing to apply an unusually ambitious pressure to see it come about.

■ ■ ■

Noguchi's first step was to bury himself in reference books for some days to learn the requirements for becoming a doctor. It appeared that he had been born too late—up until the 1860s all one needed to do was to be hired on by a practicing physician. Once the apprentice went through his years of on-the-job training and earned his mentor's stamp of approval, he was free to hang out his own shingle and treat patients himself. But after the fall of the Tokugawa shogunate this apprentice system was rejected by the new Meiji government, which enacted a law requiring would-be doctors to hold a medical license. This was available to those who had graduated from the government-established medical schools or passed the state licensing examination; anyone practicing without a license was breaking the law.

This was a considerable stumbling block for Noguchi. He couldn't possibly pay the national school tuition, and he had no idea how to begin preparing for the licensing test. His future grew murky. What could he make of himself, if not a doctor?

Noguchi went to his teacher for advice. Kobayashi had been giving the same problem some thought himself, and he told his student the conclusion he had reached: "The way I see it, you have three choices. You can be a local official of some kind, you can be a teacher, or you can become a doctor. . ." At this Noguchi's head snapped up. Kobayashi saw the intensity with which the young man now looked at him and paused. He had urged Seisaku to enter his school, and he had helped him get to where he was today, but this next step was a more important one. It wouldn't do to lead his charge down the wrong path, Kobayashi thought, as he went on carefully: "Medicine, you may not know, is called the 'benevolent art.' It is . . ."

But Seisaku was not about to sit through a lecture; his mind was already made up. "Sir, I *want* to be a doctor! I'll do whatever it takes. I'm ready to work my head off for this."

"Medicine isn't something you just pick up on your own, Noguchi." The teacher told him to calm down and consider the situation. The ideal course of action was to study the material at a college, but this was also the most expensive course, and Kobayashi personally could not offer much financial assistance from his monthly salary of just eight yen. How, then, could Seisaku build the solid foundation of knowledge he would need to pass the state exam?

Kobayashi had thought about this as well. He advised Noguchi to seek a houseboy position under a doctor so he could do his research on the job. Medical knowledge was best learned in a medical setting, and the teacher even had a particular setting in mind. "Go to the Kaiyo Clinic and talk to Dr. Watanabe. He knows you, and you'll be able to ask him for a job. Any job, mind you—office boy, receptionist, anywhere he can use you. Be humble and sincere, but be sure he knows that you're eager for this work. See what he can do for you."

Seisaku thanked him for this advice and prepared to go to see Dr. Watanabe at once, feeling certain he was now on the right track. In fact, he ran the entire distance to the clinic. But, far from feeling confident in a place where an operation had restored his confidence, he shook with nervousness when he arrived. For all his intelligence he remained a shy boy from the countryside with little experience in the wider world, and when he thought now of the favor he had come to ask of Dr. Watanabe he was filled with anxiety: what if there was no work for him here? The doorkeeper was friendly as he showed him into the waiting room, but time passed very slowly as he waited for Watanabe to see him.

At last the doctor called Seisaku into his office, the same room where he had first examined his hand some months earlier. Watanabe sat in a low armchair looking over some patient charts. The boy bowed deeply to him, took a deep breath, and began by thanking the doctor for repairing his hand. He went on to talk about his hopes for the future, picking up courage as he went, and soon he was asking for work at the clinic.

Watanabe listened with an expressionless look on his face, nodding now and then at the boy's speech. Before long, though, he was chuckling at this barrage of words. "All right, Noguchi, all right. I don't have much need for another houseboy right now, but I'm sure I can find something for you to do. Come to the clinic whenever you're ready to begin."

The boy didn't have to mull over this offer for more than an instant. "You mean there's a place for me here? Thank you sir!" Even as he finished thanking the doctor, in his mind he was already working at the Kaiyo Clinic.

So it was that Noguchi first entered the medical field in the early summer of 1893. His mother celebrated this by making her sixteen-year-old son a new cotton kimono and a sash to go with it. Akiyama, too, greeted this news with pleasure, giving Seisaku a formal skirt to wear over his robe. The young man was now outfitted properly for work in the city. Nevertheless, he had never lived anywhere but in the tiny community of Okinajima. Wakamatsu was the fulcrum of the entire region, politically and culturally. The very language spoken by its residents called to mind the courtesies of the samurai class—nothing like the rough lingo of the villages in the hills surrounding the Aizu plain.

Seisaku came down from these hills and went to live in the city. He was young and bright, and at last he was making progress. The road to becoming a doctor was a long one, though, and there were few who thought he would see its end. Many ridiculed his move to Wakamatsu. "But how is a cripple like Seisaku going to be a doctor? It's like saying the sun'll come up in the west tomorrow!" These comments annoyed Seisaku's friend Daikichi when he heard them in the streets of the village, but even he had to admit there was a grain of truth to them. Even doctors had to use their hands in their work, and while Seisaku's hand was in much better shape following his operation, it wasn't completely healed. Common sense said that this young man would have a hard time of it.

Common sense can easily become commonly held prejudice, however. In later life Noguchi would rail against this sort of uninformed bias. "I'm perfectly happy to listen to people's comments when they know what they're talking about. But if there's one thing I can't stand it's the ones who go on and on as if they know a thing when they don't have the first idea about it!"

■ ■ ■

In the end these grumblings in the village meant nothing. Noguchi started work at the Kaiyo Clinic, finding four or five other young assistants living and working at the facility, with a young man named Hyosaku Hasenuma at their head. One of these assistants had even graduated from the Jikei Medical School in Tokyo (today the Jikei University School of Medicine). Some of these young men enjoyed considerable support from their families, bringing food and pocket money from home to ease their lives at the clinic. Noguchi, meanwhile, was depending entirely on his work here—and there was a lot of work to do. He served as a receptionist, he mopped the floors, and he stoked the fire to heat water. He ran errands for Dr. Watanabe around town and helped him with his tasks in the clinic. Since he was the youngest and newest assistant to join the staff, he also had to do chores for the other young men.

On top of all this work, he had to learn all the medical knowledge he could. The state licensing exam was administered in two stages, the first a written test covering medical knowledge and the second a practical exam that was open only to those who had passed the first. Solo study might give a student like Noguchi a chance at passing the first stage of the test, but the practical experience tested in the second stage could only be gained through work at a medical clinic or by attending a school like the Saisei Medical School, a private institution in Tokyo that offered classes to students with no university background. For a serious student, neither of these options left much time for leisure activities as well as studying. Hasenuma and the other assistants spent their evenings after work chatting and playing cards, but Noguchi made no move to join them. This led to cool relations between them and the newcomer; but solitude was something Noguchi wasn't unfamiliar with, and he wasn't particularly bothered by the gap between them. His studies had always been his escape.

When he had a goal in mind, Noguchi worked with dogged persistence until he achieved it. One Fukushima doctor today who has studied his life has this to say about his efforts: "There are plenty of people with the brains to succeed. But the ones who produce truly brilliant results with that intelligence are those who can also endure the hard work it takes. This combination doesn't appear very often in people who grew up in well-to-do homes."

Seisaku wrote in the back of one of his books: "Others may while away their hours, but not one minute will I waste." True to this credo, Noguchi allowed himself to sleep no more than three or four hours a day. He got his rest wherever and whenever he could—he was once found sleeping soundly under Dr. Watanabe's desk. No ordinary person can keep up this pace for long before the body breaks down, but Noguchi stuck to this schedule for much of his life. One scholar has turned to Chinese medicine for a theory explaining this capability: the burn on Noguchi's hand, he claims, may have affected his nervous system like a moxibustion treatment, relieving him of the need for sleep even for days at a time. This may or may not be true, but certainly the man had the vitality seen in many Tohoku natives. Combined with astonishing strength of will and a desire to do better than the able-bodied people around him, this characteristic is probably the simplest explanation for Noguchi's behavior.

For some time he remained the newest addition to the clinic staff, avoiding the company of those above him. His solitude came to an end, however, with the arrival of another young man with a farming background, Kiichiro Yoshida. He hailed from a large family living near Kitagata, a town some twenty kilometers from Wakamatsu that had been the site of one of Japan's earliest popular rights uprisings in November 1882. In many respects, meeting Yoshida, who was also small, energetic, and quick-witted, was like looking in a mirror for Noguchi. Unlike the other houseboys, he had not been sent by his family to the Kaiyo Clinic to get an education, but had run away from his cattle-tending duties to learn here. The two youngsters hit it off right away, and soon were spending all their free time together, studying.

Dr. Watanabe noticed this and decided to give them some space apart from his other helpers. The next thing Noguchi and Yoshida knew, they had left the crowded dormitory behind for a spacious room on the clinic's second floor. This thrilled the two teenagers. Free at last from the noise their companions made, they were now able to lose themselves in their reading for hours on end, rarely speaking to each other. Watanabe would wake up deep in the night to use the toilet and find his assistants sitting at their desk, poring over some medical tome. He was not the only one to note their diligence. People in the neighborhood noticed as well and talked about the lights that never went out upstairs at the Kaiyo Clinic. They talked about the boys so engrossed in their studies that they wouldn't snuff out the lamps when mosquitoes came swarming into the bright room, but instead set up a kind of tent with cloth hung over the table's edges, poking just their heads out and turning the pages with their mouths as they continued their reading.

■ ■ ■

This was a pivotal point in these young scholars' lives. The late teens are a time when the environment a person finds himself in can shape the rest of his life. Noguchi and Yoshida were lucky to spend this phase under Watanabe's roof. The clinic's shelves were loaded with row after row of Western medical texts that invited exploration. Permitted to take down any of the books he wanted to read, Noguchi was particularly attracted to these thick, challenging volumes. Dr. Watanabe normally had little time for the endless questions of the clinic's young assistants, but he was willing to explain the difficult English medical terms these two asked about.

His tutelage did not last long, though. Watanabe was an energetic, outgoing man still in his thirties. Tapped by a group of local citizens to run for public office, he took gladly to the political scene—indeed, he was a natural politician, a bright, well-connected man who counted among his friends people like Yukio Ozaki, who would eventually serve as mayor of Tokyo and the nation's education minister. Campaign activities came to take up a good deal of his attention.

Noguchi and Yoshida wasted no time in finding others to guide them. They peppered another physician who came to the clinic periodically with their questions. They also went to learn English from a graduate of Tohoku Gakuin who lived in the neighborhood. The latter was a demanding instructor, but these two students mastered the material quickly and before long had finished reading biographies of Thomas Carlyle and Lord Clive. Noguchi now moved on to a reading and conversation school run by a Christian missionary living in Kitakoji with his wife. This was a fairly advanced program attended by numerous students from Aizu Middle School—then, as now, known for its excellent academic record.

But German was the language of medicine in the nineteenth century and a requisite for anyone studying in the field in Japan. Fortunately Wakamatsu, being a major center of learning in the region, provided classes in this language, too, and Noguchi started taking special lessons from a teacher at Aizu Middle School who had earned an advanced degree from prestigious Tokyo Imperial University (and now earned a higher salary than the school principal).

Seisaku did not stop at German, though. He had heard about a Catholic church in Ninomachi, a neighborhood near the clinic, where three French missionaries worked, so in order to learn their language as well he began attending church there. (This landed him in trouble one day when a passerby caught him climbing over the wall to get into the church grounds; an early riser as always, he had arrived for his lesson before the gate opened.) At first there was only one other student there to study French, but the two of them were soon joined by a crowd of Aizu students and assistants from the Kaiyo Clinic. From this growing circle of acquaintances, Noguchi borrowed science books and notebooks.

In his impatience to get on, Noguchi next turned his attention to yet another field of study when he learned that Akiyama, the friend from his own village, was taking lessons in Chinese. To find the study materials he needed, though, he didn't even have to leave the clinic: one day Yoshida found stack after stack of books in Chinese in the clinic's storehouse. This was Dr. Watanabe's father's library, and it was filled with reference works on Chinese herbal medicine and anthologies of classical Chinese poetry.

The two students were delighted at their discovery.

Noguchi's studious nature did not go unnoticed and unrewarded. Watanabe relieved him of his receptionist's duties and brought him into the clinic's pharmacy, where he began to learn medicine on the job. The doctor even looked into the possibility of getting him into a top-flight high school in Sendai, the precursor to Tohoku University. This application was rejected, though. One book on Noguchi's life claims that this rejection was due to his physical handicap, but a more likely explanation is that the student had only graduated from an upper elementary school. Still, despite his having no middle-school diploma, academically speaking he was more than the equal of students at Aizu Middle School, among whom he now counted a number of close friends; indeed, more often than not, *he* was the one helping *them* with their studies.

Studying came naturally to Noguchi, and he was most efficient when he explored a subject on his own. His academic prowess even came to the attention of the Wakamatsu Medical Society. One of many learned groups in Aizu, this society sponsored periodic medical lectures, attended by doctors and medical students alike. Noguchi made a name for himself with the complex questions he asked at these gatherings. Some of his queries involved subjects so advanced that only Kogen Saito, the famed internist, and the ophthalmologist Seiichiro Unayama were able to answer them, leading Unayama—another Inawashiro native—to predict a great future for him and to compare him even with Toyotomi Hideyoshi, the great warrior who united Japan in the late sixteenth century

■ ■ ■

Fortune's wheels continued to turn in his favor. Noguchi was soon thrust along a new path in his career by an outbreak of relapsing fever in the region, an acute illness borne by mosquitoes, fleas, and lice. The fever itself is caused by a spirochete, a member of the phylum of bacteria that cause such diseases as syphilis and Weil's disease, or leptospirosis. Patients with relapsing fever suffer from chills and bouts of shaking accompanied by high fever; their temperature goes back to normal over the course of a week or so, after which the fever and shaking return.

This was the first time that the disease had been seen in Aizu. Dr. Watanabe was nonplussed for a while, but one day he decided to put a new tool to work: his 1200x magnification microscope, which had just arrived from Germany. This was a state-of-the-art instrument for that time, and it had cost an astounding 120 yen. Physicians who used equipment like this in their diagnosis were few and far between in the Japanese countryside, but Watanabe proceeded to take blood samples from his patients and examine them at high magnification.

This paid off almost right away. He spotted foreign bodies in the blood and excitedly called the clinic assistants to his side. The five young men crowded around the microscope as he told them to look at what he'd found. The microscopic world is not an easy one for the unpracticed eye to decipher, and each of them took some time to spot what the doctor was so excited about; but at last it was Seisaku's turn to peer through the lens.

At first he made out the blood cells in the slide, but then he too saw the spirochete—a long, spiral-shaped body topped with slender appendages. Noguchi gazed into the eyepiece at this creature no more than a micron long—a thousandth of a millimeter—with unexpected emotion. This tiny thing, invisible to the unaided eye, was the cause of disease! He knew this from books, of course, but looking at the bacterium threw his learning into a new light. There it was, moving under the lens of the microscope. He was now standing on the cusp of a new age of scientific exploration and confronting one of humanity's oldest nemeses. This experience shook Noguchi, an intelligent man at an impressionable age, to the core. The first time people experience something new they have little on which to base their perceptions of it, and they tend to fall back on instinct. Noguchi's response to this bacterium seems to have been almost instinctive: he knew then and there that this would be his life's work.

The image of the spirochete swam before his eyes as he spoke: "I'm going to be . . . a bacteriologist one day," he said to nobody in particular in a far-away tone of voice.

Always one to lose himself to the outside world when he had found something that interested him, Noguchi let a long time go by before one of the crowd—Hasenuma—urged him to give up the eyepiece. "Hurry up and give Yoshida a turn at the microscope," he said. Then, to bring Noguchi out of his reverie and back to earth: "And quit your daydreaming. With a hand like yours you can't even use the thing properly, can you?" A couple of others laughed at Noguchi's prediction, though Dr. Watanabe seemed to take it seriously. Poor Yoshida, however, got tired of waiting for his turn and glumly left the room, saying "It's all right, Nogu, I can see it some other time."

Noguchi gazed at the microorganism for a few more moments until the meaning of Hasenuma's comment sank in and he stood up from the equipment and followed Yoshida out. Yes, his hand still wasn't normal. He had forgotten about it for a time—indeed, in the clinic he no longer expected to hear people speak of his injury in this way—but the fact remained that it was not a perfect limb.

Later that evening he spoke to Yoshida about it. "Listen, about my hand... You know how a person who loses one sense can expect his others to grow stronger to make up for that loss? I believe the same thing about my fingers. What do you think?"

"Look, you don't have to pay any attention to what people say," Yoshida told him forcefully, but his voice faltered as he said it. Yes, perhaps Noguchi's other abilities had increased to make up for the handicap, but it was this very change that drew his friend away from other people and deeper into his own interests. . .

One day not long after this Noguchi went to Dr. Watanabe and asked if he could borrow a book: *Methods of Pathological Histology* by C. von Kahlden. He wanted to study the work and translate it into Japanese. This was perhaps not such a surprising task for a young man in Meiji Japan to take on. The nation was on the road to modernization, a path that called for resourcefulness in Noguchi's generation. Change was in the air. The first session of the Imperial Diet opened in 1890, and Watanabe was running for a seat in this new body. In 1891 the Tohoku Line was completed, connecting Tokyo with the northern reaches of Honshu; in 1894 the city of Fukushima saw its first electric street lamps. That same year, Japan went to war with China.

This was Japan's first war with another nation since the Mongol invasions in the thirteenth century. In due course, Watanabe was called up to serve as a medical officer in the First Field Hospital Unit, Second Army Division, which meant making arrangements for the clinic to continue operating during his absence. This obviously imposed a limit on the medical care it offered. There would accordingly not be enough work for all the assistants and students, and many of them were turned loose to seek positions elsewhere. Yoshida, for example, found a spot at the clinic run by Kogen Saito. Noguchi, however, was one of the few to remain at the Kaiyo Clinic, whose day-to-day operations

Watanabe asked him to take over. The doctor went so far as to tell the young man to keep his books while he was away, and he gathered his family and the clinic staff to inform them of this decision.

■ ■ ■

Watanabe did Noguchi an honor in tapping him for these tasks, but the appointment caused problems almost right away. Hasenuma was another assistant who was to stay on at the clinic, and he was far from happy with this new state of affairs. He had been with the clinic since it was run by Dr. Watanabe's father, and he had long been in charge of all the assistants and houseboys. Although he had a rather weak constitution Hasenuma was a cheerful person, and generally well liked. But now the cheer was nowhere to be seen as he argued with the doctor about his choice of Noguchi as clinic manager. His arguments fell on deaf ears, though: Watanabe trusted firmly in the younger man's abilities and character.

Once the doctor left for the front, Hasenuma and the others persisted in their dissatisfaction. "There's a certain way of doing things at the Kaiyo Clinic, and Noguchi doesn't know enough about that way," they muttered. "Are we going to let this place be managed by a little guy like that?"

The older members of the staff began opposing Noguchi in every decision he made, ignoring his orders. Yoshida was no longer there to offer a shoulder to lean on. Then even Dr. Watanabe's family became embroiled in this conflict. It was a sticky situation: in addition to his wife, Watanabe had a mistress whose housing he also provided. This was still an age when a man of means could enjoy a reputation as a good provider even if he had additional lovers living at his expense. Now that Watanabe was out of the way, open strife broke out between this mistress and the wife in the main house. Noguchi's allegiance was to Watanabe's wife during this time, and the mistress saw everything he did in a negative light. When the older assistants joined in and took her biased side, Noguchi found his position even more difficult to sustain.

He was just eighteen years old; he had been in the city for less than two years. He was far too young and inexperienced to face problems like the ones he was up against now. He had never been a patient person in the face of criticism, and the criticism he got from others in the clinic hit him hard. Before long he was entertaining thoughts of drastic measures: "There's no reason I need to stay here and put up with this. I can go to Tokyo and work as a rickshaw driver to put myself through school there. There are other ways for me to become a doctor," he told himself.

Noguchi, knowing he couldn't leave the clinic without getting permission to do so from the teacher who had helped him get there in the first place, wrote to Mr. Kobayashi. The reply was a disappointing one: Kobayashi told him to put up with the present problems, avoid disagreements with the others at the clinic, and get on with his job.

This answer did not sit well with the letter-sender. He wasn't even a relative of Dr. Watanabe; why did he have to be dragged into these family fights, and why should he put up with it without fighting back? He wrote again and again to Kobayashi—every day at first, and then twice a day—to tell him how tough things had become at the Kaiyo Clinic.

Kobayashi wrote a single stern reply to these impatient, whining letters. Noguchi, as young as he was, had been selected from among all the assistants to handle the clinic's affairs during the doctor's time in the army. He couldn't turn his back on this honor and fail to do the work entrusted to him—not for any reason. This was no ordinary time for the country. Japan was at war, and the Japanese had to do their part. Dr. Watanabe was aiding the nation as an army surgeon; he had willingly left his family behind and gone to war. Before going he had taken Noguchi into his confidence; Noguchi was now indeed part of his family, and it was his duty to serve that family until Japan emerged victorious in the war and the doctor could come home once again. Noguchi had ahead of him a long road, certain to be filled with tough challenges. If he couldn't endure the little problems that faced him now, how could he hope to tackle the greater problems he would encounter later in life? Finally, Kobayashi asked Noguchi: if he truly wanted to make something of his life, what better way was there to spend his youth than in tough training of this sort?

These were tough words for Noguchi to hear from his old teacher, but Kobayashi knew him well and had his best interests at heart. Traditionally, warrior families like Kobayashi's had raised their children to understand that some situations can't be changed, but must be accepted and endured. This warning from his mentor opened Noguchi's eyes. He had been so wrapped up in his resentment that he had forgotten the obligation he had to the doctor who had allowed him to join in his work. Reminded once again of this duty he promised himself that he would put up with whatever setbacks came his way, secure in the knowledge that he was doing the right thing for Dr. Watanabe.

It wasn't easy to maintain this focus, though. Each time he heard some new attack on him, he found it harder to maintain his composure. It may have been this that led him on April 7, 1895, to get baptized as a Christian. He was only the second Japanese to become a Christian at the local church. Before, he had attended services there mainly to get access to French lessons; but his baptism came long after he had started that, and appeared to mark a real spiritual change in him. Perhaps the treatment he suffered at the clinic in the doctor's absence drove him to seek comfort in faith. Yet it was a faith that seemed real enough. He began handing out cards inviting others to attend Sunday school, and when Christmas came around he pitched in to help with the church's preparations and joined in the singing of carols. Church membership was no longer just a way to learn a language, but something he actively took part in.

■ ■ ■

Directly across the street from the Kaiyo Clinic stood a miso and soy sauce wholesaler called Fukunishi. The family that ran this shop were patients at the clinic, and Noguchi had become friends with them. He would often head across the road in the afternoons to spend time with Zengoro, who was about eight years older than him. The two of them would chat and the younger man would borrow their newspaper. There were few homes in Aizu that took a paper. The clinic did receive the *Tokyo Kokumin Shimbun*, but Fukunishi subscribed to another newspaper, the *Yomiuri Shimbun*, which Noguchi preferred.

One day Noguchi was sitting in the front of the shop reading the paper when something caught his eye: a young woman, a student, walking down the lane. She wore purple *hakama* over her kimono, and her hair was done in the *momoware*, or "split peach," style, parted in the middle and bunched high on the back of her head. This fashionable hairstyle topped a face with plump cheeks and lively eyes. There was a sense of dignity about this girl as she strode along, her face cast slightly downward. The young man was intrigued. He set the newspaper aside and stood up from his stool, gaping after her as she disappeared down the road.

When he finally returned to reading the news he found himself strangely flustered. This was the first time he had felt like this. Plenty of young female students had walked down this road before. Many of them even came to the clinic on some errand. But this chance encounter seemed somehow propitious to Noguchi, particularly when he was having such a hard time at the clinic.

He was not a total stranger to the idea of a lasting relationship with a woman. In Okinajima there had been several families willing to send their daughters to marry this bright young man with prospects as a future doctor, perhaps in the capital eventually. The parents had talked about arranging a marriage for him on a number of occasions. But these talks had held no interest for him, no matter how well-to-do the girls' families had been.

From that day forward Noguchi could be found each evening in front of Fukunishi, newspaper in hand, waiting for the student to pass by again. But the street's traffic brought only a parade of other girls, never the one he hoped to see. Before long summer crept into autumn, and after he finished his duties at the clinic there was little daylight left to look for her.

One day, though, Noguchi spotted Dr. Watanabe's daughter Natsuko sending off a friend who had come to visit her at the clinic. It was her! He hadn't been able to get this girl out of his mind and had looked for her everywhere; and now she had appeared under the very roof where he lived! He stared after her, taking in every little movement she made. He was in no shape to go up and greet her; he just stared, noticing how on closer inspection she seemed only more attractive, with the unspoiled looks of late adolescence.

After this encounter there was another period of some months when he didn't see her at all. Winter came. On Christmas Eve Noguchi was singing hymns in the church. Natsuko was there, along with a number of other young men and women from all over town. The voices raised in song and the music from the pipe organ made for a poignant atmosphere. As he sang, Noguchi sensed someone looking at him from the side. Stealing a glance that way, he almost cried out right there in the pews. It was her! She was sitting in the dark toward the edge of the hall, looking in his direction. He doubted his eyes at first—could it really be this girl he'd been thinking about for all these months?—but the more he looked the more certain he was.

Seisaku knew, luckily, that Natsuko was acquainted with this mystery student. On the way home from church he fell in with Watanabe's daughter and asked her with all the nonchalance he could muster about her friend. He tried hard to phrase his questions in roundabout ways so Natsuko wouldn't suspect anything, but she was quite direct in her replies. The girl's name was Yoneko Yamauchi. She was a student at Aizu Girls' School, and she was fifteen years old. She lived with her mother in the Ninomachi neighborhood of Wakamatsu, studying for a career that she hoped would return to her family the prestige it had once known.

The girls' school was only a few hundred meters south of the Kaiyo Clinic, not far from the church grounds. (The layout of this section of town remains unchanged to this day, although none of the original buildings have survived.) Considering the closeness of the church to her school, it is hardly surprising that Noguchi saw her there that night.

The Yamauchis were another family from the samurai caste. Yoneko's father had graduated from the Saisei Medical School in Tokyo and gone on to help establish the prestigious Juntendo Hospital, where he had worked for a time before his premature death cut his career there short. Yoneko's mother Chiyo relied entirely on her daughter to rebuild the family name after that. This explained the friendship between Yoneko and Natsuko—two daughters of doctors who shared pride in their families' accomplishments. The goal this girl had set herself was hard enough for a man to attain, much less a woman in the Meiji era.

Seisaku was impressed. He felt close to her: the two of them both faced difficult circumstances as they aimed for a career in medicine. As he walked on through the dark December night his thoughts went back again to the church. Why had she been looking at him? Did she know of him, of his own story? There was no way he could ask Natsuko this.

On returning to the clinic Noguchi tried to lose himself in his work. He began doing some translation, but he couldn't concentrate for long . . . her image kept returning to haunt him. As was the case throughout his life, once Noguchi became fixated on something, he couldn't easily be turned aside from it. He began writing a letter to Yoneko.

The letter that made its way to her was a bewildering one to receive. The return address on the envelope read "Machiko," the name of one of Yoneko's close friends, but the contents weren't anything that Machiko would have written. It began: "Please do not be startled at this intrusion. It is indeed rude of me to send a sudden letter in this way, but nobody could contend that the sender is anything but sincere. . ." The handwriting was elegant, but this was a strange salutation for a letter. It was certainly not the kind of note to come from Machiko, with English phrases scattered throughout the text. The letter remained impenetrable to Yoneko no matter how many times she reread it. It was signed with just a pair of initials: S.N. Who had written this thing to her?

At a loss, Yoneko took the letter to her mother. Chiyo was naturally upset. In those days it was completely improper for young men and women to date one another without supervision, or even to communicate through letters like this. Love affairs were considered to be hazardous, and they were stamped out whenever possible by parents looking out for the welfare of their children. This letter was a threat to Chiyo's daughter, and an unsigned one at that—a sure sign that the writer knew it was wrong to send such a thing. It was all too much for the mother to handle by herself. Chiyo took the letter to Yoneko's school and showed it to one of her teachers.

The Aizu Girls' School was the center of female education in the Waka-matsu area. Its primary aims were to produce good wives and wise mothers. This mysterious letter was a threat to these goals. Yamauchi's teacher took the offending note to the principal and explained how his student had received it. There was little the school could do to discover who had written to Yoneko, however; instead it fell back on a mainstay of girls' education in those days—warning the student against getting into a compromising situation. The teenager was called to the principal's office to receive a lecture: "The only reason you got a letter like this in the first place is because you must have invited it, spending time in places frequented by young men." She could do nothing but hang her head in shame.

While all this drama was taking place, Noguchi was hoping anxiously for a reply to his letter. He had seen her looking at him in the church; he was sure his initials would be enough for her to identify him. But his waiting brought no response. Would he hear from her soon? Was he being ignored? Emotions washed through him as he tried to plan his next move. Typically, once he fixed his mind on a goal it became the only thought in his mind, and it was no different with Yoneko; the idea that she had rejected his overture was a painful one to entertain. He was not just looking for a young woman to amuse him for a while. He wrote a second letter to make this absolutely clear, and decided to give it to her directly after his first attempt to send this message via the post fell through. This was quite a challenge, though: wherever he thought of making contact there were always other people around, and she no longer appeared in the church, where he might have caught her alone. Eventually he found out where she lived. Noguchi waited for her outside the house, but soon grew nervous, tossed his letter through the latticed window, and ran back to the clinic.

When she found the missive on the floor Yoneko took it to her mother without even opening it. Chiyo then took it straight to the school. Noguchi was disappointed when this message also failed to bring a response from the girl, but in this as in all matters he was not the kind of person to walk away from a challenge. The higher the wall, the more determined he was to climb it. He wrote still another letter—this time entirely in English, for fear that Yoneko's mother would learn his identity if a note in Japanese fell into her hands. This letter also went through the window . . . and then another.

The young man was of course unaware of the response his correspondence was getting inside the house. Chiyo was frantic with worry by this point. She went with Yoneko to school, where a teacher translated the notes. The writer was inviting her daughter to meet him at church; he also had hopes of working in medicine, and they knew his initials. These were enough clues to track down the culprit.

The girls' school had a standard response for situations like this. After investigating Noguchi's background and deliberating on the best way to prevent him from approaching Yoneko again, the principal wrote to his parish priest, explaining what had taken place and demanding that he lecture the boy on the error of his ways. A Catholic priest could be expected to take these matters seriously. Immediately a shocked Noguchi was called to the church to explain himself. He knew he was innocent—this was a misunderstanding, a misreading of the situation! But the priest's warning was stern: "I thought you were a respectable young man, so this all comes as quite a surprise. You will put an end to your letter-writing at once. You knew as well as anyone that there are certain procedures to be followed when you are serious about pursuing marriage!" He went on like this for some time before insisting that Noguchi answer him. The boy apologized and promised to reflect on what he'd done.

Over the years people have pinpointed various reasons for this setback to Noguchi's love life. His appearance was too unappealing, they say, for him to be viewed as a real candidate for Yoneko's hand; his clothes too shabby, his family too low in society. These details are all incidental, though, to the main issue: this was simply not an age when young men and women in rural Japan were free to select their own partners.

So Noguchi abandoned his attempts to woo her, though he couldn't just shut off his feelings for her, and she remained in his mind for a long time afterwards.

■ ■ ■

In the spring of 1895 the Sino-Japanese War drew to a close, and Watanabe returned to Aizu. Noguchi gave him a full report on how the clinic had done in his absence, presenting the doctor with a detailed ledger, written in English, of the business accounts for the previous year. Watanabe examined the entries, which listed everything from payments for rice and other produce right down to notebooks and the very last stamp. His trust in this young man had been well placed. Watanabe thanked him for his thorough, faithful service.

It had been a difficult nine months, but at last Noguchi was done with his caretaking duties. He felt almost lost in his newfound free time after all the hard work. He also felt restless. Nearly nineteen years old, he had spent three years at the Kaiyo Clinic—and three years felt like enough. It was time to move on. But where could he go?

Luck smiled on him once again. Into his life now came Morinosuke Chiwaki, a man who would be his mentor and supporter in the years to come. Many great figures in history seem to meet the right people at the right times. It is hard to find one for whom this is truer than Noguchi.

A friend of Dr. Watanabe, Chiwaki was a freshly minted dentist who had just passed his licensing examination in April and started working at the Takayama College of Dentistry in Tokyo. Dr. Watanabe had invited him to spend his summer vacation in Wakamatsu. At the time the city had no trained dentist resident there. When Chiwaki learned this, he took an extra room in an inn just behind the Kaiyo Clinic, where he opened a temporary dental office. This proved popular. People lined up from early in the morning to be treated by this sharp young dentist educated in the capital.

After a long day with his crowd of patients, Chiwaki would usually stroll over to Watanabe's clinic to chat with the doctor late into the evening. The two men were linked in their opposition to traditional medicine and in recognizing the importance of bringing Japanese medical science into the modern age. Chiwaki was particularly passionate on the subject. While he was there, however, he couldn't help noticing the young man reading quietly in the same room, unperturbed by the spirited conversation.

Noguchi got Chiwaki's full attention when the dentist asked him one evening what he was studying so single-mindedly. This poor-looking assistant in a medical clinic stuck away in a remote corner of the country was reading a work on pathology so advanced it would likely give trouble to serious medical students in Tokyo—and he was reading it in the original French!

"Where have you picked up the language skills to read a book like this?" he asked, unable to hide his curiosity.

Noguchi raised his eyes from the book and looked for the first time at Chiwaki, this dentist just six years his senior who would play such an important role in his life. "I go from time to time to learn from the priest at the Catholic church. I also get lessons from a teacher at the middle school, sir."

"That's hardly enough to let you read a book like that, though. . . ," Chiwaki muttered wonderingly, then left him to his studies.

When the dentist asked his host about the assistant later that evening, Watanabe laughed and gave an explanation that amazed him: "Ah, Noguchi, he's a real polyglot. He's already learned English, German, and French. Every once in a while he'll ask me a language question, but he picked up most of it on his own."

Morinosuke Chiwaki had shown no shortage of talent and ambition in his own life. He was a quintessential Meiji man, an energetic intellectual with a drive to succeed and achieve new things. He had been born in an inn in the town of Abiko, Chiba, and was raised by his father after his mother died while he was still quite young. Abandoning his family name, Kato, for the surname Chiwaki, he had headed to Tokyo to study at two institutions that would later become Meiji Gakuin and Keio University. After graduation he entered the world of newspaper journalism, but he only lasted a year writing for the *Tokyo Shinpo* before moving to Niigata to teach English. It was from this position that he had made the even bigger jump to medical training and dentistry.

Noguchi warmed quickly to this man. The questions he asked the dentist were often penetrating ones that took all of Chiwaki's advanced training to answer. The latter—a fair-skinned young man with a narrow face below a smooth, intelligent forehead—came to feel he had discovered a diamond in the rough in Noguchi, the kind of mind someone from the capital never expected to find in a small Fukushima clinic. Eventually Noguchi spoke to Chiwaki of his own desire to become a doctor. Like Sakae Kobayashi, another passionate young educator, Chiwaki found himself moved and inspired by the man's circumstances and his obvious talent. He, too, wanted to give him a helping hand.

"When you come to Tokyo, be sure to come and see me at the Takayama school," he urged Noguchi. "I'd like to do what I can to help."

Noguchi thanked him for the invitation. Who can say how important these words were in the course of his life? Without the chance to go to the capital and the assistance he would receive there from this dentist, the situation would certainly have been very different for a country boy with no knowledge of Tokyo, in an age without scholarship systems for deserving students. He might have found some way to get a medical license, but without connections in the field he wouldn't have gone far in his career—certainly not far enough to gain international recognition. Seen in this light, Chiwaki was a key figure in his development, and his friendly words at their meeting in 1895 marked a felicitous start to their relationship.

Noguchi was anxious to hear what his teacher, Kobayashi, had to say about the dentist's offer. His meeting with Chiwaki had touched off new feelings in him—a confidence that he was ready to pass the first stage of his licensing exam and a desire to go to Tokyo to test himself in the schools there. Kobayashi was a careful man who would take his future seriously—he might even tell him it was too early to think of going to the capital—but the young man had to know his opinion. He therefore wrote a letter to him.

Noguchi did not have to wait long for a response, and he found it a surprising one. Kobayashi praised him for staying at his post during Dr. Watanabe's absence and for plugging on with the job even as he continued his studies. He then urged him to talk to Watanabe to get his permission to go to Tokyo and find the success he deserved there.

Heartened by this message, Noguchi immediately went to speak to Dr. Watanabe. The doctor also welcomed his plan. "You won't learn much more by hanging around the clinic. It's time you went to Tokyo and learned all you can there. First, of course, you'll need to get past the preliminary stage of the test, but I can give you some money—just a bit—to get you that far."

Dr. Watanabe was as good as his word, and proceeded to coach him not only on what to expect in the licensing test but on how to deal with the various problems of living in the big city. The doctor also wrote a letter for Noguchi to deliver to Chiwaki. Finally, he presented him with ten yen to cover his traveling expenses. A deeply moved Seisaku thanked him again and again. That same day he wrote his application for the first-stage exam and mailed it off.

Soon afterwards he spoke to the doctor's daughter, Natsuko, who had some exciting news for him. Yoneko was also heading to Tokyo! She planned to get a job as a nurse initially and continue studying to become a physician herself. "Isn't she amazing?" Natsuko enthused. "I could never do something as tough as that."

But Natsuko's news aroused an oddly competitive reaction in Noguchi. So Yoneko was also going to the capital to become a doctor . . . he couldn't let her reach that goal before him! With this thought as the final goad he began preparing to leave Fukushima.

■ ■ ■

Before heading south, Noguchi had to return home to Okinajima. As he packed his belongings and made ready to leave the Kaiyo Clinic, Dr. Watanabe's wife and Natsuko grew somewhat emotional at the prospect of his going. But the young man made his goodbyes short ones here; there was another place he wanted to go on his way out of the city. The road took him past the Yamauchi home.

He was hoping to speak to Yoneko and let her know that he too was off to Tokyo, but the girl was out shopping in preparation for her own move, and it was her worried-looking mother who came out to see what he had to say for himself. She must have found this a very strange visit. Noguchi remained convinced that his feelings for Yoneko had been honorable, and that nobody could possibly think him a threat to her well-being; so, bolstered by this self-induced confidence, he chatted away blithely about his personal plans. The mother, presumably, found it awkward to respond to this odd young man, who eventually said goodbye, leaving her—and Wakamatsu—behind.

Back in the shadow of Mt. Bandai, he found his entire family waiting for him. His mother Shika was there with his younger brother, Seizo. Inu, his sister, was back with her husband Zengo and their son, Sakae. Even Noguchi's father was back in the village during a break from his work in the mountains. Sayosuke was sober at the time—an unusual state of affairs—and he solemnly congratulated his son on his service at the clinic in town. The whole family celebrated the boy's first trip back home since he had gone to Wakamatsu. The village mayor came out to see him, greeted him warmly, and wished him the best of luck. His old friend Daikichi pressed three yen into his hand to help send him on his way, although business was hardly going well at Matsushimaya. And other villagers came out of their houses to hand the young man a few coins, too.

This treatment was very different from the way they used to behave. The reason for the villagers' new friendliness was quite clear to Noguchi, though: he was off to earn his fortune, and once he'd become a doctor and returned home he would be an important man to know. These people were trying to get in his good books now in order to benefit from his acquaintance later.

One of his last acts before leaving was to take a small knife and carve a message into a pillar of the family home's main room: *I will not set foot in this place again until I have achieved all my goals.* This carving is still there, an attraction for the tourists who come to visit the house in which Noguchi was born. To head out into the wider world and achieve lofty aims was a common aspiration among the Japanese of that age, and a young person leaving his rural home to seek his fortune in the city carried with him the burden of his village's expectations. This carved pillar in a Fukushima farmhouse encapsulates perfectly those dreams and duties of the children of peasants in Meiji Japan.

The next day Noguchi went with his mother to the Kobayashi home. His teacher welcomed him with great cheer and sent him off with even greater generosity. Kobayashi's wife prepared a feast for the boy to enjoy on his last day in his hometown, and the teacher presented his former student with ten yen—almost all of his salary for an entire month. He also gave him a last dose of sound advice: "When you falter in your studies, Seisaku, remember your mother and all her hard work in Okinajima." With these words he sent him out the door.

It was 1896; Seisaku was almost twenty years old. There was already an autumn chill in the air of the Bandai highlands on the day he left this poor mountain village behind. There was no train station nearby—the Ban'etsusai Line would not be completed for almost another twenty years. It was more than thirty hilly kilometers to Motomiya, the nearest station on the Tohoku Line that led to the capital. Noguchi rose before dawn and tied his straw sandals firmly to his feet, before saying farewell to his family and friends who saw him off in front of his house. Kobayashi and his mother accompanied him for part of the way. He looked up at the mountain sparkling in the cool morning air. Even as thoughts of Tokyo filled his mind, he took in the view of lakes and hills as though it was his last. His mother stayed at his side as he passed through the next village on the road . . . telling him she would walk with him just to the next town, and then just halfway to the next. Seisaku picked up his pace and left her behind; he couldn't let her walk all day to the station with him.

She watched her son grow smaller on the path ahead of her, stopped, and called out to him one last time. "Be careful! Be sure to write to us and let us know once you get settled!"

"I will, Mother. Take care of yourself too."

He nodded to her and continued on his way. She stood in the road looking after him for a long time, perhaps waiting for him to turn around and wave to her one last time. He didn't do so. She waited until he disappeared over the next hill, and then turned to walk back to Okinajima.

TO TOKYO

When Noguchi stepped off the train in Ueno—Tokyo's terminal station for lines coming from the north—there was nobody there to greet him. He carried a single wrapping cloth containing just a change of clothes and the books he needed to prepare for his medical exam. Taking this first step into the capital was something he had dreamed about, and here he was at last—in a bustling city where the streets were filled with rickshaw traffic and people in kimono. Today visitors to Tokyo from rural Japan don't find the city very different from their own hometowns, but in the late nineteenth century it was like stepping out of the preindustrial past into a rapidly modernizing world. Bewildered by the crowds and noise, Noguchi had trouble finding his way around.

He did manage to make it to the Shitaya district not far from Ueno, however. Then, after securing a place in a cheap lodging house next to a quiet pond, he got down to business. The medical licensing examination was only offered in nine places around the country at that time. The first stage of this exam was a written test covering basic subjects from physics and chemistry to physiology and anatomy. Judging from the practice questions in the textbooks he was studying, Noguchi felt he had a good chance of passing. He had another advantage in that the three years he had spent working at the Kaiyo Clinic satisfied the requirement of a year and a half of medical training for each stage of the exam.

In October he took the first test, passing it on his first attempt. This was a major step on the way to becoming a doctor and solid proof of his talent in this field; people were generally expected to take about three years to pass this stage, and fully seven to get through the second. But the second-stage examination, and the time it took to prepare for it, involved more of a challenge than merely its difficulty. Noguchi was running out of money.

He had left home with about forty yen, and at this point he was down to about half of that, with nothing much left over after he paid his rent. Dr. Watanabe had promised to send ten yen a month, but Noguchi had yet to hear from him. (The doctor had, in fact, lost control of his clinic's finances after he broke off relations with his mistress and was forced to pay a considerable settlement to her. He was later able to send money to Noguchi only once while he was in Tokyo.) Luckily the medical trainee proved good at making friends in the capital, and he knew a few people in town who hailed from his own village. But despite having this group of acquaintances willing to give him a place to sleep, he ran out of cash in November, a considerable time before he could hope to take the next test.

Noguchi found himself in the nation's capital penniless and unsure what to do. This would have been a desperate situation for anyone, and was especially so for a young man from the countryside overwhelmed by the big city. There were guidebooks available, but they tended to be out of date and inaccurate. Though sure-footed in his studies, Noguchi was in over his head in Tokyo—even the limited part of the city that he actually got to know himself.

■ ■ ■

In the late nineteenth century forty yen was not a small amount of money, and it would require fairly extravagant spending habits—well beyond the realm of train tickets and lodging costs—to get through it all in just two months. And Noguchi's excessive spending didn't come to an end with this first sum, either; he continued to impose on a string of people from his hometown and new acquaintances throughout his time in Tokyo. While this aspect of his life never received much attention in biographies written in the past, more recent works on Noguchi have begun to focus on his spending habits, although observers tend to treat the subject in varying ways. Some point out that his tendency to rely on others for his personal needs developed early on, when as a young pupil he received free school supplies and other forms of aid. Others argue that a childhood and adolescence spent in the straits of poverty had given Noguchi a single-mindedness that carried over even to the way he overspent. Some cast Noguchi in a negative light, others seek to defend him. Both approaches, however, fail to get below the surface of his personality.

The image of the country bumpkin from northern Honshu who can't hold onto his money is a common one in popular ballads and folk songs of the past. This is not an entirely fictional image: there have, in fact, been many who fit the stereotype. Sayosuke, Noguchi's father, drank away any money he earned himself, and was apt to do the same with any cash his wife made when he ran out of funds. And Sayosuke's father before him had been the same way.

This is not to say that Noguchi's ancestral traits were all negative. The Kobiyama family was known in the area as "the scholars' clan" for the phenomenal powers of memory they showed. One person from this family who got a job dealing with family registers at the local government office is said to have memorized the personal details of every member of all the families in the village. This mental acuity, luckily, seems to have been a quality Noguchi shared with his ancestors.

A person cast in this northern Honshu mold tends to grasp immediately at things he wants, with little thought for the consequences. This attitude affects the way he spends his time—he will sleep late, drink from before noon, and spend hours in the bath at inappropriate times of the day. Money coming into his possession is soon gone and, with empty pockets, he will seek loans from his friends rather than rein in his spending. But despite all this, Sayosuke and others like him remained likable figures. Noguchi, too, must have drawn people to him in this way, or he would not have profited from their generosity. In part, they may have felt sympathetic toward him because of his injured hand, but he doesn't seem to have taken advantage of this. He was himself a generous friend to those he knew when he came into some wealth later on. Essentially, his behavior at this time, taken together with the way he acted later in his life, suggests a man with little conventional regard for money or possessions. This trait can lead to the ruin of an average person, but in Noguchi it comes across rather as a sign of character.

■ ■ ■

Though at first unwilling to approach Dr. Chiwaki in case he appeared to be desperate, on November 3 Noguchi made his way to the Takayama College of Dentistry in the Mita district of Tokyo. Kisai Takayama had established this, Japan's oldest dental school, in 1890. The school occupied the former Spanish embassy, a two-story wooden structure in a quiet neighborhood that included various cemeteries and temples. Noguchi cut a suspicious-looking figure when he arrived there, with his long hair and unwashed face and the impoverished air of someone from the back country. But he was well-spoken, and he did have a letter of introduction. The gatekeeper showed him in just in time to meet Chiwaki, who was about to head out on an errand. "Ah, it's young Noguchi! How good to see you again!" the dentist exclaimed.

Noguchi found this friendly greeting comforting after the hardships he'd experienced so far in Tokyo. He told the older man of his success in the examination and related how he had been spending his time in the city. Chiwaki was pleased with this news, but pointed out that the second stage of the test would be a far bigger obstacle to overcome.

It was then that Noguchi made his request: "That's actually why I came to see you. I need some income to live on while I study. Can you give me a job as the school rickshaw driver?"

"What? Rickshaw work? You won't last long doing that!"

"But I need some sort of part-time job until I pass that second test."

"Hold on, then," replied Chiwaki. "I'll talk to Dr. Takayama and see if I can get you a position here at the school."

Takayama had graduated from the precursor of Keio University before going to the United States, where he earned his dentist's license. After returning home he got a Japanese license to practice medicine and set to work, eventually founding his own school in addition to a clinic. The academic bent of this pioneer of Japanese dentistry made him a coolly rational man, though, quite different from Chiwaki. He asked whether there was a pressing need for a school secretary right then, and when Chiwaki admitted there wasn't one, his reply was straightforward: "Well, hire him later when there is such a need. Now, about that other matter we discussed earlier . . ."

Chiwaki was an extrovert, energetic to the point of excess. He would later get involved in politics in an effort to gain more respect for the dental profession in Japan, and became famous for punching a National Diet member in the head after the politician sneered at his choice of work. (This made him a perfect match for Noguchi, who was also idealistic and had little interest in social decorum. These two would go on to form a formidable team in later years.) Now, though, Chiwaki went beyond simple kindness, showing an almost parental desire to take care of the young man from the north. "I can't just send him away like this," he muttered as he thought about what to do.

Chiwaki then came up with the idea of approaching the elderly couple who ran the school dormitory and asking them for help. Fortunately, they agreed to take on the young man for a time, and Noguchi began work there right away. He had no bedding of his own, so he commandeered a futon left behind by a student who had gone home due to illness, and took up residence in the dorm. He must have felt as though he'd been spirited into this shelter in secret, since he kept quiet and out of the way at first. He noticed, though, that the custodial staff members were getting on in years and tended to require considerable time off. Seeing a gap to fill, Noguchi filled it. He began by ringing the bell at the dormitory entrance to mark the hours, and gradually expanded his duties, making himself an indispensable presence in the building, available for everything from cleaning the toilets to polishing the lamps. He would later recall that he found this last task particularly irksome. The lamp chimneys would slip out of his grasp when he steadied them with his left hand, and the only other option—clasping the lamp between his feet as he wiped away the soot—put someone with a surprisingly strong sense of style in a distinctly unstylish position.

■ ■ ■

One of Noguchi's weaker subjects was German, and when he heard of a woman in the neighborhood who taught the language he told Chiwaki of his desire to learn from her. But the one-yen monthly fee wasn't something the dentist could easily come up with when his own salary each month only amounted to four times that. At the risk of undermining his position further in the clinic by making excessive demands, he went to discuss the matter with Dr. Takayama again. The school head, recognizing that Chiwaki's pay was relatively low compared with others working at the college, promptly raised his salary on the spot, and so Chiwaki started giving Noguchi two yen out of the seven he now earned.

Noguchi did not let this windfall go to waste. As an indication of his application, it is said that he spent enough time drilling each new word of German into his memory to walk fully three times around Shinobazu Pond near Ueno, one of his favorite spots to study in. He became so engrossed in his reading, in fact, that he would sometimes forget to sound the school bell, leaving students and instructors stranded in their classrooms well beyond their allotted times and causing quite a stir among the school staff.

But this sort of behavior was only to be expected of Noguchi, who shared with Chiwaki a tendency to keep his eye on some grand goal rather than worry over little things. One evening Hideji Okuda, a friend from his old hometown who was studying political economics at Keio, paid him a visit. Familiarity led Noguchi to ask a major favor of this friend: he needed a copy of a rare and expensive German medical text. Medicine was not Okuda's field, though, and he hadn't the money to buy the book anyway, but Noguchi's charisma—an ability to bring people around to his point of view, as well as an obvious passion for learning—appears to have prompted Okuda to do something to help. He then remembered that an acquaintance of his had the book in question, one Yutaka Terauchi, and he promised Noguchi to borrow it from him.

Noguchi leapt at the chance. "Let's go and get it now! I'll come along."

"What are you talking about? It's already ten at night, and he lives all the way over in Koishikawa."

But distance wasn't considered a problem. "That's in Tokyo, right? Well, we're in Tokyo, too. I need to get hold of it as soon as possible—tonight, in fact. Let's go!"

Japan's capital at that time was not crisscrossed by subway lines as it is today, and needless to say these two students couldn't afford a rickshaw. There was nothing for it but to walk the many miles from Tamachi up to Hongo. They arrived at Terauchi's place very late that night. A native of Fukushima in the north, Terauchi was in the capital to study medicine at Tokyo Imperial University. He would later become a respected professor at Keio, but now he was just a bleary-eyed student confronted by two young men who had walked across the city to pound on the door of the place he lived in and make the gatekeeper show them to his room.

Terauchi listened as Okuda introduced Noguchi, who was already crouched in front of the bookcase looking at the selection of reading matter.

"I can't let that go!" Terauchi said as Noguchi lifted the book he wanted off the shelf. "I'm using it for a class now. What does he need it for anyway?"

"He's studying for his second-stage medical exam. Come on, let him have it."

"But what am I supposed to do without it?"

"You've got the money to buy as many books like this as you want! Come on, Noguchi, it's late. Let's get going." And with that, their scavenging over, the two ran out into the night.

Remorse soon set in, though. "Look, Noguchi, we really owe Terauchi for this. . . Whatever you do, for his sake, make sure you ace that test."

"I certainly will. . . To make it up to him, I'll do whatever it takes to pass."

■ ■ ■

Noguchi flung himself into his studies. As a result, however, he grew even more forgetful of his dormitory duties: his bell-ringing and other routines fell by the wayside, and an angry group of students would storm down the college hallways looking for their houseboy. More often than not they would find him in the library. He was not hiding from anyone: there he was, in plain view, with his feet propped up on a stack of books, reading. This came to be expected behavior from this extraordinarily focused, single-minded man.

But not all his behavior was expected. Living in Tokyo did change him considerably. He took to going out on the town and staying out late. He took note of the urban fashions of the day and began wearing his kimono in the casual style of the capital, without the formal *hakama* skirt normally worn with it. He even began to walk like a born-and-bred Tokyoite. This sense of style was no sign of decadence, though; he remained as studious as ever. He might spend half his waking hours slouching around the city, but the other half saw him working harder than anyone else. Noguchi was a studious dissipate—a difficult person to pigeonhole.

It is natural for any young person to look for some sort of stimulation in his life, and the energy that goes with youth is often enough to push them off the straight and narrow. But it is difficult to fit Noguchi into this mold: rather than jumping straight from a rural existence into the pleasures Tokyo had to offer, he had found the capital not quite the splendid place he'd expected. He tended to brood about the disappointing aspects of his present circumstances—the mocking he endured from the dental college students, the menial tasks he had to perform to earn his pay. He began to consider ways to extract himself from this situation.

Noguchi again went to Chiwaki for help. He had to absorb a considerable amount of material for his second exam: surgery, internal medicine, pharmacology, optometry, and obstetrics, not to mention the clinical trials one had to complete. He would never be able to do this on his own—he needed to enroll in a school program. Tokyo offered a perfect one for him: the Saisei Medical School. A doctor famed for his powerful personality and unkempt appearance had established this institution out of a desire to bring learning to Japan's less fortunate citizens. Most of its instructors were Tokyo University lecturers earning a little money on the side. Their ordinary teaching schedules left only odd hours for their classes at this school, which were held at the crack of dawn or late in the afternoon.

■ ■ ■

Noguchi couldn't hope to make it to these classes on time, but the combination of the rent needed to live near the school and his tuition brought the total money required to fifteen yen per month—well beyond his mentor's means even after his recent raise. Chiwaki knew Noguchi needed assistance, yet he couldn't see any alternative but to ask the young man to wait for some new development.

Noguchi had prepared for this: "I've thought of a way to take care of things."

"Well, that's good news. What's your plan?"

Noguchi explained his idea. The Takayama school had a medical clinic attached to it where Chiwaki saw patients in addition to doing his teaching. Dr. Takayama was unhappy with this setup; the clinic was bleeding money. Noguchi had looked at the figures, however, and was sure it could be made more profitable. He suggested that Chiwaki approach Dr. Takayama and offer to take over the clinic's management.

This was a bold plan, and not without its drawbacks. Dr. Takayama would almost certainly react angrily to it. But Chiwaki himself had actually been toying with the same idea for some time. He was sure he could handle the business side of things. Now, seeing no other options to speak of, he went to confront the school head.

This being a serious matter to broach so suddenly, Dr. Takayama said he needed time to consider it, but at least he took it seriously and didn't reject the proposal out of hand. After a while, and with some adjustments to the original plan, he agreed to make Chiwaki business manager of the Takayama clinic. And that very day the dentist made his first decision: calling Noguchi into his office, Chiwaki informed him that he would be given fifteen yen a month for his tuition and board at Saisei.

Once again luck had smiled on Noguchi. His talent seemed to open doors for him wherever he went. Chiwaki found the young man a spacious room in a lodging house just ten minutes from the school, and in early 1897

Noguchi once again became a full-time student.

■ ■ ■

The Saisei Medical School had only two large lecture halls, not nearly enough for the thousand or so students on the rolls to attend class at once. But the school was marvelously equipped otherwise, boasting an array of microscopes and other machinery to rival the epidemiological facilities at any other laboratory in the nation. Instruction began before dawn, with students learning diagnostic techniques by the light of gas lamps. Courses were taught year-round at this school with no breaks: once the teachers had covered their course material, they would return to the start of the syllabus and begin again. Students could matriculate at any time, and the only graduation to speak of was when they managed to pass their national licensing examination.

Noguchi had not been long at the school when Yoneko Yamauchi—who was also living in the area and studying there—spotted him practicing his German vocabulary on a blackboard. She found this presence from back home a comforting sight, but for the time being she chose not to renew any contact with him.

At first Noguchi was a conscientious student. To the amazement of the people sitting nearby he took down his lecture notes in English, translating the material as he went along. But at some point he stopped taking notes altogether. Soon he began arriving late to class, and before long he was skipping lectures entirely. Even when he did attend, he would ignore the open seats, choosing instead to slouch at the back of the room, looking down on the crowd. Not surprisingly, the other students saw Noguchi as an increasingly eccentric figure.

Noguchi was in fact quite disappointed with the instruction at Saisei. The haphazard teaching methods and the number of untalented students bothered him. One day, though, as he was glaring down at the lecture hall, he was jolted out of his disdain by the sight of Yoneko Yamauchi. Women were a rare sight in the school, and she stood out all the more in her seat toward the front of the hall. Noguchi felt a rush of emotion as he gazed down at her.

As rare as women were in the medical schools of the era, it wasn't surprising that two students who had come to Tokyo from the same area to study medicine should cross paths at Saisei. Nor was it surprising for Yoneko—a cheerful and attentive student—to be sitting at the front of the class. She had first come to the capital to work as a nurse at Juntendo Hospital, a position secured by a helpful cousin of hers, but her ambition to become a doctor was greeted with active discouragement there, and she left the nursing job behind, attending Saisei with financial help from a friend of her father.

Noguchi fretted over his injured hand as he took in the sight of her, but was encouraged by the relative freedom that sharing a classroom now gave them. After considering various ways to approach her, he obtained a specimen of a human skull and presented it to her to aid her in her studies. The two began exchanging small talk when they met in the hallways. She had grown into an attractive young woman, and she was as intelligent as ever. Before long she was asking him for help with the more difficult sections of her textbooks. Noguchi, for his part, was more than happy to share his solid understanding of the material with her, and he proved to have a gift for explaining it. Yoneko found herself learning more quickly from Noguchi than she did from the crowded lectures.

Social convention at that time, however, dictated that it was unseemly for young men and women to spend time together in this way. It was unusual even for Yoneko to be asking a man questions about her studies, and the two refrained from going beyond this level of interaction. This actually suited Yoneko, whose attitude to their relationship seemed to be more practical than he might have liked. Like any man placed in a situation where a woman appeared to be counting on him, he mistook that reliance for something more emotional. But she saw in him a mind with a talent for medicine, and in her fierce desire to become a doctor she sought nothing more from him. (Indeed, his slovenly appearance at this time could hardly have led her to hope for more.)

Noguchi was quick to see this as yet another rejection by the opposite sex. He was no stranger to this emotion, having felt it on a number of occasions. Once, for example, a group of students got together to play *karuta*—a game where the players listen to a snatch of a classical poem and try to be the first to grab the card depicting that verse. The young men and women paired up and began the game. Noguchi had an excellent memory and quick reflexes, and one by one his team's cards piled up. After they won the first game, though, his teammate said she wanted to change partners.

Noguchi took this to heart. He had been so focused on the poems and cards that he forgot to conceal his left hand, which he usually did. Surgery had restored its use but it was still visibly deformed, and his partner's eyes had inevitably been drawn to it in the course of the game. There are few things more painful for a young man than being rejected by a woman because of his physical appearance.

As his thoughts returned to Yoneko, he wondered whether she too was avoiding him on purpose. He badly missed the presence in his life of a woman who openly accepted him, and he blamed it all on his twisted hand.

■ ■ ■

There was more to it than his hand, of course. At this point he was taking very little care of his appearance. His kimono was disheveled and dirty, his hair was long and unkempt, and it was a rare occasion when he spent his money on a trip to the public bath. On weekends he would return to the Takayama college and stay with Saburo Ishizuka, who had taken over the receptionist's position from Noguchi and who would be a lifelong friend. On Sunday mornings they would wake up, fill a large basin with well water, and leave it out in the sun all day. By late afternoon the water was nice and warm and the two would bathe right there in the yard. This "solar hot spring" was an old tradition among poor Japanese; everyone can afford sunshine.

Naturally, Noguchi could not be expected to maintain this tradition when the temperature dropped, and women could scarcely be expected to enjoy his company when he bathed only once or twice a month during the winter. And he avoided paying for even these infrequent trips to the public bath. When he couldn't stand it any longer, he would grab a filthy towel and borrow the money for a bath from some compliant friend.

Bathing was not the only part of Noguchi's life where he sought to avoid expenses. The letters he sent his friends around this time rarely came with stamps affixed. He used to scrawl "postage to be paid by recipient" on the envelope, adding a note thanking the friend for taking care of the charge. Just about everyone who received one of these letters paid for the delivery. This sort of mutual reliance is common enough among students in any age, but the fact that Noguchi resorted to it at all makes one wonder how he was spending the fifteen yen he received each month.

■ ■ ■

Yoneko gave Noguchi an introduction to her cousin, Ryokei Kikuchi, who was working in the Kojimachi Police Station just west of the Imperial Palace, but was also an aspiring doctor. The two quickly warmed to each another and became good friends. Kikuchi was deeply impressed by Noguchi's medical knowledge, which was remarkably advanced for his age, and Noguchi, on his side, was impressed by Kikuchi's English. British and American medicine was far from the mainstream in those days, the Japanese medical establishment being dominated by doctors groomed in German at the better public schools. The two young men felt a special solidarity because of this. Noguchi's eyes would shine when he spoke of his plans: "Kikuchi, let's go to America, not Germany! English is going to be the language to know, I tell you."

As time went by, the two spent more and more time together. When either of them had a little money they could be seen walking together in the entertainment districts looking for a place to drink, dine, and talk deep into the night. They were physically a study in contrasts—the tall, thin Kikuchi and the more compact Noguchi—and their behavior differed as well. Noguchi would continue ordering sake until he was completely out of pocket, while Kikuchi would keep enough cash for a ride home.

Noguchi at this time seemed to be trying to drink away thoughts of the unattainable Yoneko. He began frequenting the brothels of Fukagawa and Yoshiwara, Tokyo's red-light districts, and even let himself be dragged off to Susaki, a particularly seedy area, by a questionable acquaintance. Being young, energetic, and interested in the opposite sex, he saw his spending spiral well beyond his means. Money disappeared as soon as it came into his possession, and eventually he was in debt to nearly all his friends.

Noguchi was a passionate young man unwilling to do anything only halfway, and now this trait showed an ugly side as he completely ignored the concerns of those around him—even Chiwaki, who was bending over backwards to support him. People began asking the dentist why he went on funding the activities of such an unproductive member of society. Everyone knew of Noguchi's profligacy by now and believed Chiwaki was only bringing shame on himself by supporting it. What could he possibly see in Noguchi?

Two or three people approached Chiwaki to warn him about his misguided patronage. This was done less out of any urge to criticize his judgment than out of genuine concern about the situation. But the furthest Chiwaki was prepared to go was to split Noguchi's monthly stipend into three payments to keep him from spending it all at once. He saw this behavior more as a product of Noguchi's youthful vigor than of some fundamental flaw in his character. And indeed, in some respects Chiwaki appeared to be right. For all the time Noguchi spent in the pleasure quarters of the city, he was never without a medical text in his pocket. For every tale of Noguchi's wild drinking there was another anecdote of the hours he spent with his nose buried in a book until the sun rose and it was time to attend the morning classes.

The truth is that if Noguchi had been nothing but a self-centered libertine he would certainly not have enjoyed the friendship of so many people unwilling to turn their backs on him and his habits. One of those friends would later sum him up as a man who threw himself wholeheartedly into everything he did—both his work and his pleasure—and transcended the usual constraints of Japanese convention through his sheer intensity, an intensity that never really flagged in the runup to his licensing examination.

Noguchi was not entirely confident going into this exam, though. The clinical care test included a section on percussive diagnosis, in which the doctor places his left palm on the afflicted part of the patient's body and taps the back of that hand with his right. Subtle differences in the sound of those taps serve as clues to the patient's condition. Nowadays doctors have electrocardiographs and other tools at their disposal, but a century ago it was the stethoscope and this percussive technique at the core of diagnostic medicine. A lot rode on doctors' experience and their "feel" for a case, and percussion was an important skill for any MD to master.

"But how is a cripple like Seisaku going to be a doctor? It's like saying the sun'll come up in the west tomorrow!" Those taunting words from his old village came back to haunt Noguchi now. He was determined to pass the exam, but percussion was a problem—not only were the fingers on his left hand too short, he had trouble straightening them out into the proper position. He practiced the technique on Kikuchi, but it didn't go well. A deeply worried Noguchi went once again to consult Chiwaki.

"You should have realized this earlier," said the dentist. "There's not much time left until the test. . . Ah, I know, let's see if Dr. Kondo can help!"

Again, Chiwaki's extensive network of acquaintances and his willingness to make use of these connections would prove invaluable to the young man. He introduced Noguchi to his friend Tsugushige Kondo, a professor of surgery at Tokyo Imperial University, and explained the situation. Dr. Kondo was a kind man. He examined Noguchi's hand and told him there was a chance another operation could give him more flexibility—enough, even, to make percussive diagnosis relatively easy to do.

This would greatly improve Noguchi's chances of becoming a doctor, but it wasn't a cheap procedure. Kondo's university hospital, however, had a system whereby surgery performed as part of student instruction cost nothing. Noguchi went under the knife, and a group of elite medical students looked on as the surgeon worked to restore his hand to a far better condition than the Kaiyo Clinic operation had. Dr. Kondo followed up this treatment with personal instruction, teaching Noguchi percussion and other techniques that he could now cope with. This was all an extraordinarily heartening experience for the young man.

■ ■ ■

The second stage of the licensing exam, which took place over two days in October, tested applicants in two areas: theoretical comprehension and practical techniques. In preparation for this, Noguchi took a rare trip to the barber and came out of the shop almost unrecognizable to those who knew his previous appearance. He also borrowed a *hakama* skirt from a friend, having none of his own to wear over his kimono, and then went off to face the first day of the exam.

On this occasion Noguchi once again displayed his willingness to help those around him in need . . . as well as his lack of caution where his own affairs were concerned. On entering the examination hall he met another young man, who had forgotten his stethoscope. This was a person he'd never met before—and a competitor for the same limited slots he was trying for—but a sympathetic Noguchi handed him the instrument right away, saying "Here, take mine. I'll be taking my surgery test today and I won't need it. Good luck!"

Needless to say, the other man was surprised by his sudden offer—one of what would become a chain of memorable episodes when Noguchi's generosity came to the fore, but also an example of his disconnection from the requirements of the real world. So it was Noguchi's turn to be surprised when he entered the exam hall—to find that today's test required a stethoscope! As he looked down at the patient lying on the examination table, he resorted to something not many would have had the wit to do: he approached one of the proctors for that day's test and explained what he'd done, asking if he could borrow a stethoscope for his own use. With a spare instrument in hand, he then went back to the patient. The case was a complicated one, but Noguchi asked a series of questions as he examined him, before making what proved to be a correct diagnosis.

Ten days later the results were announced. Of the eighty who had taken the secondary exams, only four had passed and earned their license—and Noguchi was among them! He was just twenty-two years old and he had been studying in Tokyo for just over a year. And now he had passed a test that took the average student three years for the first stage and seven for the second. As a son of Fukushima peasants, his achievement was even more impressive given the dominance of the samurai class, which maintained a grip on most positions of power and prestige even after the formal end of the class system some decades earlier. Sure enough, Noguchi was the sole farmer in the group: the other three hailed from respectable samurai houses. But when the four newly licensed doctors went together to a nearby photo studio to get a picture taken commemorating their success, the expression on Noguchi's face looked somehow more in keeping with their background rather than his own—more dignified and lively than the slightly smug appearance of these descendants of warrior clans.

Afterwards, Noguchi went straight to his benefactor Chiwaki's office to report his success. Almost overcome by the news, Chiwaki could only stammer out: "Really? That's terrific! Now everyone will see . . . see how right I was about you." Indeed, this was a victory for both of them.

The word of his success went north by telegram, and the news spread through his home district like wildfire. This put an end to the mutterings of those who had made disparaging comments in the past. Everyone congratulated his mother: "Why, Shika, now you're certain to get rich together." Indeed, it was only natural for mother and son to join forces at this point, for Shika herself had begun a medical career of sorts. She was standing in for an elderly woman named Kuma, who was famous throughout the area as a midwife. On top of her farming chores Shika had been assisting her, watching and learning her techniques. Now Kuma was growing too old for this work. Clever as well as hard-working, Shika soon took over as a full-fledged midwife in her own right. This made her a welcome presence in the district. And everyone expected to see young Noguchi—who was her eldest son and the family heir, after all—return to his mother's side and lead the family to new heights of prosperity.

■ ■ ■

But now that Noguchi had his license to practice medicine, he found himself confronting a novel problem—his reluctance to enter the clinical medical field. For one thing, he didn't present a particularly healthy figure himself, which could hardly inspire confidence in his patients. There was a possibility of starting his medical practice with Yoneko Yamauchi by his side . . . but this wasn't likely. When he paid her a visit and told her of his triumph he learned that she hadn't even managed to pass her first-stage exams. Apparently, despite her disappointment, Noguchi couldn't conceal his own satisfaction in front of her, which people have interpreted as insensitivity, yet seems rather to have been the natural exuberance of an unsophisticated young man from Japan's rural north.

At this time in Japan there were two main ladders to climb in the medical establishment. One was the reserve of elite researchers who had received a high-grade medical education at Tokyo Imperial University. The other was for doctors who had passed the licensing exam and who generally went on to take over a family medical practice. Rather than a practice, Noguchi was now considering a research career, but he was on the wrong ladder for this, and it sparked in him a fierce sense of rivalry with the established elite. A series of events had already prejudiced him against it. Once, for instance, he had sat in as a patient for the university students to practice on, where he had undergone the humiliating experience of having his ruined hand poked and probed by these soon-to-be-doctors, with their shining academic credentials.

Soon Noguchi had a position as an instructor in pathology and pharmacology at the Takayama College of Dentistry—gained, once more, through the help of Chiwaki who, seeing his potential in the research field, found a way to keep him from having to return to Fukushima. But this first job as a licensed doctor brought him up against others who thought he was unsuited to the position—his students. "He's too young to be at the lectern!" they protested. "He doesn't belong here. What do they mean, assigning him to teach us?" Since their new instructor had just a few months earlier been cleaning their toilets and ringing the bell to mark their class hours, it is hardly surprising that they reacted in this way.

Unfazed by the muttering, Noguchi stepped to the front of the room and began his first class. As his heavy Aizu accent filled the hall the other voices died down, and before long the students were won over by his confident teaching style and his mastery of the material. He had gone abruptly from playing a bit part to a central role at the school. He would later describe his satisfaction about this to a friend: "I've been through a lot of things in my life, but the best time for me was those days teaching at Takayama. I went from janitor to professor, just like that! The surprise on those students' faces was a wonderful thing to see."

He would go on, of course, to climb still higher, going from janitor to world-renowned scientist. This was not the kind of life one could lead by progressing steadily along a beaten track. A fire burned within Noguchi, urging him to make unusual efforts toward whatever goal he set his eyes on, and making him restless once it was achieved. And, sure enough, he soon tired of the Takayama teaching position and began plotting the next step to take.

"College professor" sounds like a grand title today, but Noguchi's position wasn't in fact that prestigious. He was teaching night classes, and the material he covered offered him little scope for extending his own skills and knowledge. He asked Chiwaki whether he could get him a position at Juntendo, the foremost private hospital in the nation. This had been the first institution to bring "Dutch medicine," as foreign techniques were known in the mid–nineteenth century, to Japan. Chiwaki had his contacts, and was particularly close to Tetsuzo Sugano, one of the Juntendo staff. He asked for Dr. Sugano's help in securing Noguchi a post at the medical center, which would give the young man far more opportunity to excel than the dental college. Noguchi got his chance in the following month, November 1897, when Sugano offered him a job as an assistant.

The hospital occupied a one-story Western-style building north of Ochanomizu Station. Many of Japan's best surgeons worked there, and Noguchi, still wet behind the ears, was not likely to make a name for himself in their company. To begin with, he was given editorial work on the *Juntendo Medical Research Journal*, which involved him walking all over the hospital, looking into the patients' rooms and writing reports on the more interesting cases. He was also assigned to read the latest medical papers and introduce their findings in the journal.

This work was a far cry from bacteriology, where Noguchi's true interest lay. But he found himself enjoying it—what better way was there for a young man to get his name listed in the medical journals of the day? He produced at least two articles a month under the name Sei Koryu (whose characters— "willows growing at the lakeside"—he chose in honor of the years he spent living near the shores of Lake Inawashiro). The writing skills he learned in this period would serve him well later in life, when he became known for producing academic papers at a prodigious rate. Sugano, delighted with the promise Noguchi showed in this work, soon placed the editing of the twice-monthly journal entirely in his hands.

The job was ill paid, however—just two yen a month plus board. Even in those days this was exceptionally low. Still, Noguchi was better off than other researchers at Juntendo—even some who had graduated from Tokyo Imperial University's elite program—who went unpaid.

■ ■ ■

Noguchi was soon joined by a familiar face. Ryokei Kikuchi came to Juntendo with the help of introductions from his uncle and Noguchi. He was assigned to a patients' ward, where he also took on some research duties, and the two friends were once again together.

It is easy to imagine how they spent their time together after-hours. Noguchi would receive his monthly pay one day and would rarely have any of it left the next morning. To be fair, two yen was not a difficult amount to get through in an evening of wine and women, but this spending pattern still wasn't one that most people would choose to follow, and it left Noguchi without a single sen to his name for the next twenty-nine days. Indeed, it prevented him from obtaining his actual medical license—the certificate cost six yen, a sum he had yet to see all at once since passing his tests.

Once again he found himself begging Chiwaki to speak to the hospital authorities about his salary. This—seeing his shabby appearance, and knowing him to be worth more than two yen a month—Chiwaki promised to do. In a smaller voice, Noguchi spoke again: there were other expenses he wanted to cover as soon as possible. He pointed to his hair, which was badly in need of cutting. Once again the older man showed his paternal affection for him: "Take this," he said softly. Noguchi bowed deeply as he accepted Chiwaki's purse. He opened it later to find the considerable sum of twenty yen inside.

One of Noguchi's concerns at this time was what to wear. Most of the staff at Juntendo made their rounds in Western-style clothes or in fine kimono under formal *hakama* skirts. Noguchi's wardrobe contained none of these things, and he generally wore a surgery cloak over a simple kimono. This served him well enough in the surgical wing of the hospital, but the classier *hakama* was de rigueur in the other rooms. Noguchi took to borrowing a *hakama* from a friend when he needed to look the part, but his general appearance soon caught Dr. Sugano's eye, and he received several warnings about it.

One day Noguchi found himself explaining to an acquaintance from Aizu, who had come to visit Juntendo, why he wore no Western clothing. On returning home, this man informed Shika of her son's situation, which led to her scraping together some money from relatives and sending it to Tokyo, though it only amounted to three yen or so. Still lacking the clothing he needed for the job, Noguchi next took his predicament to Toshi Tahara. This was the doctor who had urged Chiwaki to study dentistry when he had been a junior high school teacher in Niigata, introducing him to doctors like Takayama and Watanabe. Noguchi didn't ask for help outright, being someone who was conscious of his family's poverty and his mother's efforts. But Tahara, a sympathetic man, promised him some of his own clothes which he no longer needed.

This news eventually got back to Chiwaki, resulting in a stern letter to Noguchi. He had been more than generous to him so far, overlooking all his faults and believing in his qualities when nobody else would, but Dr. Tahara was an important figure in Chiwaki's own life, and he was losing face by having Noguchi go to Tahara with his requests for help—not to mention the face he had already lost due to Noguchi's behavior after-hours, which earned him nicknames like "the Male Geisha."

Chiwaki was straightforward in his letter. "You seem to be concerned about losing your dignity as a doctor if you don't have the right clothes to wear. Well, why haven't you stopped to worry about the dignity you're losing by going to people you barely know personally and begging from them? If there was something you needed, why didn't you think of coming to me for help first?" Noguchi, however, couldn't understand why asking for help getting some clothing should provoke this outburst. He had worked hard and done well academically, after all—surely he was more than just a scrounger?

His response was perhaps a sign that he had grown used to this way of obtaining what he needed, having relied on charity since his childhood. Nevertheless, Chiwaki had always been a lifeline to Noguchi, and he rushed off a letter of apology, filling it with all the overblown prose he could come up with. But Chiwaki saw through the florid phrases to the insincerity behind them, and the letter went straight into his wastepaper basket.

Noguchi had his room and board provided for him. He now made three yen a month at Juntendo, and he also had his teaching income from the Takayama college. There was no reason he couldn't live a frugal life on this. But he just couldn't bring himself to think ahead; money was spent as soon as he got his hands on it. Being small in stature himself, he set his sights on tall, attractive women, and his youth made it harder for him to deal with the setback that poverty represented in his pursuit of their company. To avoid any appearance of hardship he behaved as flamboyantly as possible. He would drink and dine with a fierce energy, and awake the next morning in tears at his lack of restraint the night before.

Knowing that he could no longer depend on Chiwaki to support him, he turned his attention again to people from home. He wrote a long letter to Yasuhei Yago, a classmate from his Inawashiro days. In it he apologized for remaining out of touch for so long, related what he had accomplished and where he was working, and explained his desire to enter a university and do research work. To do this, he wrote, he would need fifty yen; he asked Yago whether he could get it for him.

This was a considerable sum for anyone to come up with, especially Yago, whose family pharmaceutical business was not doing as well as it might have done. But the letter had its effect. Yago had always looked up to Noguchi, and here he had a note from him saying how much his hero trusted in him. The writer had couched the letter in a way that made the recipient feel as though the young doctor's successes were his own, and Yago argued with his father and his wife until they relented and agreed to send the money to Tokyo.

This wasn't the end of Noguchi's begging, though. He wrote again asking for just another twenty yen to get him through a tough spot . . . and then again, and again. He wrote probably a dozen letters in all asking for money. Eventually even he realized that he needed to help himself out as well, and he began translating foreign medical texts into Japanese for a fee. One was the von Kahlden book, *Methods of Pathological Histology*, which he had borrowed from Dr. Watanabe before; another was a textbook on the preparation of medical specimens.

As noted above, the popular image of Noguchi has tended to ignore or misinterpret his improvidence. When this aspect of his life is set against the great strides he made in the field of medical research, they tend to become the two opposing facets around which simplistic descriptions of his life are built. He did indeed have a remarkable inability to manage his finances. Even when he admitted this to himself and tried to change his ways, the attempt never lasted long. His environment may have molded him to some extent into this kind of person, but there is doubtless a genetic factor here as well.

In some ways Noguchi's was an artistic temperament—a person whose creativity overrode any conscious, balanced moral sense. Indeed, there is a genuine artistry even in the letters he wrote begging for money. He was a skilled writer of classical-style Chinese poetry, and he would later develop a talent for oil painting. In an ethical sense he was quite different from men of firm principles like Kobayashi and Chiwaki, but this difference may, ultimately, have made it all the easier for them to be taken in by his curious personality.

A BUDDING MICROBIOLOGIST
AND A NEW NAME

At this point Noguchi was beginning to think that he was stuck in a rather pointless position. It was 1898, and he had been in Juntendo for several months—not a long time by any stretch of the imagination—but he already had the frustrating feeling that his work was going nowhere. While he was glad to be in a center of medicine like this, where there were new things for him to learn, the training he was receiving was not taking him in the direction he wanted to go.

Dr. Sugano agreed that Noguchi's talents might be better directed elsewhere when the young doctor came to speak to him during a break from his duties. "You aren't really cut out for clinical medicine, I have to say. . . Perhaps you'd do better as a medical researcher."

Noguchi had his answer ready: "Sir, I'm interested in bacteriology. Juntendo doesn't offer many chances to study in this field, unfortunately. I'm not sure what I should do about this—do you have any suggestions?"

Noguchi had been fascinated by microbiology ever since the day he peered into the Kaiyo Clinic microscope and saw the relapsing-fever spirochete for the first time. That experience had made a deep impression. He had also observed Dr. Watanabe's modern methods of treatment and the way they contrasted with the style of medicine to be learned from old Chinese texts; and his study of C. von Kahlden's book on pathology had further confirmed his desire to acquire an up-to-date knowledge of Western medicine. As the nineteenth century drew to a close, microbiology was becoming a major focus of medical science, and Noguchi wanted to be a part of it. A new discovery in this field would secure professional recognition for a researcher, as any young medical student knew.

Sugano let Noguchi explain his interests before saying: "If it's bacteriology you want to study, there's no better place for you than Kitasato's laboratory. But it's not an easy spot to get into. Just about everyone there is an Imperial University graduate."

Again Noguchi had to face this fact: graduates of this institution had doors opened to them that were closed to most other people. The only real options for someone in the realm of microbiology at the time were the Tokyo University laboratory and the Kitasato Institute, as the epidemiological research laboratory headed by Shibazaburo Kitasato was known. Dr. Kitasato had left his native Kyushu to attend Tokyo Imperial University. After graduation he went to Germany to work under the famed Robert Koch, a seminal figure in the science of microbiology who had discovered *Myobacterium tuberculosis*, the bacterium that causes tuberculosis, in 1882. (He would win the 1905 Nobel Prize for this discovery.) While in Germany Kitasato made his own mark when he successfully grew a pure culture of *Clostridium tetani*, the tetanus bacillus. He returned to Japan in 1892 to set up a research institute, which would itself be the scene of significant discoveries: just five years later Kiyoshi Shiga, a researcher under Kitasato, identified the bacillus that caused dysentery. With the best alumni of Tokyo Imperial University trying to get positions there, a doctor who had passed nothing but the state exams had next to no chance of getting in.

Sugano remained hopeful, though, and said he would ask the head of Juntendo Hospital, who knew Kitasato well, to approach Kitasato about a possible opening.

As always, Noguchi charged straight toward the goal he had set for himself, paying little attention to conventional wisdom in his drive to move up in the field. Indeed, his lack of the qualifications expected among medical researchers only made him more determined. With that brashness of approach which seemed at odds with the studious introspection he more commonly showed, he decided that Sugano alone would not be enough of a bridge to get him into Kitasato's laboratory, and he next went to his long-suffering mentor, Chiwaki. Chiwaki had every reason to tell him to back down from this overambitious plan; after all, he had barely spent any time either teaching at the Takayama college or working at Juntendo. But, surprisingly, the dentist offered to relay his request to a close friend of Kitasato who was connected with the *Japan Weekly Medical Journal*.

This meant, eventually, that Noguchi not only had a letter of introduction from Juntendo Hospital's director, but the backing of Chiwaki's extensive network of personal acquaintances.

■ ■ ■

In October 1898 Seisaku Noguchi was formally admitted to the Kitasato Institute as a research assistant. This was a highly unusual appointment, but Noguchi's timing was good: Kitasato seemed to be beginning to rebel against the overbearing presence of the national university in the academic field, and along with Noguchi another man was hired that year without a diploma from Tokyo Imperial University. Sahachiro Hata would later go to Germany and gain international fame for creating Salvarsan, a treatment for syphilis.

Noguchi was only twenty-one years old. To come from the mountains of Tohoku to the capital without any real academic background and make his way into the national center of microbiological research in just two years was quite a feat. Nevertheless, his first tasks there were mundane ones. Kitasato put him in charge of the library, where he earned twelve yen a month writing abstracts of foreign texts and editing articles for publication in medical journals. Indeed, it was Noguchi's language skills that had got him in; people who could read and understand the foreign literature that came pouring into the country in this era were few in number and much in demand.

It was a nervous assistant who entered Dr. Kitasato's office to meet this pioneer in the Japanese medical world for the first time and thank him for the post. Kitasato was a large, sturdy man with a neatly trimmed moustache. He rose from his armchair and examined the young man standing in front of him for some time before speaking. "You're going to have to work very hard here." he told him. "You'll have a good chance to continue your research overseas if you can make it through five years at my institute—but I warn you, you'll need to stick to it. I have little patience for people who leave this place before their time is done."

The institute itself was a simple affair housed in a two-story wooden building. But the staff members were first-rate scientists with impressive academic backgrounds, many of whom would go on to become pillars of the medical establishment in Japan. Compared with his new coworkers Noguchi was largely self-taught, and he had spent next to no time in laboratories. Yet they treated him well enough, walking him through the laboratory, carefully explaining about all the equipment and its uses. He returned this courtesy by coaching them in English. Surprisingly, there were no cliques in the Kitasato Institute based on academic records. There were, however, a few researchers who looked down on him for his very limited formal training.

Dr. Kitasato was not among them. He had perceived that this was no ordinary young doctor, and he had admitted him on the strength of the potential he sensed in him. When other people claimed that "experimentation and proof are the only tools a scientist has," Kitasato disagreed. "That may be true," he claimed, "but there's more to science than those tools. Before a scientist even begins his experiments he has to go through a long process of searching for ideas; of curiosity. It's these talents—curiosity and insight—that are most important for a scientist. Experiments are nothing but the last step in the process."

It may be that Kitasato sensed a similar approach to discovery in Noguchi. Since his days in Fukushima, Noguchi had known that a bit of extra effort could take him beyond his classmates, but steady progress was not the same as making a breakthrough of some kind. He could absorb endless amounts of knowledge from books, but what sort of name would that make for him in the end? Like Kitasato, Noguchi believed in the flash of insight that might lead to something entirely new.

He had a close friend in Hata, who had entered the institute at about the same time. But he could not shake off the feeling that he was somehow inferior even to this person. Noguchi reacted strongly not only where the results of his medical experiments were concerned; he was moody in general, and found it hard to keep his balance emotionally. His mood swings were soon widely known. When he felt good he would fling himself energetically into his work, but when his humor headed south he stayed away from the laboratory entirely. His temperament was similar to his father's in this way.

Once, for instance, he put in an order for thirteen guinea pigs to use in a new set of experiments, only to have Dr. Kitasato cancel the transaction as soon as he got wind of it: "Noguchi's just an assistant. He hasn't even completed his training period. What on earth is he doing trying to get lab animals for himself?" It was entirely in character for a talented young scientist like Noguchi to try to leap ahead in his work with moves like this—to bend the rules.

A similar episode followed a short time later. A new piece of equipment arrived at the Kitasato Institute: a state-of-the-art German microscope outfitted with a camera. The researchers had all peered through microscope lenses dozens of times before, but this was the first they had seen—perhaps the only one in Japan—that could record what they saw on film. There was one problem, however. The instruction manual was entirely in German, and no one could decipher enough of the highly technical descriptions to operate this tool . . . no one, that is, except Noguchi. Noguchi worked his way through the manual, informed the section head that he now understood its workings, and prepared to take some photos.

"What do you think you're up to?" cried a voice that stopped him in his tracks. "Assistants like you don't have permission to use gear like this!" The voice belonged to the lab chief in charge of equipment. No newcomer was going to be the one to break in the microscope. Noguchi felt the blood drain from his face, but was obliged to give in. Here was just one of the innumerable ways in which life in his country was hemmed in by regulations small and large. Like many people who went on to greatness later in their lives, Noguchi spent much of his early career honing his desire to succeed on the whetstone of frustration.

■ ■ ■

Noguchi had been in Tokyo for more than two years by this time. He was still teaching classes at the Takayama college, and he had his position in the Kitasato Institute. He now decided to take a break from these jobs and return to Fukushima for the first time since he'd come to the capital.

One of the first friends he visited was Yasuhei Yago. It was common in the Meiji era—particularly among country folk—to hold ambitious, talented people in high regard, so the Yago family was thrilled to have a Tokyo-trained physician as a guest in their house, and proud that he had been in the same class as their son. The prestige associated with Noguchi was enough for his mere presence at their table to bring them pleasure.

Noguchi made claims at this table to match that prestige. He was planning to serve one day as one of the Meiji emperor's personal physicians, he said—an exalted post for a doctor in the days when the emperor was still revered as a living god. Yasuhei and his parents listened to him go on to describe the poverty his mother still had to put up with and his need for financial assistance to make his way in the medical field. The other men he worked with wore decent clothes each day, and his standing suffered in comparison with them. The Yagos had already been kind enough to send him fifty yen, some of which he had used to buy one presentable suit. But one suit was not enough: his limited wardrobe was keeping him from moving ahead in his chosen career.

Was this simply a case of a talented young man letting his confidence get the better of him, or was he actually telling these tales in order to lead the Yagos on? It is hard to tell. Most biographies present this incident as an example of duplicity, but at some level he probably believed the claims he was making. Noguchi was not one for moderation in his speech or behavior, and he shared with his mother a strong sense of pride and an unwillingness to adjust to other people's expectations. When much of what he stated on nights like this one at the Yago home came from sincerely and confidently held conviction, it is not easy to accuse him of fraud. But it also isn't easy to ignore the fact that his inflated claims did bring him the clothes he wanted. Over the next three days the Yago family put together a complete suit of clothes for him—a new lined kimono, a *hakama* skirt, a silk coat to wear over the kimono, a cloak, and even underwear, a hat, and a pocket watch—to complement his salary of thirteen yen a month (and free lodging in the Juntendo boarding house).

On his return to the capital he wrote a thank-you letter to Yasuhei and his parents, again touching on the bold plans he had for his future. "My emotions as I write these words of thanks to you are stronger in their ardor than any flame. . . I solemnly promise to become the kind of doctor of whom you who have done me such great kindness can feel jusifiably proud. I will be no ordinary physician. . ." He went on like this at length, sprinkling Japanese verse and quotations from the Chinese classics throughout the pages.

At around this time Chiwaki announced he was going to China. During his absence Saburo Ishizuka would take over the medical tasks at the Takayama clinic, but he needed help. Noguchi, who was still working as a lecturer there, left the Juntendo boarding house and moved back to his Takayama lodgings to be on hand. Now that Chiwaki was leaving, though, he found himself worried at the thought of his mentor's absence. Chiwaki had taught him a lot and knew him better than anyone—all his strengths and weaknesses—and he had helped him out of any number of difficulties. Noguchi sat with him for a commemorative photograph and saw him off with a farewell meal.

This send-off was interrupted by news from the north. Noguchi's old teacher, Kobayashi, wrote to tell him that his wife was seriously ill. The young man wanted to go to Inawashiro as soon as he heard the news, both as a doctor and as someone who had benefited from Kobayashi's friendship and instruction, but he had only recently joined the Kitasato Institute. This wasn't his own mother on the sickbed; Dr. Kitasato wouldn't see this as an emergency requiring Noguchi's presence. Naturally, Noguchi was dismayed at his inability to take a long vacation and go to look after his teacher's wife, but he did what he could from Tokyo, consulting with the senior members of the institute's staff and writing prescriptions to send north along with advice on treatment. He asked for frequent reports on the patient's progress, and was disappointed to learn that her health continued to deteriorate.

Eventually he made up his mind to take as many days off as possible and go to Inawashiro. She was under the care of a Dr. Rokkaku there, a trusted man who had been practicing in the community for many years. After examining the patient, Noguchi made the same diagnosis he had—serious kidney disease—and immediately offered to help. Using both German and Japanese, the two of them discussed Mrs. Kobayashi's condition and ways to treat it. Noguchi conferred with the pharmacist about the medicines to be used, and even lent a hand with cleaning the hospital room and shopping for his teacher. He was at once doctor, nurse, and servant.

■ ■ ■

Some time passed with no major change in her condition, but gradually the illness abated. She was getting well again. Now that he had less to do, Noguchi picked up a book to take his mind off things: Shoyo Tsubouchi's *Tosei shosei katagi* (The Life and Times of a Modern Student). Tsubouchi was one of a new breed of writers who scorned the simplistic moral preoccupations of Edo-period literature, stressing the need for realism in art. This tale painted a convincing picture of student life in Tokyo, and was widely read in the provinces as well as the capital.

Noguchi casually began to read it, but soon found himself turning the pages tensely, his eyes glued to the text. The main character was called Seisaku Nonoguchi—a gifted medical student who had come from the countryside to study in Tokyo. The similarities continued to mount: Nonoguchi worked hard at his studies until, enticed by the city nightlife, he started frequenting its red-light districts. With growing nervousness, Noguchi read quickly ahead, only to find that his fictional counterpart, so like himself in everything including the name, went steadily downhill, until he ended up taking his own life.

Noguchi was shocked. Who else could have been the model for a character called Seisaku Nonoguchi? The book brought all the sights and sounds back—the drinks lined up on the table, the voices of the women. . . He was sweating, certain now that the book was based on his own experience.

He took the book to Kobayashi to ask him what could be done about it.

"It looks as though Tsubouchi spotted you up to no good and wrote it all up," said Kobayashi simply.

Noguchi was reluctant to let the older man know how he had actually behaved in Tokyo. "It can't be me. I never did all these things, and this can't be how I'll end up. . . But even so, it makes me so angry—using me as a starting point, without ever asking me."

"Well, it certainly is a strange coincidence, all these similarities between you and this character."

Noguchi wouldn't let the matter drop, determined to take some kind of action. But what *could* be done? There was little chance of a successful lawsuit against the writer for damaging his reputation. Kobayashi told him he'd like to think about it.

Three days later he came to Noguchi with a solution. "The only thing to do is to take a new name. I've thought of one for you: Hideyo. The *hide* is a character that's been in use in my family for generations—it's a good one, meaning 'to excel,' and you find it in words like 'hero.' And *yo* means 'the world'—that's another grand character to have in a name. What do you say? Is it too good for you? Will you be able to live up to it?"

"It's a wonderful name, sir," Noguchi replied. "I'd be honored to bear it. And I promise to try to live up to its meaning."

This was how he came to be known as Hideyo Noguchi. It didn't happen overnight, of course—the rules governing name changes were designed to prevent them occurring for frivolous reasons, and he had to wait until the following year to become Hideyo, when another family in the area named a newborn baby Seisaku. Avoiding confusion was a valid reason to take a new name. It was officially registered on October 21, 1899.

Years later, after Noguchi's death, Kobayashi wrote to the novelist to ask him whether he had actually based this tale on his former student. The answer was a surprising one: the plot and the character's name had been a product entirely of the writer's imagination. He had written the book in 1884 or 1885, when Noguchi was less than ten years old. Any similarity between the two was entirely coincidental. Tsubouchi knew plenty of other young men who might have served as material for his writing—in those days Tokyo University was full of medical students with a keen eye for women and drink and with flashy spending habits. In *Tosei shosei katagi* he was merely attempting to lampoon those students in general, not one in particular—and certainly not one who wouldn't arrive in Tokyo until more than a decade later.

But the book's influence on Noguchi's life went beyond forcing him to take a new name. It made him take a closer look at the way he was living his life. Spending more money than he could afford on his own amusement, he wasn't so different at all from the dissipated character it portrayed, and he saw it as a prescient warning. He would not let himself end up wrecked like Seisaku; he would strive instead to be Hideyo—heroic, making his way onto the world stage.

■ ■ ■

Noguchi had now spent some two weeks back home. He had left his work at the Kitasato Institute behind, but he couldn't ignore it for long; there was also his work at the Takayama clinic to consider. Ishizuka, who had been handling much of that work on his own, now got ill and sent a telegram urging Noguchi to come back quickly.

Luckily Ishizuka's illness was nothing more serious than a bad cold, but it was still enough to keep him from his duties, and Noguchi's help was badly needed at the clinic. Early each morning he and one of the college clerks went out to take the rain shutters off the windows and sweep the grounds. Once the college and clinic were ready for the day's activities Noguchi headed to the Kitasato Institute, where he performed his duties as an apprentice researcher. These lasted until the evening. He would then return to the college to teach his classes there. After these lectures he still wasn't done: he had his editorial work for the Juntendo journal, published twice monthly. Then there was the Takayama college's own dental journal, which he edited together with Ishizuka. Finally he had his translation of the von Kahlden text to keep him busy late into the night. It was rare for Noguchi to get to bed before two or three in the morning. And at six he arose to begin it all again.

At times he felt his eyelids growing heavy before the day's work was over, but as he nodded off right there at his desk, Ishizuka would call out to him: "Hey, don't go to sleep just yet! Tomorrow's the deadline for the journal and I need ten more pages. Can you help me put something together?"

"What? Oh . . . sure, I'll have ten pages for you by the end of the night." Hideyo would shake his head to clear it and will himself back awake. Tokyo seemed absolutely still at this hour of night except for these two.

Thanks to this perseverance, Noguchi found time between his teaching, research, and editing duties to complete his translation of *Methods of Pathological Histology*, which he gave a difficult-sounding title to match the specialized knowledge it contained. This was its first appearance in Japanese, and it marked Noguchi's first major achievement in the realm of medicine. The great pathologist Katsusaburo Yamagiwa checked his manuscript for him, and no less an authority than Dr. Kitasato provided the preface for the work—or, more accurately, attached his name to the preface, which Noguchi wrote himself.

Soon after Noguchi wrapped up work on this project he was delighted to receive a visit from Kiichiro Yoshida, his friend from the Kaiyo Clinic days. He proposed a night out on the town, but alas—as was usually the case—he had no cash to spend on dinner and drinks. He knew a way to get some, though. With his finished manuscript tucked inside his kimono he led Yoshida out into the city. Soon they reached Kanda, where Noguchi ducked into one of the many bookstores there—Handa Booksellers, a shop specializing in medical texts—and emerged after a while with thirty-five yen in cash. He was disappointed that his translation had not fetched more—he had hoped to get a hundred yen or more—but he didn't complain that night. With money in his pocket and his friend by his side, he was in high spirits. They headed for a fancy tempura restaurant to celebrate their reunion.

Jean-François Millet is said to have burned his paintings to warm a visitor in the depth of winter. Now Noguchi was following his example, cheerfully exchanging a precious manuscript on which he'd worked for years for some cash to entertain his friend. Handa Booksellers later published this translation, so he did at least see his name in print.

Soon after this Noguchi heard news of another old friend. Yoshiji Akiyama, his classmate in Inawashiro, was in Tokyo, and seriously ill. He had been traveling around Japan, even climbing Mt. Fuji, after the onset of the illness.

Normally healthy, Akiyama was now in pain, with a high fever that Noguchi decided was no ordinary infection.

"There's probably nothing to worry about, Akiyama. But I'm just starting out in this business, and it'd be best to get you looked at by some top physician. I'll take you to Juntendo tomorrow."

The next morning Noguchi took a break from his work and went to collect Akiyama in a rickshaw. As soon as he learned the diagnosis—typhoid fever—he arranged for his friend to be hospitalized at the clinic attached to the Kitasato Institute. Here he could receive more specialized care from experts in epidemiology. Whenever Noguchi found a few free moments in his schedule he would pop over to Akiyama's room to check up on him and do whatever he could to put him at ease. In this he was merely repaying a kindness—this was, after all, the boy who had stood by his side while Dr. Watanabe operated on his hand and then run to tell his mother that the surgery had been successful. Noguchi was indebted to him for this; he would do anything he could for him now.

Noguchi was a man hard to admire for some of his personal habits, but in his devotion to his friends there were few more admirable than him. Akiyama regained his health completely.

TO GO BEYOND JAPAN'S SHORES

After Japan opened its doors to the outside world in the middle of the nineteenth century, the nation soaked up as much knowledge and culture from the advanced nations of the West as it could. This was especially the case in the medical field, where any doctor who really wanted to make a name for himself was expected to travel overseas and study in the leading institutions of the day.

Noguchi remembered Kitasato's prediction—"You'll have a good chance to continue your research overseas if you can make it through five years at my institute." But this proposition sounded more like an anchor chain than a boat ticket to him now, considering all the researchers at the institute who were ahead of Noguchi in line for a trip abroad. He was just a lowly assistant. He fed the guinea pigs, washed the test tubes, and made sure the laboratory dogs were properly muzzled. He was on an even lower rung of the institute ladder than his friend Hata, who had started just before him. With all these people above him, Noguchi would be well into middle age before he got his chance to go.

While he was brooding about this, he got word that Saburo Ishizuka was also heading to China. Chiwaki's dentistry had proved hugely popular on the continent and he needed assistance with his practice there. Noguchi's added duties at the Takayama College of Dentistry, on top of the drudgery at the Kitasato Institute, only reinforced his doubts about his own future. His life seemed to be going nowhere. The year 1898 drew to a close.

Politically and culturally, this was a time of sweeping change. Japan was carving out a position for itself among the world's nations. It had been pressed into treaties with many global powers following its long seclusion, but these had been concluded when it was comparatively weak. Following its victory against China Japan moved to rewrite these treaties and improve their terms. This newfound confidence on the world stage was matched by confident progress in all domestic fields of endeavor: the Japan Art Academy was founded around this time; Kiyoshi Shiga discovered the dysentery bacillus; and Jokichi Takamine successfully synthesized the chemical adrenalin.

Eventually this age of discovery and development brought Noguchi into its orbit as well. In April 1899 the Kitasato Institute was designated a national research facility under the aegis of the Interior Ministry. Its staff members were now public servants, and Noguchi's monthly salary jumped to fifteen yen. This was a welcome development, but that same month the young researcher would see something far more important happen to him when he met another man who would greatly affect the course of his life: the American Simon Flexner.

■ ■ ■

Professor Flexner taught pathology at Johns Hopkins University and was part of an American team on its way to Manila, currently in the grip of a dysentery epidemic. The team stopped off in Japan before reaching the Philippines, since Flexner wanted to visit Dr. Kitasato's institute and talk to the man who had discovered the bacteria in question. The Americans checked in at the Teikoku Hotel and sent a message to the institute requesting an appointment to view Shiga's research results.

Noguchi spoke English better than anyone else at the institute, so he was tapped to go to the hotel and meet the foreign team. His language skills came in handy again when he brought the visitors back to the laboratory and guided them around. His interpreting was of course far from perfect—his Aizu accent was thick in both languages, and he had learned English almost entirely from books, not by actually communicating in the tongue—but his vocabulary was surprisingly well stocked. Dr. Kitasato led the group around his facility with Noguchi at his side.

That evening the Japanese side held a banquet to welcome their American visitors, and Kitasato and other high-ranking staff members filed into the dining hall. But Noguchi was not included in this party. Seething with resentment every time he heard a round of applause at some speech, he was left waiting outside. Wasn't it he who had been sent to meet Flexner and his group? Wasn't he the only person who could interpret for them? And yet here he was, left outside the doors of this festive hall while his superiors in the institute, who had done almost nothing all day, enjoyed the company of these foreign guests. Noguchi felt that he had lost the respect of the Americans by being shut out in this way.

This episode rankled with him for years afterwards. Later in life, when he returned to Japan after earning fame abroad, he would still complain: "When people come to visit from faraway countries they find themselves on strange soil, not understanding what other people are saying around them. It's damned rude to leave them without an interpreter to help them navigate around the place! Professor Flexner must have had a rotten time at the dinner that night."

At the time, though, Noguchi did not have long to wallow in this humiliation. That same night Kitasato announced that he had to take an overnight train for Osaka, where he was to make a presentation the following day, and before departing he called Noguchi in and told him to look after the Americans for the remainder of their time in Tokyo. Flexner and his team would apparently be in town for two more days, visiting various facilities; with Kitasato gone Noguchi was the only person available to guide them.

This cheered Noguchi up. Instead of waiting his turn for a ticket to Germany, he would take advantage of this opportunity to open up a way to the United States instead. This plan had in fact been growing in his mind since he first learned of the American researchers' visit. He stayed up late plotting his moves for the next two days.

First he took Flexner and his team to the Takayama College of Dentistry and Juntendo Hospital. These were places he knew well, and he was confident that the people there would show him in a positive light after all the work he'd done for them. As the group toured these facilities Noguchi spoke energetically of his interest in microbiology and his activities to date.

Flexner surprised him with an unexpected question: "What did you write your thesis on? I'd like to see what you've produced so far."

Hideyo lacked a solid body of published research. He stammered out as much, noting that he had yet to begin any real work in the field. He did show the professor a copy of his translation of von Kahlden's book and a paper on gangrene in children's feet that had appeared in a Juntendo publication. "To tell you the truth," he explained, "microscope technology isn't all that advanced in Japan. I hope to go to America and do some serious work there... What do you think of the idea?"

"I think that would be fine. I'd like to be of help if I can." Noguchi was now hanging on every word, listening for a chance to pursue his objectives. The professor continued: "Of course, my own position will be changing soon—I'm moving from Johns Hopkins to the University of Pennsylvania—so who knows if I'll see you when you make it over."

These were the polite words of a guest to his host, but to Noguchi they seemed to open up a future. The young man had so much invested in this meeting with Flexner that it is easy to understand how he could mistake what were simple attempts to make conversation for an invitation to cross the Pacific. But this misunderstanding was, in fact, what would eventually take Noguchi to the United States.

One researcher who worked with him during these years wrote later about the amazing gift he had for advancing his career: "He was like the wind—he could find his way through the smallest crack if it opened up. And he had the courage to pursue an opportunity to the end once he was launched on it."

Although the goal of a trip to America obviously wasn't something one could hope to reach overnight, Noguchi did enjoy some benefits of his time with Flexner right away. Baron Tadanori Ishiguro invited him to his mansion to receive a full report on what the Americans had observed during their time in Japan. The baron was the head of the Japanese Red Cross and the nation's surgeon general; to be invited to his home was a great honor for anyone. Ishiguro listened to Noguchi's Aizu-accented speech and revealed that he hailed from the town of Yanagawa, also in Fukushima Prefecture. The two had even more in common: Ishiguro knew Sakae Watanabe as well. When he found out that Noguchi had studied under the doctor he wrote him a letter of recommendation on the spot, praising him as "an extraordinarily sharp young man with great clarity of mind and a most promising future."

■ ■ ■

At this point all seemed to be going well for him. But he soon found a way to derail this stretch of good luck. At the Kitasato Institute he was in charge of the collection of reference materials—a job that meshed well with his bookish temperament, but that proved disastrous when combined with his generosity toward his friends. One day he loaned a valuable set of medical texts to one of these friends. The books were not supposed to be removed from the library, however, and the next time an inventory was taken they came up missing. Noguchi went to his friend to ask for them back, only to learn to his horror that all five of the books had been lost or pawned.

These volumes were too rare for the dismayed librarian to replace them simply by going out to a local bookstore. Dutifully he reported what had happened to Kitasato. This was no minor incident: since the institute had been nationalized, all its equipment and reference material, right down to the last pamphlet, were now government property. Kitasato was upset at the loss of the books, of course, but knowing the way this assistant splashed his money about in the bars of Tokyo, he suspected that he'd sold the books himself. Noguchi was relieved of his library duties immediately. After a stern lecture on the need to treat official institute property with more care in the future, the chastened young man was sent away with a promise that the matter of the missing books would be dealt with later.

Noguchi spent the next few weeks in nervous anticipation of some extra punishment. A month or so later Kitasato duly called him in for another talk. Noguchi walked into the office feeling like a condemned man. But the topic of this talk was not what he had expected: Kitasato was telling him about a new position. The government was establishing a number of quarantine stations in the nation's main ports—Yokohama, Kobe, Nagasaki, and Moji—to prevent diseases entering Japan via ships. Kitasato, who was the first person to isolate the plague bacillus, was in charge of picking the doctors to serve at these posts. The new Yokohama Quarantine Station needed medical staff, and he had recommended the multilingual Noguchi as a doctor there. Was he interested in the job?

The pay was thirty-five yen—a very comfortable salary, considering Noguchi could get by on around six yen a month for room and board. It would also give him plenty of opportunities to speak to the captains and crew of foreign vessels. How could he say no to this chance of improving his language skills and hearing first-hand news of other countries while he was saving up the money he needed for his own journey overseas? A few days later a happy Noguchi formally announced his acceptance of this position.

The Yokohama Quarantine Station was a vast facility almost a square kilometer in size, containing office buildings, lodging for visiting sailors, baths, and a separate area for medical examinations and the quarantine rooms.

Noguchi cut a fine figure in his white uniform and hat as he headed out on the station's launch to meet incoming ships, to check their cargo and crews for signs of any communicable disease.

In September Noguchi made a name for himself at the station. The *America* sailed into port and the young doctor went out to meet the ship. On descending into the hold he came across a Chinese crewman with a high fever that alternated with bouts of shaking chills. Finding his lymph nodes swollen, Noguchi made his diagnosis: it was the plague.

This was a fearsome disease. Known in China and Europe as the Black Death, it was perhaps the most dreaded sickness of the day, and for good reason—a pandemic in the Middle Ages had killed a third of the European population. One of its most frightening aspects was its communicability: the main vector for plague germs was fleas carried by rats, but the disease could also jump to new victims via skin contact, infected mucous membranes, and even just through the air. After a week-long incubation period it made itself evident in patients in the form of violent chills, high fevers, aches and dizziness, subcutaneous discolorations, and finally, in many cases, death. And Noguchi had found this disease on a boat entering Japan.

The rest of the staff had little faith in his diagnosis. They argued instead that the Chinese sailor was suffering from blood poisoning. This was another sickness that infected the blood and lymphatic system, causing acute inflammation and toxic reactions. But Noguchi stuck to his original conclusion. He transferred the patient to an isolation hospital at Nagahama, where he examined his blood and grew a culture of the bacteria he found. The results vindicated him: it was the plague. He then reported his discovery immediately to his superiors. By becoming the first officer to spot a case of this disease at a quarantine station, he more than made up for the damage to his reputation caused by the library foul-up.

A month later, in October 1899, Noguchi received an urgent telegram from Kitasato summoning him to the institute. On arrival he learned that there was something better than the quarantine station on offer. "What do you say, Noguchi? There's a job for you in China if you want it. We've got an outbreak of the plague to deal with there."

The city of Niuzhuang in Manchuria was in the throes of the disease, and after the foreign consulates in the city had formed a committee to deal with it, a request had come via the Japanese Foreign Ministry for medical staff to provide assistance. Kitasato was a natural person to contact in a case like this, and Noguchi, who had spotted the plague case in Yokohama, was a natural candidate for him to think of.

The pay was a considerable step up from the Yokohama Quarantine Station: two hundred taels per month, some six times what Noguchi was making at his present job. He accepted this invitation immediately, seeing it as a good chance to save up some money for his trip to America, and he joined a team fifteen members strong with Shohei Murata, a senior researcher at the Kitasato Institute, at its head. Everyone but Noguchi was an Imperial University graduate.

Once the young man's decision was made, his thoughts turned to Yoneko Yamauchi. Knowing he would have to return his uniform when he left the quarantine office, he was keen to show the girl at least once what he looked like with some gold braid on his jacket. He was also anxious for her to see him in his new capacity as a member of Japan's official international medical team, thinking that it might influence her feelings for him to some extent.

It was late in the afternoon when he set out for Tokyo's Hongo district. Yoneko was visibly surprised by this sudden visit, not to mention his uniformed appearance, but she welcomed him into her room. Noguchi liked the way she was casually dressed. He greeted her politely, suppressing the urge to boast about his new position, and she politely expressed her disappointment at losing the guidance he'd been giving her in her studies. When, however, Noguchi realized he didn't have all that much time before the last train for Yokohama, he launched into a hectic presentation of his plans for the future, speaking breathlessly about China and an eventual move to America. It was only when he noticed how uncomfortable this monologue was making her that he abruptly changed the subject, asking about her preparations for the licensing exam. Altogether it was a clumsy performance.

"I won't be seeing you for a while," he told her finally. "Would you accompany me as far as Shimbashi Station tonight?"

Yoneko seemed unnerved by this request. "I'd like to, but it looks as if it might rain, and anyway I really ought to go to bed soon, with my tests coming up. . ."

Noguchi had come to see her in the hope of forging some sort of bond between them. Now that time was running out, he was willing to try anything. "If I can't have the pleasure of your company as far as the station, might

I ask for a picture of you to take with me on the trip to China? It would be a great comfort to me in a strange land."

"I don't have any photographs of myself here. . . When I get one taken I promise to send it to you, though." Yoneko was well aware of the significance attached to a photograph given at a time like this.

Noguchi pleaded with her. "If you don't have one, then let's go and get one taken! We can go to a studio and sit for a portrait together." He was beyond caring about the discomfort he was putting her through; he was almost frantic by this point.

"But then you'll miss the last train to Yokohama!"

Noguchi was tenacious, but his efforts came to nothing. Luck was not on his side, at least not in this area of his life. He may have been able to move ahead professionally in leaps and bounds, but he couldn't find a way into Yoneko's heart. As he walked away, alone, on that rainy night, he gazed gloomily at the ground. The next day he had to get ready to go to China.

■ ■ ■

Noguchi was given ninety-six yen to cover the expenses involved in leaving for the continent. With this money he hoped to straighten out his affairs, then make his way to Kobe, the port where the ship for China was waiting. But as word got out that he was heading overseas, his creditors all came running in an effort to get their money back before he left. Noguchi wasn't the kind of man to hide any of the funds he had on hand—when someone asked him for repayment he cheerfully handed over the full amount—and in no time he was broke again.

Now needing money for his train fare to Kobe, he began making the rounds of his friends in search of a quick loan. Nobody, though, was willing to lend money to a man on the point of leaving the country. The rest of the medical team departed for Kobe, but Noguchi was still frantically running around Tokyo looking for loose change.

Following a pattern that had worked for him all too often in the past, he turned to his old benefactor, the dentist Chiwaki, who had returned from China by now. The problem was, Chiwaki had recently married, and most of his money had gone into his wedding preparations and the wedding itself. In yet another act of amazing generosity, however, he pawned his wife's wedding kimono. Any other person would have taken Noguchi to task for his complete inability to hold on to money, but Chiwaki quietly handed over the fifteen yen he'd made from selling one of his wife's most cherished possessions.

At this Noguchi broke down and cried. Taking only five yen, he returned the rest, refusing again and again to accept the whole amount. "No, please, keep it. I just need to get as far as Kobe; after that I can manage on my own."

Unable to convince Noguchi to take the remaining ten yen, Chiwaki instead presented the young man with a parting gift: an old traveling bag of American make. Noguchi then went straight to a nearby used-clothing store and got himself a summer kimono—not the best choice for mid-October, but a cheap selection. With his rain cloak draped over his shoulders he was now ready to go. He couldn't leave from nearby Shimbashi—there were too many loan sharks around the station who might be on the lookout for him— so he headed for Shinagawa, with Chiwaki accompanying him for much of the way.

Noguchi made it to the ship in time. The other members of the team were busy studying Chinese in preparation for their time on the mainland, their noses buried in Mandarin-Japanese dictionaries. Noguchi chose a different linguistic route: he went down into the hold to meet the coolies. Whenever and however he could, grunting and gesturing with his good hand, he began communicating with these Chinese workers. Before long he had picked up a few words of their tongue—and then a few more. By the end of the voyage he was holding simple conversations with the Chinese on board. This gave him a head start on his dictionary-wielding countrymen, who could hardly recognize one single word in the phrases chattered at them as they stepped off the ship at Niuzhuang. It was perhaps thanks to this newfound talent, along with his skill in German and French, that Noguchi earned a spot immediately under Murata, the head of the Japanese delegation, at the central medical office.

Niuzhuang (also known as Yingkou) was one of Manchuria's key ports, at the mouth of the Liao River. The harbor bustled with shipments of soybeans from further inland and railroad ties imported from Japan. The constant influx of traffic from abroad had brought a less welcome guest, though: the plague. By late October, when the Japanese team arrived, the disease was rampant in Niuzhuang. The doctors had no time to set up labs and do research; they were needed in the sick wards. With their advanced Western training, the Japanese physicians were much in demand, but more than anyone it was Noguchi who was most sought after. He may have had little practice in clinical medicine, but his experience of poverty had given him something his university-trained colleagues lacked: sympathy for the dirt-poor people who crowded around them. He spoke to the Chinese in their own language, and examined them patiently and thoroughly. Even the upper-class women of the city, usually too modest to remove their clothes before a doctor, seemed willing to obey the orders Noguchi gave in his examination room.

Noguchi also found time to visit the opium dens and study the effect of the drug on addicts. Experiments on the plague bacterium and its resistance to deep cold were carried out as well. Noguchi wrote up the results of these tests and sent a copy of his report to Professor Flexner along with a letter describing his activities, asking whether this paper could be published in the University of Pennsylvania's journal covering pathology and bacteriology. He also told Flexner once more of his desire to go to the United States, to work with him at the university. Could the professor find him a suitable position there as a researcher, or even get him admitted as a student? He sealed up these requests and mailed them to America.

He didn't forget Yoneko in his letter writing, either. To her he sent a ring inscribed with her name. Along with gifts and medical information, he filled his letters with observations on the political situation in China, views on the moves other nations were making to protect their interests in the country, his ideas about what the Japanese should do for their nation's newly gained continental territory. To learn more about the situation around Niuzhuang he contacted the local governor, and soon the two of them were exchanging Chinese poems in their letters to one another.

Noguchi also spent a fair amount of time in more frivolous pursuits. One of his goals in coming to China had been to save up some money for the trip to America, but all the cash he received quickly disappeared in a fog of drink and women. Niuzhuang was a walled city with the pleasure district outside the city perimeter. Noguchi lost track of the time on many evenings, leaving the drinking places well after the town gates had been closed. Needing to get back to his quarters to be ready for work the next day, he would often scale the city wall. Once a police officer caught him climbing over, and it took him until the following morning to convince the authorities that he was a member of the Japanese medical team and thus gain his freedom.

Noguchi was not the kind of worker to remain cooped up day after day. Every evening when he had money in his pocket was spent outside the city walls. In the end it made no difference that his pay had risen from thirty-five yen to two hundred taels—it vanished just as quickly. Eventually he came around to seeing the need to set some money aside for future travel expenses, but by then it was too late: most of his team were already preparing to return to Japan after their half-year stint in China.

Noguchi did not return home with the other Japanese. The plague outbreak had died down, but a Russian team asked him to stay and continue health-monitoring activities in the region. Noguchi enjoyed a key position in this group as well as a considerable raise in salary. He was now making three hundred taels a month—and was actually managing to save some of it. Having some spare cash to his name made him no wiser about handling money, though. When an acquaintance asked for a considerable loan he gave him two hundred taels in exchange for nothing but a signed IOU. Needless to say there was no sign of it ever being repaid, and when the Boxer Rebellion made Niuzhuang a dangerous place for foreigners to inhabit, and the Russian group left Manchuria, Noguchi too fled China and returned to Tokyo—without his money.

The young doctor came back without the funds he had hoped to amass, but he had gained valuable expatriate experience in the field, rubbing shoulders with Western doctors and getting a feel for life outside his own country. More importantly, he had made something of a name for himself in the international medical community through his energetic and wide-ranging work in Manchuria. It was a more confident Noguchi who came back to Japan to plan his next move. He had no job—he had quit his post at the Yokohama quarantine office rather than do the paperwork for an extended leave of absence—but he did have enough money to live on for two or three months. After landing in Osaka, Noguchi fell in with his friend Sahachiro Hata. Relaxing by day and drinking with Hata by night, he spent around ten days considering what to do with himself.

■ ■ ■

His next move was to return to the capital, where he headed for Chiwaki's house near Kanda. Noguchi was not the only young man borrowing a room in the dentist's spacious home—the lodgers kept noisy company with each other late into the night. Once he had settled down, though, his thoughts turned again to Yoneko and the disappointing way they had parted before his departure for China. Things were different now. He was a qualified doctor with international experience under his belt, and her attitude would surely have changed. He found a room closer to where she was staying. One fine summer day he made his way to her place to see her again and tell her about his time abroad.

Yoneko, having read Noguchi's letters, was painfully aware of his feelings for her. She knew that any continued contact with him would give rise to gossip about the two of them, which went against her sense of propriety. The ring he had sent her remained in the desk drawer into which she had tossed it. Not looking forward to another meeting with him following his return, she spoke to the lady running her boarding house, asking her to fend off the amorous young man should he come to visit.

The older woman did her job well. Noguchi came calling, sure enough, and asked to see Yoneko. From the front of the house he could see her figure through the screen she had lowered to shut out the afternoon sun; she appeared to be studying with a friend. But when he entered the building and moved toward her room the landlady stepped in front of him, stopping him in his tracks.

"Excuse me, but I'm here to see Miss Yamauchi."

"I'm sorry, sir. She's not in at the moment."

Noguchi peered into the gloom behind the woman with growing irritation. "I can see her moving about in her room. What do you mean, she's not in?"

At last he realized the truth of this situation: Yoneko didn't want to see him; she had no wish to be with him. This was the last visit he would ever pay her. Years later, Yoneko's granddaughter would relate that Yoneko had never appreciated his tiresome interest; nor, perhaps, did this woman with medical aspirations of her own relish the idea of a life in which she was bound to play second fiddle to the talented Noguchi.

Tokyo felt cold now, and Noguchi decided to return home to Fukushima, attracted by the prospect of being reunited with old friends and villagers who *would* be interested in his stories of life in China. His spirits lifted at the thought of going home a hero.

Since he had left for Tokyo in 1896 the Gan'etsu Line had been extended

Noguchi's father, Sayosuke.

Noguchi's mother, Shika.

The Fukushima farmhouse where Noguchi was born.

Noguchi as a student.

In May 1878 Noguchi burned his hand in this hearth.

Sakae Kobayashi, teacher and mentor.

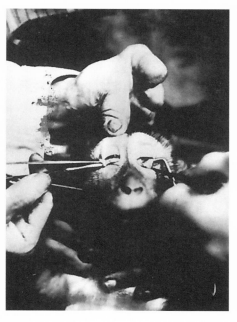

Kanae Watanabe gave Noguchi the
use of his hand again.

Surgery restored the use of his fingers, but
they remained stubs.

Morinosuke Chiwaki, Noguchi's benefactor.

The epidemiologist Shibazaburo Kitasato.

Simon Flexner (seated) with Noguchi.

Silas Weir Mitchell guided Noguchi's early career in America.

Mary Dardis Noguchi, Hideyo's wife.

The photo of Shika that brought Noguchi back to Japan in 1915.

Posing on the deck of the *Sado Maru*, November 1915. From left to right: Watanabe, Noguchi, Ishizuka, Chiwaki, and Kobayashi.

The Shandaken cabin, a retreat from the summer heat.

Noguchi with members of his laboratory staff at the
Rockefeller Institute.

Posing among his laboratory equipment in 1926.

Sergei Konenkov's 1927 bust of the doctor.

as far as Wakamatsu, with a stop at Okinajima. Noguchi got off the train and began the four-kilometer walk to his house. He crested a hill and saw his hometown lying there ahead. The last time he'd been back it was as a freshly minted, struggling physician; now he was a top-notch doctor with foreign experience.

Daikichi at the Matsushimaya store, elated to see his old friend again, ran around the village telling everyone he could that Noguchi was back in town. Naokichi Nihei also helped round up the people who knew him from childhood, and soon there was a party underway at a restaurant in the village.

"Look at what you've done with your life!" they told their old classmate. "Only twenty-three years old and already important. . . It's a big thing for us just to say that our village produced a doctor."

"You were always a bit different from the rest of us, Seisaku—ah, Hideyo. Look, you can't expect us to get ahold of your new name when we knew you for so long by your old one."

It was a happy reunion. These country folk weren't as polished as the citizens of Tokyo, but they showed a warmth lacking in the city. Tohoku people tend to like their drink, and this group was no exception. The more bottles they emptied the less they held back. Soon Noguchi was putting on a show for them, doing the songs and dances he'd learned in the Niuzhuang bars and brothels. Everyone cheered and rolled on the floor laughing until the sun rose on them all.

The next day, Daikichi approached his friend with something more serious on his mind. Would he use his medical skills to treat the village people? "Look, you might have become one of the best doctors in Tokyo," he said, "but what does that mean if you won't even treat the people you grew up with? Some of them never thought you'd make it as far as you have—you should do this just to show that they were always wrong about you, if nothing else."

"Yes, but not all doctors are the kind who examine patients."

"But that's just what you were doing in China, isn't it? Come on, Sei. Do this for me."

Noguchi couldn't say no to this old friend, and proceeded to set up a makeshift office in a room at Daikichi's store. As word got out that he wasn't charging anything for seeing patients, the villagers began lining up. Then the mayor, seeing what was going on, invited Noguchi to perform this service in a more spacious room in the village hall as part of a summer health-awareness campaign. Though something of a local hero—the doctor who had gone to the capital to train and all the way to China to practice—Noguchi was down-to-earth in his examinations, and the locals liked his thorough but lighthearted approach. Several people came to him with serious illnesses. These he correctly diagnosed, sending the patients to the Morikawa Pharmacy in Wakamatsu with carefully written prescriptions. They all saw their conditions improve.

To these poor villagers it seemed as though Noguchi had returned to work medical miracles among them. A few biographers have written doubtfully about his accomplishments in that temporary medical clinic of his: some of the ailments he is said to have cured were not the sort to go away after a single checkup and a dose of medicine. But certain facts remain. Those he treated went on to live long, healthy lives, and the stories of grateful villagers remain to this day in what was then Okinajima. Long years may have polished the praise they had for their doctor, but the praise was heartfelt and genuine.

Noguchi looked again at the pledge he'd carved into the pillar at home: *I will not set foot in this place again until I have achieved all my goals.* Now a full-fledged doctor, tested overseas and popular at home, he could certainly boast of his accomplishments. But his future still worried him. He needed to get to the United States; he needed money. Once again he headed to Yasuhei Yago's house.

The two men sat on the veranda. Coils of fragrant incense kept the summer mosquitoes away as they talked. Noguchi's determination was clear as he spoke of his need to be in America to further his career. As was often the case when he listened to his friend, Yago found himself daydreaming along with Noguchi. Of course he should go to the United States. He had done all he set out to do so far, hadn't he?

"I suppose it'll take a little money to get there, right?"

"It's more than a little, Yasuhei. I think five hundred should do it."

"Five hundred yen?" Yago paused at this. Then: "I figure I can get that much together for you."

"Really? You don't know how grateful I'd be!"

When Noguchi left to share this news with his old teacher, Kobayashi, the response he got was unexpected. "I see. . . ," was all Kobayashi had to say. Unnerved by his teacher's silence, Noguchi asked whether he'd done something wrong. The reply made him rethink his decision to accept Yago's money: "Something wrong? Well, I'd say you need to give some more thought to what you're doing. . . This is no easy task you're talking about attempting, Hideyo. You can't expect to make a success of it if you're going into it with this kind of easygoing attitude. Yes, you do need travel money. But if you start off by getting other people to give you everything you need, how can you expect to get over the problems you'll face later on your own?"

Noguchi, still a student to this man, listened to him carefully. Kobayashi told him to rely on himself alone—to act as though he were on the brink of disaster, and to make the kind of effort that would save him from it. "You've got to work as though your life depended on it. With the proper spirit I'm sure you'll manage."

This advice hit home. Later, a more subdued Noguchi told his friend Yago of his change of heart. Yago, predictably, was shocked: "You mean you really don't want the money? But I was looking forward to being able to help you out. . ." Noguchi reassured his friend that he was grateful for the offer, but he was afraid that having so much money placed in his hands would actually be bad for him; he wanted to achieve his goals on his own. This Yago could understand.

Before leaving for Tokyo, Noguchi remembered his friend Ryokei Kikuchi, who was now in Wakamatsu, so instead of heading south to the capital he boarded a train going north to meet up with his old drinking partner, who had once shared so many late-night talks about the prospect of going abroad.

Kikuchi showed Noguchi into the examination room of his medical clinic. A steady stream of patients sat waiting for their turn. When the day's work was over, Kikuchi called a rickshaw and the two headed for an inn near the Higashiyama hot springs, where they raised cups to old times.

Noguchi had been amazed at the crowds in the clinic. "With that many patients to care for you aren't going overseas any time soon."

"I know, it's frightening, isn't it? With a parade of sick people like that I've got no time to study new fields like psychiatry or forensic medicine . . . things I'm really interested in."

"It really is too bad, Ryokei." Kikuchi's dilemma was one that Noguchi, too, was personally aware of from his own recent experience at home.

■ ■ ■

Again in Tokyo with no work, he found himself, as usual, heading for Chiwaki's house. The dentist was now head of the Tokyo School of Dental Medicine, the successor to the Takayama college. The new school was not yet situated in a building of its own; Chiwaki had borrowed space on the second floor of a middle school to hold evening classes. Here there was work for Noguchi to do right away. He began teaching pathology and pharmacology in a lamp-lit classroom, the students perhaps smirking every once in a while at his northern accent.

During this interlude, Noguchi's linguistic skills served him well once again. The school had a copy of a new French text known to be an authoritative treatise on dentistry that would certainly come in handy in lectures, but none of the other instructors could read the language. Noguchi got straight to work on it, producing a simple translation for use in the classroom. Many of the anatomical terms he coined for this translation are still in use today in the field of dentistry in Japan.

As always, Noguchi did not take well to the idea of settling down, and America was behind this restlessness. The problem was, with Yago's offer no longer a possibility, he hadn't any other sources lined up. Saving up the funds himself was out of the question; even if he were capable of this it would take far too long to amass the amount in question. Comparatively speaking, it was much more expensive to travel abroad a century ago than it is now. Could his other friends help? No, they hadn't even been willing to loan him the few yen he needed to get to China in late 1899.

In situations like this, Chiwaki was the only person at all willing to listen to Noguchi. No matter how many times he got derailed in his career, he seemed to be able to count on the dentist's trust in him. Chiwaki, on his side, remained convinced that his talents would be wasted as just another country physician in Japan; he wanted to see Noguchi go as far as he could. And he was willing to go the whole hog to send him to the States. Even though they were only six years apart in age, Chiwaki's loyalty to the younger man was an extraordinary example of almost fatherly devotion.

The dentist was in no position to offer financial support himself, though; having just taken the top position at the new school, he was hard pressed to meet all his own bills. Once again he went to Motojiro Kawakami at the *Japan Weekly Medical Journal*, who had helped get Noguchi into the Kitasato Institute. When it came to the outside world, Kawakami was one of the more knowledgeable men in Japan at the time. Chiwaki consulted him about likely places for a young doctor to go to continue his research; Kawakami then wrote a letter asking for financial help addressed to a friend of his—Eigoro Kanasugi, Japan's foremost ear, nose, and throat specialist, and a man who would go on to be the first president of the Jikei University School of Medicine.

Kanasugi greeted Noguchi quite warmly, considering the nature of the letter he brought with him. "A request from Kawakami is certainly worth honoring," he told him. "But I have a request for *you*, young man. You're working under Dr. Kitasato at the moment, and I don't want to leave him without an assistant unless he's in complete agreement that you should go. If he approves of this trip of yours he'll be willing to pay for half of it; if he does that, I'll gladly pay the rest."

Noguchi dutifully went to Kitasato with this request. But his boss refused to put up any money at all for this venture, much less half of this considerable sum. His reason, though, was not a reflection on Noguchi's personal prospects; rather, he was unwilling to do someone a favor that would be grossly unfair to those who had worked in his institute for years ahead of him.

This setback made Noguchi begin to consider other ways of making it to America. Accordingly, he came up with the idea of working his passage across the Pacific—as a ship's doctor. He had one connection who might help him get him this post: one of the lecturers he knew from his Takayama days, Tamao Fujishima, whose uncle was in charge of hiring on-board medical staff for the ships of the Nihon Yusen line. Noguchi learned that the sole requirement for becoming a ship's doctor was the certificate showing the candidate had passed the state licensing exam. Now Noguchi realized that he had yet to pay the six-yen fee to obtain this document. He did so immediately and went to speak to Fujishima's uncle, license in hand.

The latter, however, quickly put a stop to this plan. "But Dr. Noguchi, don't you realize that being a ship's doctor means serving on board from the time the vessel leaves Japan until it docks again at a Japanese port? You can't just get off and stay in America!"

He was back to square one. His situation seemed hopeless. As the year 1900 drew on into autumn, Chiwaki invited him to the mountain resort of Hakone to spend a few days at the Tonosawa hot springs. He did this out of simple kindness, to help take the younger man's mind off his troubles, but the trip turned into a major event in Noguchi's life.

There was a billiards table in one room at the spa, and once Noguchi started playing he focused on nothing but the game for hours on end. Any other guests at the inn who wanted a game played against him. He should have been tired after a solid day of pool without stopping even for meals, but when evening came he began reading. With the same phenomenal energy he had always shown, he lost himself in his books at this Hakone hot spring, remaining awake deep into the night.

The other guests inevitably noticed the young man's behavior. One of them, a person named Fumio Naito, was visiting from Tokyo's wealthy Azabu district with his family. He and Chiwaki spent a while chatting together during the days they were there. At one point Naito and his wife went to Chiwaki's room to continue their conversation, in the course of which Mrs. Naito remarked on the dentist's studious companion. Chiwaki then told them all about him and his dream of studying in America.

Noguchi and Chiwaki returned to Tokyo soon afterwards. This, however, was not the last they would see of their new acquaintances. Some days later Mrs. Naito came to visit Chiwaki at home with a proposal for him: that a marriage be arranged between her niece and Noguchi. The dentist tried to convince her that the idea was ill advised. Noguchi was an unsuitable hus-band—a lowly medical researcher with no money to his name. The woman would not be turned aside, though. Eventually Chiwaki told her he was unwilling to make any decision in this matter without asking Noguchi him-self what he thought of the proposal.

Chiwaki had hoped to put a stop to her matchmaking with this last state-ment, but she took it to heart and went straight to the prospective "groom" with her offer. Noguchi, however, was even less open to her overtures than Chiwaki had been. Only interested in ways of getting out of Japan, he paid little attention at all to a proposal that would leave him tied to a wife here. Mrs. Naito was perceptive, though, and saw a way to overcome his resistance: "You know, there's no need to marry my niece right away. Get engaged now, and we can have the wedding later after you've been to America to study. Oh, and of course we'll be paying for that. Take your time thinking about this offer."

Her words made him sit up and listen. "Do you mean this? You'll pay for my trip? That would be perfect!"

"Shall I take this as a yes?" the woman said with a smile.

Noguchi saw this as his last, best chance to get to the United States. When he went to Chiwaki with news of the proposal, the dentist advised caution. "It isn't just an engagement we're talking about. Once you accept that money you're into it for much more than that." Chiwaki knew that marrying the girl in the end was the only honorable way to take the money. Noguchi may have been uniquely talented, but he knew little about the ways of the world.

"I realize what's involved, sir. But I have to take this offer. There's no telling when I'll be able to get to America otherwise."

"If you're sure of what you're doing, Noguchi, then I won't stand in your way. But remember that the Naitos are as serious as you are about this deal, so make sure you keep the promises you're making!"

Thus was a marriage of convenience arranged between Masuko Naito, whose family saw Noguchi as a promising mate for her, and Hideyo, who had found his ticket to America. As it turned out, Masuko had known of Noguchi for some time—she had often gone to the Kaiyo Clinic to pick up medicine from him. What was more, she was also aiming for a medical career of her own; a talented young man like Noguchi was a natural target for a family looking to make a good match for a young woman with professional aspirations.

■ ■ ■

Noguchi returned to Fukushima again to say his goodbyes and make his final preparations for the move to America. His family was not in very good shape. His father was as usual deep in the bottle, leaving the household finances in a sorry state. His grandmother, now well over seventy, could no longer do any kind of work. His younger brother Seizo was a student at the upper elementary school, which added to their expenses. His sister, Inu, should have been a help to the family by this stage, but the man she had married turned out to be just as much of a drunk as their father, and she had her hands full supporting him.

As always, this left only Shika to manage the Noguchi home. She was nearly fifty years old, though, and her white hair and wrinkles were far more evident than her son remembered. She shrugged off his concern, though: "Ah, I'm still healthy. You don't need to fret over me. You go on and keep studying. You'll be an important man, and I want to see you go as far as you can!"

Her first thought was for her boy's success, as it always had been. As the eldest son in the family Hideyo knew better than anyone the hardship she had gone through to raise this family. Was he unkind in leaving his mother behind to pursue his dreams abroad? No, this wasn't really so. He cared deeply for her, and she for her part blessed his venture despite any extra difficulties it may have brought the Noguchi home. That night Noguchi stayed awake thinking long after he had crawled into bed.

The next morning he went to see his old teacher, Kobayashi. He couldn't bring himself to tell the man how he had obtained the money that would take him to America; he explained that Dr. Chiwaki would be helping him. Kobayashi lit a candle on the Buddhist altar in his home in thanks for this good news. He noticed, though, the worried look on Noguchi's face.

"I've still got one serious problem. . . When I think about it I wonder whether I should be heading to America at all."

Kobayashi asked at once what the problem was. The young doctor explained: if he went abroad, he felt that his whole family might fall apart if his mother were to collapse from overwork without him in Japan to come and help out. He felt he faced a terrible choice: to turn his back on his family or to give up on his own hopes of carrying out research overseas. His mother had told him not to worry about her, but he couldn't ignore the hard life she had to live. He'd been up all night thinking about what to do.

Kobayashi had reassuring words for his student. "It's good of you to be worried about your family, and you're right to think about your mother. But I want you to go, and go through with what you've set out to do without this at the back of your mind. I'll look after your family and make sure your mother is all right. Whatever I can do for the Noguchis I will."

It was another generous gift from his mentor. Noguchi thanked him again and again.

"Yes, I'll keep an eye on them and give them a helping hand if they need it. I want you to walk out onto the world's stage without a worry in your head."

Noguchi started crying. After a while he looked up and said: "Sir, I'd like to ask . . . whether you'd let me call you Father."

Now it was the teacher's turn to be moved. In tears, the two men forged a bond that would last a lifetime. Jaded modern observers might find this exchange maudlin; indeed, some have suggested that it was all just a ploy of Noguchi's to earn sympathy and perhaps financial gain. But the parties involved treated it as a formal thing, with Kobayashi calling his wife in to be part of it. Noguchi's behavior later in life made this seem an honestly forged bond of affection between him and the Kobayashis, whom he called "Father" and "Mother" for the rest of his life. His real father had never been much of a presence in his life, and Kobayashi filled an emotional void for him. His real mother, meanwhile, became "my mother in Okinajima."

To celebrate this new relationship, and to send Hideyo off to America properly, Mrs. Kobayashi presented him with two hundred yen she had made raising silkworms. This was an astounding sum—far more than her husband made in a year as a teacher—and it had been earned with hard labor among the mulberry bushes where the worms made their cocoons. The gift shows the extent to which she had let this young man into her heart—her new son and her only child, the Kobayashis having no children of their own.

Noguchi's teacher also congratulated him and then gave him a fatherly lecture. There were three things he must not forget during his time away. "First, you must always remember your mother in Okinajima with love and respect. Second, you must give thanks to Kannon for what you've achieved. And third, you must always remember this. . ." He grabbed Noguchi's left hand and raised it up before his eyes. "Don't forget what you have done, and must continue to do, to overcome this handicap. If you keep these three things firmly in mind I have no doubt that you'll do admirably wherever you go in the world."

As soon as he made it back to the capital, Noguchi was swamped with preparations for his trip. He went to the Foreign Ministry and the American Embassy to get his travel documents in order. He also learned all he could of the situation in the United States so he wouldn't be completely lost on his arrival there. His coming departure did not go unnoticed by his friends, especially those from Aizu who were in Tokyo at the time. Soon they gathered to hold a farewell party for him. In all a dozen or so young men gathered in a room above a shop in Kudanshita to celebrate their friend's departure. It was a simple get-together, but they sent him off warmly, with high hopes for his success overseas.

Three days later the Naito family visited Chiwaki and presented him with three hundred yen wrapped in ceremonial paper. Before long this money was in Noguchi's hands.

Before his boat sailed, Noguchi thought he should say goodbye to his colleagues at the Quarantine Station in Yokohama. He had enjoyed a lot of food and drink at their expense, and he was now in a position to return the favor. The money from the Naitos was burning a hole in his pocket. When he met up with them, the first thing he said was: "What do you say? Your friend's leaving Japan—let's have a feast to celebrate."

Needless to say they welcomed the idea, but they proposed a low-key celebration at a nearby restaurant, a going-away party being something they felt they should treat him to. But Noguchi had a purse full of money and wouldn't hear of it. "No, you treated me to all those meals during our time together. Now it's my turn to take you all out. Tonight is on me!" For someone who was prone to blow a whole month's salary on one evening's drinking, this was a risky proposition. He may have been capable of great things in the laboratory, but when it came to everyday life he had less sense than a child.

Noguchi had three hundred yen on him, a vast sum, not likely to be dented by a night of drinking with some friends. The group readily agreed to his generous invitation. They began telling other friends about the party that evening, and before long several dozen people had gathered to send Noguchi off in style. The happy doctor led them to Jinpuro, supposedly the finest restaurant in Kanagawa Prefecture at the time. With three floors of banquet halls and an atmosphere that came straight out of some Chinese classic, the place had a constant line of rickshaws waiting outside for the wealthy customers who dined there.

The raucous quarantine crowd piled into Jinpuro and began eating and drinking with gusto. In due course they called for geisha to entertain them. The view the restaurant offered of Yokohama's harbor, with its brightly lit steamships from around the globe, roused everybody to singing and dancing, and of course more drinking. The young men's cheers and laughter rang out into the night.

■ ■ ■

There was no laughter the next day, though. The bill was a long one, and when the restaurant manager had finished adding it all up it came to nearly everything Noguchi had on him. He was left with just over thirty yen to his name. A day earlier he had been rich. He had made some purchases to prepare for his trip with the two hundred yen from Mrs. Kobayashi, but those hadn't cost much at all. With the cash he had received from the Naitos his total funds had been nearly five hundred yen yesterday. In the course of a single night he had gone from an optimistic young man setting out to conquer the world to a dejected pauper with no future. He could no longer afford to go to America. He hadn't even bought his ticket yet.

The next few hours were like a nightmare. He stood motionless for a long time, his mind in a state of shock at the reality he now faced. The faces of his mother, of Kobayashi, of Chiwaki came to mind. . . All of them had dreamed with him of success in the United States, and he had smashed those dreams in a single night. He was broke. What was he to do?

He slowly made his way back to Tokyo and at last stood before Chiwaki. Down onto the floor he went, his hands on the ground. He told his benefactor everything that had happened. He cursed his own stupidity and apologized over and over again. "I didn't think it would cost more than a third of what I had last night. . . I had no idea the bill could be so high for a single party. I had no idea. . ."

Chiwaki was speechless. He had overlooked a lot in his dealings with Noguchi over the years, but this time the man had gone too far. Yelling at him now would not bring the money back. Indeed, the problems that he faced were not the kind that could be fixed with any number of stern words. Chiwaki calmly and quietly presented the facts to him: if this had been his own money, he could spend it as he pleased and go to America later. But it had not been his money to spend. He was bound by duty to travel abroad, study, and return to his waiting fiancée. The ship he should be on was leaving for San Francisco in three days' time, and at most he would be able to put off his departure for a month or so. Any later than that and he would be guilty of fraud. It was imperative that he find the money he needed to buy passage on another ship within that month.

This was Noguchi's responsibility, but Chiwaki knew that he was caught up in this problem, too, as the go-between in the marriage talks. As much as he wanted to, he couldn't leave this young fool to his own devices. But this was a difficult time for him financially—the dental school was still in its infancy and not on a firm financial footing. He did not have the resources to bail Noguchi out himself. But he did still have his network of connections in the medical establishment. He went to several acquaintances and asked them for help. With his reputation Chiwaki should have had no trouble putting together two or three hundred yen, even at short notice, but the news of Noguchi's last extravagance spread rapidly, and nobody was willing to offer Chiwaki anything if it was going to a man like that.

When it came to money Noguchi was a walking disaster. But Chiwaki couldn't bring himself to walk away from him. He had to help him; he knew he had talent and he knew it could lead to a brilliant future for him. In later years he would recall that it was a sense of duty that made him go on supporting him. And so, for the first time in his life, the dentist found himself walking into the office of a moneylender to obtain another three hundred yen.

When Noguchi learned how Chiwaki had come up with the money he wept openly. Shaking with sobs he thought of the deep debt he owed—a debt of more than just money—to the only person who was there for him when his own family couldn't help.

Noguchi made arrangements for passage on another ship and went one last time to the Kitasato Institute, where he said goodbye to its founder. This was an encouraging visit. Dr. Kitasato wished him all the best and wrote several letters of recommendation for him to take with him. One of these has survived to this day. In it Kitasato wrote in German to Simon Flexner: "Noguchi, who worked as an assistant at my institute, wishes to study under you. I entrust him to your kind care."

The day of departure arrived at last. Various friends accompanied Noguchi to Shimbashi Station. Among them was Masuko Naito, dressed in formal kimono to see off her future husband properly. Noguchi approached her and her mother just before his train left, bowed, and said: "Well, I'm on my way. I will see you when I return." The Naitos knew nothing of the party in Yoko-hama that they had inadvertently funded. As far as they were concerned, Noguchi was going abroad on their money. He knew differently, though, and he knew that he could never allow himself to slip up again.

Chiwaki, who was all too painfully aware of how this trip was being funded, accompanied Noguchi as far as Yokohama, where he paid for the ticket and handed it to the traveler. He gave him another valuable gift at this parting: an introduction to Midori Komatsu, who was traveling on the same ship to serve in Japan's embassy in Washington. Chiwaki asked Komatsu to look after Noguchi during their voyage. The three men approached the *Amerika Maru* as the last cargo was being stowed. The dentist accompanied Noguchi on board, where he stopped, faced him, and spoke to him of his obligations and the tasks that lay before him.

"Now listen to me. In the time that follows, your actions will determine whether you are a man with the true gift of genius or one who sinks without a trace. When you set foot on American soil you will have nobody to look after you and catch you when you fall. Understand that you will be on your own."

Noguchi listened intently to these instructions.

"No matter how tough things get, you must persevere. You must go on, to the very limit of your strength. Become the kind of man who has nothing to fear when he returns to Japan. They say that three days after a lioness gives birth, she takes her cubs to the edge of a cliff and pushes them off. Only the strongest is allowed to live. That's the way I feel about you now. Do not forget it."

This was a stern lecture, and coming from Chiwaki, ordinarily so friendly and forgiving, it hit home with more than usual force. Noguchi clasped his hand firmly once as they heard the gong that told visitors to leave. Without a word Chiwaki walked down the gangplank and watched the ship head out to sea. With Chiwaki's speech still ringing in his ears, Noguchi despondently waved his hat at the figure on the dock. Now he was beyond help. All he had to rely on were his youthful energy, his desire to succeed, and his tenuous connection with Flexner, a man he had met only once.

On December 5, 1900, Hideyo Noguchi left Japan for the West. He was twenty-four years old.

A NEW START IN AMERICA

Not long after the *Amerika Maru* left Japan's shores it ran into a violent squall. Fierce winds tore the railing from the deck and even the lifeboats vanished into the waves that came crashing over the ship. A superstitious traveler might see this as an ominous way to begin a journey to America, but Noguchi rode out the storm quite calmly with his nose in a book as usual.

He had chosen *The Merchant of Venice* as the first work on his reading list. Midori Komatsu noted this with surprise.

"You know, Noguchi, we're going to America, and it's the year 1900. Wouldn't a more modern book be a better choice?"

"Not a chance. Shakespeare is the foundation of all literature in English. I'm going to start at the beginning and work my way forward."

Komatsu walked away shaking his head. Either this man was an idiot . . . or a genius.

After putting ashore briefly in Honolulu the *Amerika Maru* continued on to San Francisco. Then, after more than two weeks at sea, on December 22 Hideyo Noguchi stepped onto American soil. He was one of a wave of Japanese seeking their fortune in the United States—over ten thousand of his fellow countrymen made this trip in 1900 alone. It was not such a difficult move to make. America welcomed these newcomers, requiring only that they have in their possession thirty dollars each to enter the nation. This made it a natural destination for those traveling and studying without official financial support of some kind.

Noguchi took a room on the third floor of the Palace Hotel, where he wrote a quick letter to Chiwaki letting him know he had arrived safely. He touched not at all on his first impressions of this new country, focusing instead on his plans for the future, which felt a lot closer now.

The next morning he boarded a Union Pacific train for the east. He spared little time looking out the window at the splendor of the Rocky Mountains, choosing instead to go on reading and to gaze at a sheaf of picture postcards depicting famous landmarks around America. These had been an expensive purchase he'd made in Honolulu—three dollars' worth, more than a young man taking only one meal a day to stretch his scarce funds could really afford. On the third day out of San Francisco Komatsu, who was on the same train, noticed that Noguchi wasn't eating anything and invited him to join him in the dining car. The next day Komatsu disembarked in the nation's capital, leaving the other man to make the half-day journey north to Pennsylvania on his own.

■ ■ ■

Noguchi's first move in Philadelphia was to take a carriage to the University of Pennsylvania's School of Medicine to call on Professor Flexner. The cold winds of late December blew through the campus, which was closed for the winter holidays. Luckily the professor was in his office. He looked up with considerable surprise at the Japanese man who walked into the room and handed him a gift from Tokyo before inquiring after his health.

"I told you I'd come to do research under you, Professor Flexner, and here I am. I hope you've got some work for me!"

Flexner was taken aback by this intrusion. He had never invited Noguchi to come to the United States or to work with him. This over-eager foreigner had taken his polite words of encouragement at their last meeting to mean far more than they actually did. Even if he did have some work to assign to Noguchi, he was himself a new arrival, having been at Johns Hopkins until recently, and had no authority to hire new staff himself.

"Look, young man, the other researchers at this school are all paying their own way here. Do you have any money for tuition?"

Disappointment showed on Noguchi's face. "No sir, I'm afraid I don't."

"It won't be easy to give you a spot, then. Do you have a place to stay?"

Again Noguchi shook his head.

As put out as he was by this unexpected visitor from Asia, Flexner was a kindhearted person. The son of Jewish immigrants, he had worked his way up from a shop clerk's position to become one of America's top medical researchers. Like Noguchi, he was small in stature, and driven in temperament; he had also learned medicine at a minor training institute, not a respectable university. Perhaps these similarities bred sympathy in him. The professor said he would speak to the school authorities about finding a position for him, and helped the newcomer find a cheap place to stay.

Noguchi's room was little more than an attic in a flophouse. In this cramped, musty place he waited for word from Flexner. When it came, though, it was a major letdown. The university had a general policy against hiring foreign nationals; the professor advised him to give up trying for a position there. This wasn't like Japan, where foreigners were unusual visitors whose knowledge of a more advanced world was often highly valued. America attracted countless immigrants from other countries, and people were quick to gauge their value to an organization in terms of their qualifications and their ability to use the knowledge they'd acquired. A man like Noguchi, with limited command of academic English, had little chance of finding university work.

This news was devastating. Noguchi had come thousands of miles in the belief that Flexner would have a job for him. With this hope gone, he had nothing but the twenty-three dollars in his pocket. And this did not last long. Alone and penniless in a strange town far from his own country, Noguchi floundered around, looking for a lifeline of some kind. If he could only make it to New York, he thought, he could be among other Japanese again—he could find help there. He wrote at once to Komatsu, one of the few people he knew in America, offering to make use of his language skills at the Japanese embassy in Washington or at the consulate in New York. The English spoken in Philadelphia was not what he was used to, and he would certainly do better in the bigger cities. Noguchi carefully avoided mentioning that Flexner had no work for him, being aware that the news would reflect poorly on his mentor Chiwaki, who had supported his bid to do research in America. Instead he finished his letter with two requests: an introduction to a job—any job at all—and some money to pay for train fare.

This letter met with a cold response. If Noguchi were sick, or if he had already completed his studies and needed a new position, Komatsu could do something to help, but he was under the impression that Noguchi still had a position waiting for him in Pennsylvania, and this message from him seemed merely like the selfish request of a frivolous young man looking for a free trip to New York. Komatsu made it clear: this was the kind of attitude that could make the embassy send a medical student, who was supposed to be picking up knowledge for the good of his fellow countrymen, straight back to Japan.

So this was the choice Noguchi now faced: he could either be sent home in the deepest shame or he could slowly starve in the cold city of Philadelphia. His lack of knowledge had led to a lack of caution, his naivete to the brink of disaster. With these thoughts in his mind he flung himself down on the floor of his tiny attic room and lay there motionless. The late December chill seeped into his bones. What options did he have in this strange new country? What could he do?

After some hours of this, he sat up, took a piece of paper lying nearby, and began to sketch a picture. In it stars sparkled in a broad sky stretching over a stormy sea. Toward the edge of the paper he drew a skull lying on its side. There are plenty of possible interpretations of this drawing, but whatever it really meant to Noguchi, it left him feeling better. He thought back to the words that Chiwaki had used on the deck of the *Amerika Maru* before it left port, about persevering "no matter how tough things get . . . going on, to the very limit of your strength." Pulling on his jacket, he burst out of his room into the Philadelphia winter. This was America's fourth largest city at the time, and its streets bustled with large, fair-haired people. Among them walked this small Asian, urging his steps along as he headed toward Flexner's office.

"I stand before you," he shouted in Flexner's presence, "ready to work harder than anyone. Please give me something to do!"

The urgency in his voice seemed to jolt the professor into action. Promising he would do what he could for his determined visitor, he sent him away. It was New Year's Eve when he summoned him back. "Have you ever worked with snake venom?" was the abrupt question Flexner put to him. Noguchi was flustered. The way he answered this might decide his fate in America—and the best response required specialized knowledge that he didn't have. He did, however, remember seeing an older researcher at the Kitasato Institute working with the *habu*, a pit viper native to Japan. He had merely looked on from time to time at his experiments, and asked a question now and then.

"Yes, sir, I do know a little about it. I'd like the chance to learn more."

"Well, that's fortunate. I'll take you on as my personal assistant in my research on poisonous snakes." And with this generous offer, Flexner gave Noguchi the opening he'd needed. "There isn't much money in it for you," he went on. "You'll only get enough to cover your meals—about eight dollars a month. You'll need to speak to people in your own country about getting what you need for things like housing and clothes."

Noguchi now had a way to stay in the world of research abroad. From the start, he hadn't been entirely on the level in his efforts to land this position— his English résumé referred to him as "a graduate of Tokyo Medical University" rather than a former research assistant at Kitasato's laboratory who had passed the medical licensing examination—but whether this was deliberately misleading or an innocent mistake, it had helped him find a job, and that was what mattered most to him now. On January 4, 1901, he appeared for duty at the medical school. He was given a small space in a pathology classroom with the equipment and materials he needed to carry out his investigations.

■ ■ ■

As Flexner had suggested, Noguchi wrote to his sponsor in Japan again seeking funds to keep him clothed and fed. The reply came some time later, but it wasn't a very encouraging one. With the new dental college in its early days, Chiwaki was scrambling to keep the school afloat and ensure its success. He enclosed a money order for a hundred yen, but said it would probably be the last he could send him. Hereafter, the letter told Noguchi, he would have to rely on his own hard work if he wanted to continue his activities in the United States.

Noguchi took the money order and dashed to the post office to exchange it for dollars. But when he got there and thrust his hand into his pocket to hand it over, it was gone. Had he dropped it along the way? He ran back to his lodgings, searching the ground in between for the slip of paper. But it was nowhere to be seen, and though he turned his room upside down in the search he couldn't find the thing. Feeling unable to tell his benefactor about this, he wrote a letter thanking Chiwaki deeply for his generous gift.

When he returned dejectedly to the post office to mail this off, he decided to press his case with the staff there. He *had* received the money order, even if it wasn't with him now. And after several hours of persistent negotiations with the post office clerks he finally managed to get the money.

With this his life seemed to be on a more even keel. Yet this stability did not last. Soon Professor Flexner was called away to Washington. There had been an outbreak of the plague, and the government had ordered him to help get it under control. He would be gone for about three months on this assignment. Noguchi had been lucky to arrive in America when he did—a little later and he would have failed to meet up with Flexner at all—but now he faced the prospect of being in this new place without the one person with whom he wanted to work. He felt nervous about being at the University of Pennsylvania on his own. He had always fancied himself talented in English, but it wasn't serving him as well as he'd expected. He had, after all, taught himself most of what he knew from books; without speaking and hearing practice he hadn't built up the skills he needed to communicate effectively. Much of the time he had a hard time making himself understood even by the people who worked alongside him.

Professor Flexner was active in various administrative affairs in addition to his own research. When the government wanted to establish a new laboratory, he was the man to set it up, finding people to staff it and helping to develop new fields of research. This took him away from the university for much of the time. Now he placed Noguchi under another doctor in his absence—Silas Weir Mitchell.

Mitchell was a well-known figure in American medicine, with a number of key discoveries to his name. He was over seventy years of age and no longer active on the "front line" of research and treatment, but he was a renowned neurologist, a long-term professor at the University of Pennsylvania, the president of the College of Physicians of Philadelphia, and an accomplished writer and poet. His father had been a pathologist with a deep interest in snake venom, and Dr. Mitchell had carried on that research to become an authority on toxicology as well.

Noguchi asked this venerable doctor for any assistance he might be able to give regarding the venom studies he was working on. Dr. Mitchell took a liking to this earnest foreigner, speaking frankly to him about his research and other matters. Known to be a perceptive judge of character, he may have seen something unusual in him. Dr. Mitchell's son John would later recall that his father often talked about him. He praised Noguchi as "a most interesting young man," someone of "great spirit." The doctor's wife, too, noticed with amusement the way these two got along so well: "Look at those blue eyes and those black eyes staring into each other!"

In spite of this enthusiastic welcome, though, Mitchell did have some reservations about him. It was still far from clear how much a young Asian researcher would be able to accomplish in the unfamiliar environment of the West. At the dawn of the twentieth century it was no easy matter for a Japanese to become a fully accepted member of American society. And Noguchi was aiming to go beyond this level of assimilation; he wanted to make a name for himself as a medical innovator. His chances of success in this seemed slim, despite the special talent he had for turning wishful thinking into a powerful drive propelling him toward his goals. When Mitchell steered him toward taking "a fresh look at venoms along the lines of some new concepts in the biological sciences of toxicology and immunology," Noguchi promised to do his best, but in truth he lacked experience in any of these areas—the study of snake venom, toxicology, and immunology were all new to him. All he had was a little general experience in the laboratory. His only recourse was to plow ahead and acquire knowledge as he went along.

For some time Noguchi subsisted on nothing but quick bites of bread and glasses of water. He spent hours in the medical school library looking for every reference he could find in English, French, and German dealing with poisonous snakes. Reading through these books as quickly as he could, he made copious notes on any information of interest he found in them. In the evenings, after the library was shut, he would often make his way to the nearby home of Edward Kirk, dean of the School of Dental Medicine, whom he knew thanks to an introduction from Chiwaki. Kirk would give the hardworking researcher dinner and, if it was late, a place to stay for the night. After accepting this offer several times, Noguchi grew nervous about becoming a nuisance to his host and started taking his leave after the meal. But he was loath to return all the way to his small room in Professor Mitchell's home when he wanted to be back at the library early the next morning. So it was that Kirk's gardener was startled early one morning by the sight of a man collapsed on the veranda. Shaking him awake he found it was only Noguchi, who apologized for causing trouble and went off to spend yet another day among his books.

Some months went by, and Flexner returned from his assignment. Noguchi presented him with the results of his three months of labor in the library stacks: an amazing 250 pages of abstracted information on snakes and snake venom. An American researcher would have been hard-pressed to come up with this volume of information in just three months, but Noguchi had done it in English—a foreign language to him. This impressed the professor, who went straight to the university administration and convinced the school to hire Noguchi as an official research assistant. Now that he was no longer a privately hired researcher he could look forward to getting twenty-five dollars a month. Thrilled by this new turn of events and pleased by the trust that Flexner had placed in him, Noguchi resolved to redouble his efforts.

The research made heavy use of dehydrated snake venom. Dr. Mitchell had been providing Noguchi with most of the pale yellow powder that he used in his work. But the school laboratory's cages were home to a dozen or so types of poisonous snakes. They were a fearsome sight, these thick, coiled, venomous creatures with their triangular heads and stubby tails, and Noguchi shuddered to think of their deadliness. Some of these snakes could kill almost instantly with a bite; others would inject a poison that doomed the victim to a week of agony before death. A single spoonful of rattlesnake venom could kill more than a hundred men. Even other snakes weren't safe from these killers: a black mamba had been observed in Africa dispatching more than ten of another species of snake one by one. The first lay dead near the tree in which the mamba lived, with a line of dead snakes stretching away down the path in the order they had been attacked—a testament to the lethality of the mamba and proof that the potency of its bites decreased somewhat the more it struck.

Snake venom is a clear, yellow-tinted liquid sticky to the touch, and has no odor or flavor. It was vital to Noguchi's research, and obtaining it from live snakes was a dangerous task. An animal handler would first use a snare pole to grab the serpent just behind its head. Next Dr. Gay (who had accompanied Flexner on his tour of Japan and the Philippines) would hold the snake's body still to keep it from thrashing about. Finally Noguchi would put on rubber gloves and force the snake's mouth open, squeezing its poison glands from the sides and forcing streams of venom from its fangs into a watch glass.

Walking in wild, overgrown places, especially after dark, is a way to invite a snakebite. Once the poison enters a person's bloodstream it begins dissolving red corpuscles. Immediate treatment involves applying a tourniquet to the bitten limb to keep the venom from flowing through the entire body, and cutting open the bitten area to squeeze the poisoned blood out. Injecting serum to reduce the concentration of poison in the bloodstream is the most effective treatment if it can be done in time. The serum provides the patient with immunity, Noguchi learned. This concept of immunity, and his desire to understand it, would be a central theme of his life's work.

Immunity is the body's capacity to resist an illness or poison. Animals are born with natural immunities to some threats and can gain acquired immunity to others during their lives, as when a person becomes immune to the measles after having it once. In the late nineteenth and early twentieth centuries researchers were working furiously to develop serums and vaccines to boost human immunity to diseases. Edward Jenner had opened up this field of science in 1796 when he demonstrated a vaccine for smallpox. More recently Louis Pasteur in 1881 had come up with a medicine that prevented anthrax in animals, and in 1890 Emil von Behring and Shibasaburo Kitasato had discovered an antitoxin for diphtheria.

Now Noguchi turned his attention to the effect of snake venom on the human body. The mechanism by which the poison dissolved blood cells was not well understood, and Noguchi decided to focus on clarifying this process first, which—if successful—should lead to a better understanding of the workings of serums and broader microbiological factors as well. Dr. Gay was in charge at the laboratory, and he gave Noguchi his assignments; but in between those official duties the young researcher worked on his own experiments. He came up with his own methods, too, for this extra work. He tried introducing low concentrations of venom to thinned blood, observing the results with a microscope and his naked eye. His workspace was soon littered with used test tubes and—due to a heavy smoking habit—cigarette butts. In the midst of his experiments he would toss these butts aside without watching where they went; this earned him repeated warnings from Dr. Gay. Noguchi's response was to point to his test tubes and tell his advisor to look at the results he was getting, not the cigarettes he was smoking—and indeed, Dr. Gay acknowledged the confident progress this young man showed in his research and methods despite the short time he had been working in the laboratory.

The laboratory snakes needed to eat, of course, in order to continue providing their venom. The custom was to toss a few live rabbits into the snake cages, where they remained until a snake was hungry enough to eat one. If a snake began to feed while people were in the laboratory they would head to one side of the room, away from the cage, to give the creature some peace while it ate.

It was a nervous Noguchi who waited for the snakes to finish eating. He would mutter under his breath, unable to keep still, tapping his fingers on a desk until it was time to go back to work. Finally, unable to keep it pent up any longer, he told his coworkers how cruel he found this practice—how scared the rabbits must feel as they waited to be swallowed. This only earned him a reputation for being oversensitive, too sentimental to be a scientist.

■ ■ ■

Noguchi was finally settling down in his new life in America. He wrote frequently to Chiwaki, keeping him informed of his activities and the events around him. These long, detailed messages revealed the extent to which he had been affected by his new surroundings, as this sample shows:

> I have been living each day on its own, trying to make the best possible use of every moment I am given. I have no time to worry much about what the weather may be like tomorrow or the day after. Everyone is born with a certain destiny set out before him. It isn't possible to see what this fate may be, but I believe it is decided for us nonetheless.
>
> Since coming to America I have made some progress in my academic work. I have also come to understand, to some small extent, the true nature of this world. Fortune and misfortune, poverty and wealth, the human self, the way to live one's life so as to be satisfied with it, the relationship between the individual and society—all these things I have considered in my time here. On reflection, I have come to recognize a deep value in one's own convictions and calling in life.
>
> I am taking a special interest in the relations between the races of man—their clashes and the potential for harmony between them. I strive constantly to maintain the optimism and moral fiber required of me as a person who has been thrust into this turbulent world. Surely there can be no greater pleasure than that to be derived from one's ability to remain a moral, hopeful person in the face of adversity.
>
> I have completed part of what I set out to accomplish in coming to the United States. The tasks that remain for me are of two kinds: those

that I must complete with my own labor from now on and those that must be left to fate. I must confess that my original goals in coming to this country were horribly small-minded ones. One of them—indeed, the principal objective I had—was to gain fame and honor for myself. Now, however, this desire has receded from my mind. I wish only to dedicate my life to the pursuit of new medical knowledge through my research.

Had I remained in Japan, would I have been able to find the kind of environment that allowed me to do this? Rather than suffer the restrictions placed on my actions by arrogant public servants, I would probably have struck out on my own, becoming a quack physician or finding some other way to make a living on my own terms. But here in America I pass my days in quiet fulfillment. Some in Japan may see me as accomplishing nothing with my life; but it is enough for me to believe in what I am doing. In the end, it is not so very difficult to put into action what one's heart commands, no matter how low one's station may be...

Letters like these might suggest a wise old writer with deep experience behind his words, but Noguchi was not even twenty-five when he wrote to Chiwaki.

Along with the maturity he seemed to be acquiring, Noguchi also developed a cooler eye for judging other people. One day he discovered that some money had gone missing from his room in a local lodging house. The woman who ran the house and her daughter were his partners for English conversation practice, and even after he had narrowed down the suspects to them, he was unwilling to forgo the language skills he could pick up by speaking with them. This was the old Noguchi: trusting in people even to his own financial detriment. But after speaking to people at the university about this situation and receiving simple advice—leave that place and find a new one immediately—he reconsidered the matter. He told the woman that he would no longer room with her, and why. Her tears almost swayed him, but now a more rational, observant Noguchi stepped forward—he realized she was crying not in regret at his leaving but in fear for what this would do to her reputation with the university. This made his decision an easy one: he left right away.

In September 1901 America was rocked by the assassination of President

William McKinley. An anarchist named Leon Czolgosz shot the president on September 6, and after he succumbed to his wound eight days later, Theodore Roosevelt took over as the youngest man ever to hold the office. Flags around the city flew at half-mast. Noguchi was not a single-minded man of science; he paid close attention to political trends and ethnic shifts in America, and now his letters to Japan explained what he thought was taking place—why anarchists had appeared on the scene, the societal background to this tragedy, and even the social structures in place in America and how they differed from those in Japan. He wrote to Chiwaki that Japan's feudal history, its emphasis on vertical relations between parent and child, lord and servant, made the rise of anarchism unlikely there. Noguchi's observations and comparisons at this time mark him as a true Meiji man, examining his own nation in the light of new things he learned about other lands.

The Japanese residents of Philadelphia had a social club. After hearing of this group Noguchi began to take part in its activities as a way to maintain his ties with his own country. The members of this group took turns inviting the others to their homes. When Noguchi's turn came around he thought back to his days in Aizu, when a celebration usually meant a chicken. He bought a bird and took it back to his small apartment—little more than a kitchen and a living room—to prepare it for his guests that evening.

After putting the chicken in the oven, Noguchi was suddenly struck by some new idea related to his research. He headed for his bookshelves to check his references and lost all track of time. It took the other members of the club pounding at his door to snap him out of this studious reverie. He rushed to get the cooked chicken onto the table for his friends. It was only when he noticed that none of them were helping themselves to the meat that he recognized the strange smell that filled his room—he had forgotten to clean and dress the bird, and it had been cooked with all its organs intact. Once again he had proved himself capable of being absent-minded and single-minded all at once.

■ ■ ■

The dedication and drive Noguchi had in abundance derived from his mother. Shika had been doing well for herself during the time her son was making a name for himself in America. Her reputation as a midwife had spread, making her a trusted figure throughout Okinajima and the surrounding region. Her blossoming career, however, suffered a serious setback in 1900 when the law regulating midwives was revised to require a government license for anyone performing this work. This forced her to stop providing her services locally. Seizo, Hideyo's brother, was away serving in the house of a rich family in Wakamatsu, so she no longer needed to support him, but her husband was still a drunk, and now there were three extra mouths at home to feed—her grandchildren Sakae, Torakichi, and Eisaku. Without her income as a midwife the Noguchi family faced desperate times.

Like her son, though, Shika was unwilling to accept defeat, and she had a talent for finding a way to make it through difficult times to reach a goal. She also had allies. The village did not want to be without a midwife, especially now that the population was growing quickly thanks to an influx of laborers building a new power plant at Lake Inawashiro. The county office launched a program to train one candidate from each village in the area. The mayor of Okinajima nominated Shika to earn her license under this program. And though she wasn't truly ready to receive this training—the priest Unoura had taught her to read *kana*, but she wasn't literate enough to study the material this course involved—she nevertheless resolved to get the license that would let her continue to serve her village. Her son had made a place for himself in the world of research despite his lack of a proper academic background; she would do the same in her own field. A woman in the town of Aizu-Bange taught the classes, which gave a basic education in everything from anatomy and physiology to nursing methods. After ten days of lessons the students headed to Wakamatsu for their test. While this examination was not as difficult as the one her son had passed to become a doctor, she was still a proud woman on the day she learned she had passed it and become a licensed midwife.

Shika lacked the money to purchase the tools required for this trade—a clock, a stethoscope, and a selection of medicines. But once again the mayor stepped in to help her, taking up a collection among the people of the village, and soon she had enough to buy a midwife's kit. She hung up a sign on a dilapidated shack in town and she was back in business.

Pregnant women in other villages came to seek her services. The Aizu hills remained a poor region, though, and often the family wouldn't have the money to pay for Shika's care. But she was herself no stranger to poverty. While she did need all the money she could get to support her own family, she frequently made allowances. "I've spent my whole life depending on the kindness of other people. You go ahead and pay me what you can, and don't worry about the usual fee." She was earning respect for the Noguchi name—something just as important to her as money.

■ ■ ■

Back in Pennsylvania, Noguchi was still working on his venom research. Unfortunately, his term as a research assistant was set to end in June 1902; he did not have a permanent position at the university. Yet again his future looked uncertain. The people who shared a laboratory with him held his apparent sloppiness against him, wondering if he would ever stop making errors in his experiments. People at the school also had misgivings about his English ability. The other researchers had taken to calling his speech "mooing": when he got excited and began speaking quickly in his deep voice the words merged together, sounding like the lowing of an animal. After he gave a presentation to the University of Pennsylvania's Department of Pathology on the results of his toxicology investigations, one professor shook his head and said: "I've no idea what that man is trying to say to us. And from what I could understand, I'm not so sure I accept his findings, either."

His research did not always go smoothly. When he came up against some obstacle in his work, he reacted as though it were the end of the world. He was as always susceptible to quick shifts in mood. But often when he was at a low point one of his friends would clap him on the shoulder and say: "Hey there, Yellow Peril! What do you say? Want to go and get a drink?" This was the dawn of an age when many in the West saw the "Yellow Peril" as a very real threat. But this man used it as a term of endearment, teasing Noguchi for his intense efforts in the lab. Noguchi, for his part, enjoyed this open, accepting side of many Americans like him. The stress would drain from his face and, laughing, the two men would go out to find a place to spend the evening.

In November Noguchi got the opportunity to present his scientific findings in a most distinguished setting—the general meeting of the National Academy of Science, held that year in Philadelphia. Together with Dr. Mitchell he was to give a talk on their preliminary research on the corpuscle-dissolving component and toxicity of snake venom. This academy represented the pinnacle of American scientific endeavor—only a hundred members were admitted at any one time—and until the appearance of the Nobel Prize, given for the first time that year, membership in it was the highest honor available for a scientist in the United States.

Mitchell and Noguchi gave their presentation to thirty members of the academy, along with a group of scientific luminaries including the dean of Johns Hopkins University. Just eleven months after arriving in America, Noguchi was making his appearance before this group thanks to his work with Mitchell, a world authority on snake poison, and his connection with Flexner, chief pathologist at the University of Pennsylvania. The young Japanese was still a nameless research assistant, but this was America, where talent, not affiliation with a certain academic clique, decided how quickly one rose to fame.

In truth Noguchi did not play a major role in the presentation that day. It was Mitchell who did all the talking; Noguchi handled the equipment used in the various demonstrations. But Mitchell had words of high praise for his assistant. "It is thanks to the great efforts of this young man that I have been able to bring my thirty years of research to their final conclusion."

This compliment brought his name to the public eye for the first time. The *Philadelphia Public Ledger* carried a lengthy piece on the gathering, mentioning "Hideyo Noguchi" as one of the scientists involved in important research. After the general meeting came to a close the university hosted a dinner to celebrate the successful presentation by Mitchell and Noguchi. Later yet another party took place, giving Noguchi a chance to rub shoulders with the cream of Philadelphia society at an elegant hotel in the city.

All this pleased Noguchi, of course. But he was truly overjoyed to learn later that Dr. Mitchell had recommended him for an official position as a public researcher, making him eligible for a grant from a fund supported by the National Academy of Science and the Carnegie Institution—an amazing two thousand dollars, which would make his situation in America a stable one for some time to come.

With a preface by Dr. Mitchell, and Noguchi and Flexner as coauthors, the report on snake venom appeared in the University of Pennsylvania's medical journal. This was in fact Noguchi's first research publication, but it received attention around the world. The report, along with his appearance in a major American newspaper, also boosted interest in his work back home. Japan's *Jikken igaku zasshi* (Journal of Experimental Medicine) published the paper, and Baron Tadanori Ishiguro, who had not forgotten his encounter with the young man, wrote to congratulate him for his latest accomplishment. The great German researcher Paul Ehrlich also wrote to offer his compliments on the work. Noguchi's subsequent papers accordingly received more than cursory attention in America and elsewhere. And he saw his pay rise to a more comfortable thirty dollars a month.

This lion cub had plunged to the very bottom of the cliff, but had climbed high again since then...

■ ■ ■

At last life slowed down a little for him; he no longer needed to focus on his work every hour of the day just to keep his head above water. In the free time he allowed into his schedule he found himself thinking once again of Yoneko Yamauchi. Just as he could focus on his work to the exclusion of everything else around him, he showed himself to be subject to a powerful fixation when it came to this woman. He wrote to Ryokei Kikuchi in Waka-matsu to get some news of what she was up to.

He was not overly direct, though. In his first letter he didn't mention Yoneko at all. When this letter elicited a reply from his friend, who wanted an expensive medical text available only in America, he sent the book along with another note that asked in passing how Yoneko was doing.

The response to this letter shook him: "Yoneko is doing well. She passed her examination and is a practicing physician at last. She married another doctor, Toshio Morikawa, and they are quite happy together."

This was simply a fact, and Kikuchi had no reason to conceal it. But Noguchi didn't take it well at all. He tore the pages to shreds and composed an anguished reply. It had always been his hope that Yoneko would join him in his endeavors. He had been lucky enough to come across a woman whose circumstances and goals were similar to his, and she had been his first and only love. He wrote to his friend that he would never forget the pain he felt at this turn of events. God had given him great success in his career, but it would never make up for this failure... He found it especially painful that she had married another doctor, and it made him determined to outshine this Morikawa in their shared profession.

At least his research was going very well indeed. He turned his attention to one problem after another, coming up with perceptive discoveries in a range of fields. To date, a French serum had been considered the only reliable method of countering snake venom, but Noguchi soon proved that this serum was insufficient as a treatment for bites from North American rattle-snakes. Quick-witted and shrewd in the laboratory, he kept himself busy outside the research hall as well. He wrote an article on Japanese medicine for an encyclopedia, which brought in twenty dollars, soon spent on books and clothing. He also began giving some thought to his own health—usually overlooked in favor of sustained bouts of work. The spirit also required proper care. Books of Japanese classical poetry, to put his mind at ease after tough sessions in the laboratory, were something he asked Chiwaki to send.

During all this, he did not forget that his position in the university was by no means a guaranteed one. Once his research term came to an end there was a chance that he would have no place at the school, a constant worry at the back of his mind. Noguchi also worried about his eventual position in Japan. Studying in America was certainly proving good for him, but few in the medical establishment back home would give much weight to his time abroad unless it included a stint in Germany, the center of the medical universe at the time.

It was around this time that he met Hajime Hoshi. Another member of the society of Japanese residents of East Coast cities, Hoshi lived in New York, where he published the *Nichi-Bei shuho*, a weekly magazine in Japanese covering Japan-America relations, and an English-language journal called *Japan and America*. He would go on to found Hoshi Pharmaceuticals and become one of Japan's top businessmen, but at the time he was an energetic young man who had graduated from Columbia University. On his way back from a trip to Washington he stopped off in Philadelphia to meet Noguchi for the first time. They sat on the double bed in Noguchi's room and talked deep into the night. The doctor spoke about his need for funding to get to Germany, and Hoshi, who was always looking for material to fill the pages of his magazines, interviewed him right then and there about his research. They were both young—at twenty-nine, Hoshi was only a few years older than Noguchi. They both had exceptional drive. And once they learned that they shared a Fukushima background, they were friends for life.

In the meantime, a new project proposal came his way. The Carnegie Institution wanted to fund a new line of research, which involved extracting blood from fish and testing the effect of venom on their corpuscles. The institution asked Noguchi to come to the Marine Biological Laboratory in

Woods Hole, near Boston, for three months beginning in June. With most other researchers taking long summer breaks, the facilities would be entirely at his disposal. Noguchi was joined there by two other Japanese researchers: Naohide Tanitsu of Tokyo Imperial University and Kenkichi Sakai, who was at the University of Chicago. A fourth man—Kiichi Miyake, who was studying at Cornell University—teamed up with them for part of the summer, staying with Noguchi for the month he spent in Woods Hole. He was there to do work on thalassotherapy, the use of seawater and seaweed to treat various ailments, before heading for Germany to continue his studies.

Surrounded by bright young researchers who spoke his own language, Noguchi could have enjoyed a relaxing summer by the sea. He pushed himself hard, though. He declined numerous invitations to join the others in swimming excursions, remaining in the laboratory for long hours. Curiously, though, he did seem to enjoy taking slow walks whenever he noticed the moon was out, even if he was in the middle of some experiment.

During this summer Noguchi received sad news from Fukushima: his teacher's mother had died. This put him in a melancholy mood, and his walk along the beach was longer than usual that day. He sent Mr. Kobayashi a long letter consoling him for his loss; then another. In the second one Noguchi urged him to look beyond the reality of living and dying to some greater meaning above it all. Perhaps he was trying to convince himself of the truth of this, as he wrote with unusually deep feeling. His own distress at his teacher's news was only increased by the next reply, though: Kobayashi's wife had suffered a relapse of her earlier sickness. But as much as he wanted to return to Japan to care for her again, his present situation would not allow it.

■ ■ ■

At the end of the summer of 1902 Noguchi headed back to the University of Pennsylvania, to receive the first good news he had heard in some time. He had been promoted from a temporary research assistant to a full-time pathologist on the university's research staff at a monthly salary of fifty dollars. He had Simon Flexner to thank for this new position. The professor had been a vocal supporter of his, making the case to the school administrators that he must not be allowed to leave. According to Flexner, Noguchi had three qualities making him an excellent candidate for a permanent post: first, his clarity of thinking and avoidance of time-wasting sidelines in his work; second, his astonishing technical prowess; and third, his diligence in his duties, which went beyond that shown by anyone else.

As always Noguchi saw his duties as something to concern himself with for as many hours of the day as possible. When he was particularly focused on a project he was loath to leave the lab table even for meals, sometimes going without food all day. As evening rolled around and the others began packing up to go home, they would ask whether he was leaving too. His reply was often simply: "This is my home." The building would grow quiet as the evening drew on into night. Noguchi made plans for the next day's experiments, recording any promising line of investigation before the spark of inspiration went out. Sometimes he would thumb through the pages of old notebooks, amending the descriptions of earlier experiments in red pencil. After completing these tasks he spent the remaining hours until dawn writing letters. He was a dedicated correspondent, keeping in close touch with countless researchers, relatives, and friends. Perhaps it was his loneliness in everyday life that made him such a sociable man on paper.

The lab coat Noguchi wore during his working hours was home to a small white mouse. Mice were commonly used in experiments in the laboratory, but the one in his pocket lived a better life than the others. From time to time the other researchers would catch Noguchi chatting to this pet, noting with surprise that it seemed to respond to his words. They asked him about this mouse one day. What was the story behind it? How did it come to be living in his coat pocket?

Noguchi grinned sheepishly and replied, "In the beginning there was this one male and a dozen females. All of the mice we use in this lab are the descendants of this little guy. But now that's he's gotten on in years, he can't do that job any longer. . . But I keep him around as sort of an honorary father to all the lab mice. He's done good work for us, and I like to think he deserves a little kindness in return."

Perhaps because he was in a strange country whose customs he couldn't be expected to know, Noguchi took pains to act with proper courtesy at all times. He could be dashing across campus to get to the laboratory, but if he spotted one of his colleagues heading along the path toward him, he would stop, stand straight, and wait for the other man to approach. Hat in hand, he would bow, greet the person, and extend his arm stiffly to shake hands. The Americans marveled at this Oriental decorum. The traveler Lafcadio

Hearn had described Japanese people in his books, and here was a living character from their pages.

As proper as he was in his behavior toward other people, however, he was a disaster in terms of keeping his surroundings tidy. It was a strange trait for a man with such a keen sense of fashion when out on the town, but he seemed to have no sense of organization or personal hygiene at school. Cigarette butts littered his workspace, and it could be hard to find an untouched spot of white fabric among the paint and other stains on his lab coat. Professors in other departments regarded this with disapproval. They had never seen a man who scattered things around a room like Noguchi. They could see no future for such a sloppy scientist. Due to this behavior, he picked up an unwelcome nickname during his time in Pennsylvania—"the dirty Japanese."

The negative image he had at this time was due in part to the same failing he'd had in Japan—money problems. Even his laboratory activities could lead to financial disaster at times. Once he ordered a rare and expensive animal for use in experiments—a mongoose from Jamaica. Noguchi wanted to test whether the blood of this snake-killing creature showed any resistance to the effects of venom. Flexner told him to knock the animal out with chloroform before taking a blood sample, but Noguchi misjudged the dosage and killed the costly creature, which earned him an angry lecture from his boss. He listened without offering any excuse, then retired to a corner of the room, where he seemed to shrink into himself. Always a touchy individual, he found negative feedback upsetting. When he was particularly shaken by some critical comment, he would sometimes take time off from work to recover from the shock. Endurance was his watchword when applying himself to work, but his relationships with other people in his workplace may have been the hardest thing for him to endure.

■ ■ ■

His endurance paid off, though. One day he learned that Flexner and Mitchell had tapped him for a trip to Europe for further study. No foreign student had ever received this honor—and it was a doubly great honor for Noguchi, who knew he would never have had this chance at such a young age had he remained in Japan. In preparation for this trip, he moved from his lodgings on Walnut Street to a room in a German family's home on Sansom Street.

The two older men had a reason for sending Noguchi to learn what he could in Europe as soon as possible. The Rockefeller Institute for Medical Research was soon to be established in New York, and Professor Flexner had been nominated to serve as its first director. Flexner had a staff of dozens under him at the University of Pennsylvania, but out of all of these researchers he wanted to take only Noguchi with him to this new institute. A period of study in Europe would make his protégé a more natural candidate and add prestige to the team he was thinking of putting together.

In March 1903 the Carnegie Institution issued a grant of five thousand dollars for the publication of the snake venom research results in book form, along with an additional eight hundred dollars to cover the expense of reproducing photographs. In conjunction with this grant Noguchi was made a senior pathological researcher at the university. When Flexner informed him that after returning from Europe he would be given a position at the Rockefeller Institute Noguchi made his mind up at last. He would not return to live in Japan. His home country was a small place, where he could only dream small dreams. The work he wanted to do now would never be possible for a researcher based in Tokyo. In his letters around then he said he hoped only to be able to continue his life in America. . .

But though it was clear that he would now stay abroad, he had to face a sticky problem at home. He was engaged, and Masuko Naito was waiting for him to come back and live with her. For months all thoughts of her had been driven from his mind by other questions—would he be able to remain in America? How could he bring himself to forget Yoneko Yamauchi? But now that these other problems had been sorted out he needed to confront the matter of his fiancée. He found himself torn: on the one hand, the rational thing to do was to find a way to return her family's three hundred yen so he could do the work he had to do without being bound by his promise. But on the other hand, he was a lonely man. The thought of the woman waiting for him in Japan must have been a tempting one.

As he had done so often at difficult times in his life, he went to Chiwaki for help. But the letter he sent was unlikely to receive a reply before his ship sailed. He set out on the next stage of his life with the matter still unsettled.

BUILDING A REPUTATION

In October 1903, a month shy of his twenty-seventh birthday and less than three years after arriving in the United States, Noguchi boarded a ship for Europe. After making port he went straight to Paris, where he ordered himself a new set of fashionable clothes and sat for a photograph to commemorate his arrival in the Old World. He then went on to Denmark. His research position was not in Germany, but in the Statens Serum Institut in Copenhagen. There he was greeted warmly by Dr. Thorvald Madsen, a friend of Professor Flexner's and an authority on serums, who headed the institute.

Their friendship was not the reason Flexner had chosen Madsen as an ideal host for Noguchi during his time in Europe. The Dane was known for his modern research methods—he took a comprehensive approach to biological matters which drew heavily on the physical and chemical sciences—and Flexner hoped to see his assistant pick up as much of these broader disciplines as he could during his time away.

He would be acquiring these new skills in an intimate setting: the institute had only four researchers. It was housed in a graceful building, though, and its facilities were always kept in top condition. Madsen, a dignified scholar whose learning went well beyond his thirty-two years, had never had a foreign researcher under his care before. He knew one was on his way, but it wasn't until he actually met Noguchi that he realized his guest was Japanese. And so young! Rather than ask the age of this new arrival directly, Madsen approached the question in a roundabout manner that reminded Noguchi of the indirect way Japanese people spoke to one another: "It's difficult to tell how old a person is by looking at his face. But how old would you say I am?"

Westerners may have looked older than their actual years to Japanese people, but Madsen could only gape in surprise, and then grin, at Noguchi's reply: "I'd say you must be around sixty-five, sir." He grinned even more later, when Noguchi explained that traditionally the elderly were treated with considerable respect, and he had been trying to honor the doctor with his absurdly high guess.

Once settled in Copenhagen, Noguchi got right to work. He continued his studies of snake venom and immunity to it, using a supply of rattlesnake poison he had brought from America. He began his work at the same feverish pace he had shown in Philadelphia, but this soon changed. Madsen took a leisurely approach to his research, weighing the results of one experiment at length until he came up with an idea for his next course of investigation. With this new model to follow, Noguchi learned to relax and take more time to complete his work as Madsen told him to—slowly, surely, and precisely.

His time in Copenhagen was quite productive, all the same. Soon Noguchi and Madsen had coauthored their first paper together, a report in French on toxins and antitoxins, and the effect of temperature on their reaction rates. In all, he published ten papers while at the institute. He also traveled to England with the director to attend a conference of serologists at Oxford University.

Copenhagen was a pleasant place to be in the early twentieth century. Denmark was the land of Hans Christian Andersen, and the capital looked as if it belonged in one of his tales—a clean and decorative city, with rugged capes jutting into a white-capped ocean, green hills in the distance, bright flowers in the yards of the colorfully roofed houses, and countless church steeples rising into the clear, blue, Scandinavian sky.

The people's friendly manner matched their surroundings. Noguchi found himself charmed by the way they doffed their hats in greeting in the street, even stepping aside to let him pass. In the laboratory, too, he enjoyed the company of those he worked with—as he would describe it later, "one of the freest, happiest times I have ever spent anywhere"—and Madsen made him genuinely welcome, to the extent that he insisted on keeping a photograph of this Japanese scientist on the walls of his office from then on.

■ ■ ■

In February of the following year, 1904, war broke out between Russia and Japan. Noguchi, being one of the few Japanese in Denmark, was seen by some as the representative of a warlike, acquisitive country, even though he had left it behind years earlier and had little intention of ever returning there.

The war loomed large in Noguchi's mind. As he wrote to Chiwaki, "Day in and day out, I am troubled by the fighting. I can no longer take any pleasure in my research." He bought English, French, and German newspapers, scanning them to see how Europeans viewed the war. He also sent money to Jiji Shinpo, a Japanese news agency, to get information in his own language delivered directly to him. Luckily the small state of Denmark maintained a strictly neutral stance. Although the Danish royal family had close ties with their Russian counterparts, the public in general felt oppressed by the long shadow which the giant to the east cast over European affairs. But whatever their political leanings, the Danes—along with most of Europe—expected Russia to emerge victorious in the war. Noguchi observed all of this closely, writing a stream of letters to Chiwaki and others back home and providing a Japanese perspective on Europe and its response to the war.

This period of global turmoil was also a rocky time for Noguchi personally. He was still engaged to be married, and the Naito family had not forgotten it. Everyone had expected Noguchi to complete his studies in America in two years or so and then return to Japan and to Masuko. As the months dragged on the Naitos began pestering Chiwaki for news of their future son-in-law, and then for an explanation of his continuing absence. Before long they were demanding that he return to Japan at once. To avoid interfering with the progress Noguchi was making professionally, the dentist took this pressure upon himself, forwarding none of their angry messages and instead urging Mrs. Naito to wait. Far from returning to Japan, however, Noguchi had journeyed on to Europe, only widening the gap between his course of action and the Naitos' expectations. When he did think to write them it was always to explain that he wanted to remain abroad a while longer, or to ask for loans of four or five thousand yen to live on in the interim. These outrageous requests may have been meant in part to push the family toward breaking things off between Masuko and him. Noguchi was also disappointed with his would-be wife's inability to pass the first-stage medical exam, difficult though it was.

When Masuko learned that he had gone to Denmark rather than return to marry her she wrote him an anguished letter. She had expected to wait only two or three years before living with him, and the news that he would be away for at least two more was distressing. All she hoped and prayed for now was to be together with him as soon as possible; would he please reconsider and return to Japan according to their original understanding?

This letter hit Noguchi hard. He had second thoughts about making the Naitos wait so long to see their daughter married, and didn't welcome the idea of breaking off an engagement with someone who had done nothing to deserve such ill treatment. It saddened him to think of what she must be going through, and he felt ashamed of his failure to be kinder to her. He had still been young when he left for America, just twenty-four, impetuous and inconsiderate. If only he'd known his foreign research would lead to this . . . if only there had been a scholarship that would have let him avoid this mess! Uncertain about what to do, he sent out anguished letters of his own, asking Chiwaki for help and even begging his mother to go to the Naitos and get them to break off the engagement.

But despite his self-reproach, Noguchi had never really looked forward to the idea of marriage with any eagerness. He had no desire for children of his own. "The world," he would say, "is already filled with children who need looking after." One child affected him deeply, though, when he got word that she had died at the age of five: Chiwaki's daughter. Noguchi had played with her when she was a baby; he felt Chiwaki's grief almost as his own.

His letter took some time to compose. "Today is exactly one week since I first heard of your terrible tragedy. The loss of your daughter was a deep shock to me, and your letter left my mind awash in thoughts—of the brevity of life, coupled with sweet memories of your little child. . . With my emotions in this tangled state I have let seven days pass, considering what to write and trying to find the courage to offer my condolences. . ." To comfort his friend he quoted a haiku by the eighteenth-century poet Chiyojo, written after the death of her only son, a playful boy who loved to catch insects:

> *Hunting dragonflies*
> *How far away have you roamed*
> *In your chase today?*

■ ■ ■

After a full year in the land of fairy tales, it was time to return to America. He had been busy during his last few months in Europe, giving talks on his snake venom research in England, France, and Germany and rubbing shoulders with senior scientists on the continent. He had made a name for himself during his year in Copenhagen.

On his way back to America he went to the Japanese embassy in London to straighten out some matters concerning his passport. There his Aizu-accented speech caught the ear of one of the embassy officers, Tsuneo Matsudaira. The son of a hereditary lord of the old Aizu domain, he called this young Japanese man over and asked where he was from.

"I was born in a small village called Okinajima in Fukushima."

"I thought you sounded like an Aizu man. . . I come from there myself." And this was the beginning of a friendship that would have been unthinkable some decades earlier, between the son of a lord and a peasant.

For the time being, Noguchi left this new friend in London and headed for New York, to join Professor Flexner at the Rockefeller Institute for Medical Research. This step would be a springboard for Noguchi, giving him the base of operations he needed to achieve greatness in the microbiological field in later years.

The institute had been founded in 1901 as one of the Rockefeller Foundation's philanthropic enterprises. Men like John D. Rockefeller and Andrew Carnegie were pillars of American society, and their success made them both objects of admiration and targets for those who envied their wealth. To draw negative attention away from the fabulous fortunes they had amassed and the monopolistic ways in which they had done it, they began to divert some of that wealth into charitable operations with a humanitarian objective. Rockefeller looked around the world and saw that France was home to the Institut Pasteur; Germany had the Royal Prussian Institute for Infectious Diseases, later the Robert Koch Institute, and the Institute for Sera Research and Serum Control under Paul Ehrlich, which would later take his name; and in Japan there was the epidemiological institute under Dr. Kitasato. America lacked such a research facility, and Rockefeller had found just the man to run one in Flexner, who had both administrative talent and a passion for research. Flexner chose eight researchers to staff the new facility. They were all outsiders in the eyes of the establishment of the day—young researchers who had yet to make a name for themselves, Jews who couldn't get positions in universities, and a Japanese man. Noguchi was the youngest of them, with a healthy starting salary of eighteen hundred dollars.

For the first year and a half the team carried out its research in a rented building while they waited for the construction of the brand-new Rockefeller Institute to be completed. Once they were in their new location Noguchi found an apartment on nearby Lexington Avenue. This was a tiny place, no bigger than a single room with attached kitchen, but it was all he needed. He spent most of his hours at the laboratory and wanted little more than a place to sleep when he needed to. After the relatively leisurely pace of his work in Denmark he was eager to get back to work. This was America, and he was trying not just to make a name for himself but to show what the Japanese were capable of.

The United States was to all appearances a fiercely competitive society where one either scrambled to the top or got kicked off the ladder entirely. This ladder was especially difficult for an Asian to climb in the face of the racial prejudice of the day. The nation was already home to several hundred thousand people of Japanese birth, but their position was hardly secure. A Japanese person going to the theater was likely to be sent around to the back door, if he could get in at all; the front entrance was for whites only. Given the reality of prevailing social conditions, Noguchi resolved to work as swiftly as possible to carve out some respect for himself and his countrymen.

As hard as he had ever worked before, it didn't compare with what he put himself through now. He was like a man possessed, thinking nothing of working straight through the night for days on end. Those around him commented on his pallid appearance, even though his stamina seemed unrelenting. Flexner himself asked in wonder: "When do Japanese people sleep?" Similar questions came even from Japanese friends, like the one who on visiting Noguchi learned that he hadn't spent any real time at home in months, and their reunion was a good chance to get back to his apartment.

There were penalties to pay for this, unfortunately. Noguchi suffered from severe hemorrhoids, which he blamed on lengthy sea voyages with no access to a hot bath. It soon became a painful exercise even to go in to the laboratory; indeed, he should have been hospitalized. He was unable to sleep well even in the few hours he allowed himself to rest. His work suffered. He wrote to Chiwaki of his irritability, noting that "every little noise grates on my ears." Luckily for him, though, a lifetime of long waking hours had hardened him, and he managed somehow to make it through this spell of ill health on short, deep naps.

■ ■ ■

Noguchi had gone almost as far as he could with his snake-venom work, despite contributing a chapter on the subject to William Osler's *System of Medicine*. He needed some new topic to study—and this time, one he chose himself, rather than having it assigned. He was twenty-eight, old enough to begin carving out his own space in the medical field, and he wanted to be doing important work to match the role he now enjoyed.

For a while he focused on the study of trachoma, an eye disease afflicting millions around the globe, leading in severe cases to scarring and blindness, and especially prevalent in China and Japan. The following year, however, saw a development that would give him the direction he was searching for. In April 1905 the German scientists Fritz Schaudinn and Erich Hoffman discovered the organism that caused syphilis, *Treponema pallidum*. This was sensational news at the time, as this disease loomed as large in the public consciousness as cancer does today. Vast numbers of people were passive carriers of this sexually transmitted disease, which in many cases had an exceptionally long incubation period. Eventually, though, the symptoms would appear, generally including lesions on the skin and progressing to serious disfiguration. The fearsome disease could spread to the brain and wreak havoc on the nervous system. It could also be passed from mother to child, afflicting even newborns as a result. Syphilis had vexed humanity for centuries. Now, though, a first blow had been struck against it.

This thrilled Noguchi. He and Flexner got straight to work on tests following up what the Germans had accomplished, and soon they had succeeded in obtaining a sample of the *T. pallidum* spirochete from a syphilis patient. They promptly wrote up a report on their findings. Noguchi set aside his trachoma research and made syphilis the new focus for his efforts. He had been making little headway in the study of the eye disease, but this was not his fault—the instruments powerful enough to view the virus that caused this illness had yet to be invented.

To Noguchi's mind, he was branching out within the same broad fields of microbiology and serology. But others did not see it this way. His shift to syphilis research drew criticism from people who claimed he had abandoned a systematic approach to science, instead seeking fame in the fashionable field of the day. Japan's scientific establishment in particular placed great weight on a "pure" approach to learning. Noguchi rejected this insistence on exclusive specialization: "The pursuit of scientific knowledge is a kind of gamble. A lifetime can go by without one making a breakthrough," he wrote. Why, then, should he stick to a less than promising line of research?

He needed to look no further than Shibasaburo Kitasato for an example to back up this argument. Noguchi's former boss had learned from Masanori Ogata, a pioneer of Japanese science who had brought the theory and practice of experimental medicine to Japan. Despite his extraordinary talent and his renown in the nation's medical history, though, he had no major discoveries to his name. Ogata's student, meanwhile, had struck out on his own and had a string of findings and the directorship of Japan's top medical research facility to his name. "If I had to sweat away through long years of laboratory work without anything to show for it," said Noguchi, "I'd probably want to throw myself in front of a train."

At the moment there seemed to be little chance of this, though. John D. Rockefeller had spent over ten million dollars to establish his institute, and a steady stream of journalists visited the facility, located some distance from the center of town on the bank of the East River, to report on its findings. On their side, the researchers employed there were eager to give them something good to write about, and this meant finding cures for deadly diseases.

Noguchi's laboratory was on the third floor. He had a fine view of Blackwell Island—today Roosevelt Island—and the river. Flexner also had an office on this floor of the building, and Noguchi maintained a close working relationship with him during their time together there. He also found himself in charge of the institute's library, a position familiar to him from his days in Japanese research facilities and schools, and he had a young staff member under him to help take care of this duty.

His home by now was a spacious apartment on East Sixty-Fifth Avenue, just a few hundred meters from the institute. This was a run-down section of town, but he had plenty of room—enough to turn one of his bedrooms into a home laboratory so he could continue working when away from the office. There was a gap, though, between his public and private lives, and he wasn't happy about it. As an assistant at the Rockefeller Institute he had considerable social standing, and he worked and spoke with a confidence befitting that position; but when, exhausted, he finally returned to his room, he was a different man—silent in his bleak apartment, and solitary. "After a day at the laboratory, where I pour myself into my work, I come home drained at about six. . . It is already dark, and in my pitch-black rooms I have to grope to light the lamps myself. I make up my own bed and take care of all the little tasks a home requires. It is the lonely existence of a single man. . ."

His answer was to go out to drink. As always, he took to this pastime energetically, especially when he had a chance to treat an old friend to a night on the town. On one occasion Noguchi and Tsurukichi Okumura—a companion from his days at the Takayama Clinic and the eventual author of one of the first biographies of the researcher—walked through the doors of eighteen bars in a single night, spending an amazing thirty-six dollars on beer.

These sessions gave Noguchi a reputation around town, and led to the sort of startling conversation he had one morning in a diner as he ate a sleepy breakfast after a night in the bars. "Hey look, Noguchi, there you are in the paper," said a woman at the counter. "'Noguchi in New York'. . ." He snapped awake at this. Had he lost his wallet last night? Had some reporter spotted him as he reeled around? But the woman continued: "No, it's Yone . . . Yonejiro Noguchi. He's a poet from your country"—just somebody who happened to share his surname.

■ ■ ■

Did Noguchi need a wife to keep him on an even keel, then? This was a possibility he may have been considering at the time. With his fiancée Masuko, though, there was little hope of a solid relationship. Knowing that more than four years had passed since Noguchi's promise to the Naito family, and that her coming to New York herself would probably be a disaster, Chiwaki took it upon himself to cancel this ill-fated engagement and return the three hundred yen to the Naitos. (This ended up being one debt that Noguchi actually repaid, though it took him a decade to do it: he eventually presented Chiwaki with a portion of the prize money he received in 1915 from the Imperial Academy.)

Noguchi still had other options when it came to marriage. One well-established family in Denmark had been eyeing him as a potential partner for a daughter. Her parents were serious enough to send one of their employees across the Pacific to speak to Noguchi about it after his return to New York. Soon her portrait adorned one of his walls. But in the end his string of bad luck continued, and this Dane followed Yoneko Yamauchi and Masuko Naito in the list of women Noguchi could not and did not marry.

Noguchi had always kept himself busy, but now his workload began to get him down. He needed his home to be a place of rest and recuperation, not the dark, silent place it was now. So, resuming a habit he'd had since his days at the Kaiyo Clinic, he invited Ryutaro Miyahara, a young medical student from Chiba Prefecture, to share his apartment. Miyahara took over the housekeeping duties, which had gone neglected in Noguchi's long hours at the institute, and it was a novel pleasure for him now to come home and take a bath while his flatmate prepared dinner for them both.

The senior of the two, however, was not a particularly sociable dining companion. He had only one hand for the meal; the other generally propped up a book of some kind—often a literary work like the poetry of Heinrich Heine or some heroic tale, his particular preference. He had a powerful thirst for knowledge, and he went to great lengths to ensure that he learned more than just medicine and science. Time was limited, though, and he scheduled his reading quite strictly, with literature limited to his dinner hours.

Miyahara worried about Noguchi's health. The student warned his host to take better care of himself, otherwise the irregular hours he kept and his lack of sleep would do him in one day. Noguchi thanked him for his concern, but informed him that he couldn't take his advice to heart: "I appreciate what you're saying, and for most people your warning would be spot on. But not everyone can live his life in the same way as the next man. In the end you'll have to judge whether I'm spending my time wisely by my results. . . You just wait a while longer and see what I'm capable of."

People began to speak of the fire that burned in Noguchi—of a drive that could only be the sign of great accomplishments to come. This drive served him well in the world of science, but he developed other passions where his temperament became a liability. Gambling was a dangerous pastime for him. In a game of cards he would never back down as the bets escalated, and the higher the stakes rose the harder it became for him to conceal his emotions. His opponents could read his hand in his face; there was no way he could win.

In the summer of 1906 Noguchi and Miyahara, during a break from their work, opened a temporary medical clinic for the Japanese expatriates in and around New York. This attracted attention from the publisher of a weekly magazine for the Japanese community, who came to ask them to advertise their services in his journal and spent several evenings with them over the course of the summer. The journalist later described Miyahara as a confident, handsome young man, and Noguchi as quite the opposite—a short, sullen person with an unruly shock of hair, likely to nurse a bottle of whiskey for hours with no more than an occasional "Yep" or "Ah, I see" to add to the conversation. The summer medical clinic was barely successful thanks only to the efforts of Miyahara, who took on most of the work. This bothered the younger man, but his feelings don't seem to have had much impact on Noguchi.

Before long Miyahara returned to Japan, and Noguchi was left to his own devices again. He withdrew into a kind of shell. His coworkers named him "the blank wall" for his silence. Unable to open up and share his innermost feelings with the people around him, Noguchi—ordinarily quick to warm to others—was in emotional pain now. Was he really so oblivious to the nature of Americans and their society that he could find no way to fit in? No, Noguchi insisted: it was *they* who were shutting him out.

His parting comment to Miyahara was a fierce one. "There's a powerful anti-Japanese current in the United States today. But you just watch—I'll show these people just what we're capable of." And with these words, and an angry but lonely gleam in his eyes, he said goodbye to his Japanese flatmate and turned back to his test tubes.

■ ■ ■

Noguchi soon received a new measure of recognition for his work. In June 1907 the University of Pennsylvania awarded the thirty-year-old an honorary degree. He was now a Master of Science. This was followed soon afterwards with a promotion within the Rockefeller Institute. There were six ranks in all in the organization, beginning with full members—Simon Flexner and three others—and going down through associate members, associates, assistants, and so on. Hideyo moved up this year from assistant to associate, a post he would fill until 1909, when he was made an associate member.

He also published two books in rapid succession: his work on snake venom, for which the Carnegie Institution had provided a further five hundred dollars as a personal bonus for him, and a text that organized his previously published research on syphilis and seriological diagnosis of the disease into a solid scientific framework. His career was in full swing again.

His letters home mentioning these achievements, however, struck an oddly dissatisfied note: "It's as though I've at last got a rare flower in my hand only to find it less attractive than I'd hoped." His messages also contained harsh criticism of the Japanese establishment, which he accused of focusing on position, not ability; on academic records, not actual achievements. Noguchi had often been made to feel like an outsider in the United States, which was not his country; it rankled with him that he had been an outcast even in the medical establishment of his own land. At home or abroad, he had only his own talent on which to rely. His resentment and his restless ambition now combined to make him set his sights on academic recognition in Japan.

Noguchi took four papers he had produced to date—three in English and one in German—and mailed them off to Kyoto Imperial University along with an application for a degree. This represented a small part of his total body of work. Despite his youth he had already written ninety-three papers, and he would go on to publish over two hundred. At around seven papers a year, this was way ahead of the average university researcher's output in America, where the usual pace was one report annually. Noguchi's single-year record was an unheard-of nineteen published papers.

However, his performance in the academic field did not translate into a better quality of life for his family back home. His mother was once again close to bankruptcy. The Tohoku region had been in the grip of a lengthy cold spell. As crops suffered, so naturally did people's incomes, and nobody could pay for Shika's midwifery—on top of which, Noguchi's grandmother had recently passed away, entailing additional funeral expenses. Unable to pay her taxes, his mother was looking at the possibility of losing her fields.

A distant relative saved her from this disaster with a timely loan, but her position remained far from stable. Fortunately, Kobayashi was also there to help: Noguchi's old teacher would stop in from time to time to see how she was doing, bringing her a bushel of rice when it looked as if she needed some food in the house. Noguchi's father Sayosuke was as useless as always, his mind focused only on his next drink and unable to focus on anything else once he'd got one inside him. Bartenders would come to Shika after Sayosuke built up large tabs at their establishments, putting further financial pressure on her. Her husband was a versatile man with a talent for intricate handicraft, but he had no interest in using his skills for the sake of the household. People came to him with offers of work, knowing him to be a pleasant fellow, but he tended to turn them down unless they came with promises of free sake. At one point Kobayashi, concerned that this drunkard would ruin his son's good name without someone to keep an eye on him, took Sayosuke in to live in his own home. It did little good.

Given this family history, it is hardly surprising that Noguchi never spoke of his father. Things back home only got worse when he learned that Seizo, his younger brother, had become involved in some sticky relationship with a woman in the village and run off to Hokkaido to get away from his mistakes. All this news was painful to Hideyo—the family's eldest son, the one supposed to be holding it together at this point. He noted: "I have to say that the key is to teach children the importance of saving and living frugally while they're still young, or it's too late. For all my success in my studies, I haven't done a thing to keep my family above water financially."

With this bitter thought in mind, he sent his mother what little money he could scrounge together, and began looking for other ways to help her as well. He managed to obtain some high-quality medical equipment for her to use in her midwife's work, but then learned to his dismay that these instruments were only approved in Japan for use by licensed physicians, not country midwives like Shika. In the end his assistance was meager and short-lived. There was little difference between Hideyo and his father or brother when it came to the support he could offer to the home finances.

■ ■ ■

Noguchi had a soft spot for students who worked to support themselves while furthering their education, and before long he had found another youngster to share his apartment with him. Norio Araki had worked at the Takayama college, performing the same houseboy service that Noguchi had done a decade earlier, before coming to America to improve his dentistry techniques. Noguchi liked having another person around—especially someone like this who needed little attention and was willing to cook the sort of meals from back home, with plenty of rice, that he enjoyed.

Araki would sometimes ask him for a bit of help with the cooking. "Dr. Noguchi, would you mind watching the rice to make sure it doesn't overcook?"

"Of course," said Noguchi as he brought a chair over to the stove and continued his reading while peering from time to time at the pot. If, as often happened, he became engrossed in his book, it was only an odd smell coming from the stove that snapped him out of it, to see that the rice had burned and the meal was ruined. "Get a coat and let's go out for dinner," he'd say, throwing his hands up in resignation.

Noguchi had a particular restaurant he always went to, and he ordered the same dish every time. The waiter no longer needed to take his order when he turned up; he would show the customer to a table and bring him his food. Without a word Noguchi would take his seat and bring out some book, turning the pages without looking at the plate as he chewed on whatever he managed to spear on his fork.

His approach to research was little different. After working at the institute laboratory late into the evening he would return home and continue the work there. Midnight always came and went with Noguchi reading some text or peering into a microscope and sketching a microorganism, a cigar clenched between his teeth. At times he would collapse into a chair for a nap or topple onto his bed. He was a stranger to pajamas; he would sleep like a dead man for a few hours in his clothes, without changing.

Even conversation was a distraction—his messages for Araki were usually scrawled on a scrap of paper and left where the other person would find them. His reputation for absent-mindedness was well known. He would wipe the ink from his fountain pen with an expensive silk handkerchief pulled fumblingly from his pocket. On more than one occasion he poured a pot of steaming tea into his inkpot. Even when walking between his office and home he would become so wrapped up in his thoughts that he would bump into other passersby. This gave him the idea that New York was a dangerous place for pedestrians, and he advised Japanese newcomers to the city to take a taxi everywhere.

Noguchi's policy of self-reliance was deep-rooted by now. He even washed out his own test tubes and ground his own mixtures, the pestle gripped in his right hand and the mortar held down with his clumsy left. The lab assistants wondered why he wouldn't let anyone else take care of these minor tasks, but as he explained it, "I can't allow someone who doesn't know exactly what I'm doing here to interfere."

In his work he was a perfectionist to the extent of distrusting others. Collaborating with other researchers was not an option—indeed, he even found it difficult to accept the findings of other scientists, no matter how famed they might be or how much more they had achieved than him, and he was constantly repeating their experiments to confirm what was in their books. All this effort led Simon Flexner to describe his associate's work as "superhuman."

Noguchi often gave his flatmate pieces of advice. "You're young now, and you may not have realized it yet, but a man's life is made by what he accomplishes before his fortieth birthday. Don't believe that you've plenty of time left to make your mark!" These warnings weighed heavily on Araki, but he couldn't ignore the results Noguchi was enjoying by following his own advice. A foreigner in an unfamiliar land, he was climbing steadily up through the scientific community. He was a success.

The doctor had other tips for his flatmate. "The word 'no' must never cross your lips when you're dealing with the people above you, the ones who determine your position." When Araki asked why this was, Noguchi launched into a long lecture on perseverance—one of his favorite subjects—drawing heavily on examples from his own life to make his point. It was only by cutting back on sleep that he had made real progress in the laboratory, but when the time came to announce his research results to the world, he'd had to do so in papers published jointly with Flexner, his boss. He had shared his glory in this way three times already! Noguchi was a realist, though, knowing that it was common for scientists to be forced to deal this way with the administrators who often controlled their careers. "Do you know what would happen if I told people 'No'—if I said I wanted the credit for my own work? Why, I'd be out of a job. With no job at the institute, I wouldn't be doing the research I want to do, that's for sure."

With this example Noguchi was outlining the struggle between the academic temperament—the scientist's drive to create new knowledge for its own sake—and the political drive of others intent on harnessing that impulse for their own benefit. He personally was confident in a purely scientific role. To overcome the constraints these other people imposed, he had only to work still harder, to produce more results. Noguchi had no talent for politics and no desire to develop one. He was perfectly content to be a discoverer.

"You've got to publish what you discover, though. It doesn't matter how groundbreaking your findings are if you aren't the one announcing them to the world. It would be like leaving a jewel you'd unearthed on the floor of the mine! Whatever results you achieve in your experiments—however minor they seem—get them out into the scientific community. You let me know if you come up with something, and I'll write it up in English for you so you can get it published."

He kept this promise. Araki spoke to him about his dental studies, and Noguchi scribbled down notes as he listened. By the time these were fleshed out enough to pass as a proper report it was past two in the morning, but Noguchi's sense of urgency was unchanged. "The sooner it reaches the journal editors the better!" he cried as he pressed an envelope into Araki's hands, telling him to take it to the mailbox before daybreak.

■ ■ ■

Noguchi was not spending all his time helping younger researchers, though. In November 1906 he turned thirty. A scientist's thirties are supposed to be his golden years—a time when youthful energy and the experience of age blend to produce original results. Looking for some theme around which he could build a career, Noguchi dabbled in research on tuberculosis and anthrax. The trend of the times was for medical researchers to turn away from microbiology toward immunology and serology. The world was still home to any number of serious diseases whose cause had yet to be identified. A discovery that defeated any of these enemies of humanity would ensure acclaim for the man who made it.

One of these enemies was syphilis, a universal blight. Noguchi had been quick to repeat successfully the experiment done in 1905 by Schaudinn and Hoffman to identify the bacterium causing it. In the following year August von Wasserman came up with a serological method to test for the disease. By 1908, Noguchi decided finally to wrap up his snake venom work and begin full-time research on syphilis.

The organism that caused syphilis, *Treponema pallidum*, was a spirochete ten to fifteen microns in length and just 0.3 microns across. In appearance it was similar to the recurring fever spirochete that had sparked Noguchi's interest in the microscopic world back in Aizu Wakamatsu; its pale color caused some researchers to give it another name, *Spirocheta pallida*. Fritz Schaudinn was not trained as a physician or microbiologist, but was rather a zoologist studying amoebas, paramecia, and other tiny and primitive forms of life. He had found the *Treponema pallidum* using an innovative and unexpected method, and the world hailed him as a genius.

This annoyed Noguchi. "There's no such thing as genius!" he insisted, arguing that it was nothing more than patient study—the willingness to do three, four, even five times as much as other scientists—that allowed breakthrough discoveries like this. He now redirected his own efforts into the field of serology, where he joined a host of other researchers working on ways to make Wasserman's test more accurate and easier to perform. Noguchi's previous work had given him an understanding of the lysation of blood cells, a process that played a part in the Wasserman reaction, and he focused in particular on this new angle from which to approach the problem.

Noguchi wrote a flurry of papers on the diagnosis of syphilis. These reports included critical analysis of serological diagnostic methods for the disease, an examination of the prospects for a syphilis antibody, and the ways protein, lipoids, and saline compounds affected Wasserman test results, among other subjects. The press paid close attention to Noguchi and the Rockefeller Institute at this time, and invitations to present his findings to various medical societies began landing on his desk with some regularity. A wealthy industrialist expressed interest in funding his work in order to speed the discovery of a cure. The scientist received letters from all around the country asking about his work, and visitors came to his laboratory to see him in person. Syphilis attracted considerable attention as a threat to even the modern nations of the world, unlike rattlesnake venom, a threat mainly to the poor and the rural.

Soon his reputation attracted more than just attention from a curious public. First he had a job offer—would he become the first president of the newly formed New York Serological Society? This he turned down, although it pleased him greatly to be asked to head such a group. He did not turn down the next offer that came his way, though—one of a doctoral degree in medicine from Kyoto Imperial University in early 1909. The school judged that the papers he'd submitted merited this honor; he was the first person to earn his doctorate in this unconventional way.

And still his research continued. "Araki!" he'd call out across the apartment. "Come here for a moment. I'm afraid I need to take a bit more of your blood for an experiment, and I'm in a hurry."

Noguchi's flatmate came to dread this voice, with its request that never changed. At first he had been thrilled to be taking part in work of such obvious importance by a man so obviously dedicated to it. But as the days wore on and he saw a hundred ccs here, another hundred ccs there of blood taken from his veins, this participation took a toll on him. Araki could not bring himself to turn down the request, though, and so there Noguchi would be, needle in hand, saying—like a vampire—"I'm sorry about this, but I really just need another ounce or two. . ."

There was no question, however, that his work paid off in results. Soon he had improved the Wasserman test considerably, replacing the sheep blood used in the German's method with human corpuscles. This refinement of the syphilis test was one of two developments bringing Noguchi acclaim. The other was an entirely new method of testing for the disease that involved withdrawing a sample of fluid from the spinal column. This spinal fluid showed abnormally high protein levels in syphilitics, and Noguchi's method tested for these. The medical community hailed his butyric acid test* as a major step forward in diagnosing the disease.

■ ■ ■

Life went on, with Noguchi and Araki sharing the apartment, though their friendship sometimes came to grief. Not surprisingly, money lay at the root of these problems. Now and again Noguchi would leave a note on the sitting room table—"I need ten dollars." He required funds for his research materials, and these notes to his flatmate—whom he rarely saw, with Araki spending more time out studying and Noguchi locked away in his room most of the time—were his means of getting the cash. Araki usually obliged. Eventually, though, these small loans added up to hundreds of dollars. One evening Araki screwed up his courage to ask him to settle the bill. "Listen, sir, I've made up my mind not to lend you any more money. I think it's in your best interests for me to do this—your mental and physical health suffers when you work and drink too much, and too much of my money is going on these habits."

"I see," replied Noguchi amiably. "Thanks for your advice. I promise to keep it in mind."

"I'd also like to know when I can expect repayment of the funds I've loaned you so far. . ."

"Ah, well, it's no good asking me to do anything now, when I'm broke myself. You be sure to let me know again when I get paid next month." It must have been an odd sight, the host asking his house guest for a little more

---

* Noguchi's paper on this test is available at http://www.jem.org/cgi/reprintframed/11/4/604

time to pay his bill, rather than asking him for the rent.

In the laboratory at this time Noguchi was focusing his attention on one specific problem: the precise identity of the syphilis-causing organism that had been discovered. Its true nature was still somewhat unclear. All samples containing *Treponema pallidum* also comprised a number of other organisms, making it hard to design treatments tailored just to this pathogen. Noguchi set himself the goal of isolating this bacterium and creating a pure culture of it.

This was a relatively simple process for other diseases like pneumonia and dysentery, but the spirochete in question was a different matter, and isolating it had proven a task too difficult for numerous researchers. From time to time the medical community would be jolted by the news that someone had managed to raise a culture of the germ, but these reports were invariably followed by retractions noting that the culture was of another organism or was impure. A pure culture of *T. pallidum* was the grail of syphilis researchers. It would open the way to new areas of research on diagnosis, treatment, and prevention of the disease, as well as clarifying the ties between syphilis and other ailments that seemed to come with it, like progressive paralysis and *tabes dorsalis*, degeneration of the spinal cord.

Noguchi's experiments ended in failure countless times. At last, though, he began to get a fuller understanding of the peculiar nature of the spirochete. There were two main obstacles to creating a pure culture. First, it was difficult to get hold of a sample of the syphilis pathogen from a human host. Rabbits were the preferred source at the time. Researchers would inject a small dose of syphilis into a rabbit's testes, which in three or four weeks would begin producing spirochetes. These bacteria were then transplanted to a new rabbit. This process of repeated transplants and the very nature of the testicle served to gradually purify the mixture of bacteria, isolating the spirochete in question from the other impurities.

After achieving this somewhat purified culture of the germ, Noguchi confronted a second obstacle: the lack of an ideal medium in which to raise *T. pallidum* outside animal bodies. He tried a variety of kinds of animal blood and different types of serum as a medium. The spirochetes did not take readily to any of them, though; their growth was fitful in some kinds of serum and totally suppressed in others. Noguchi improved this growth with the addition of water to cut the concentration of his medium, but this introduced a new problem—the air that entered the mixture, destabilizing it and drastically reducing the survivability of the bacteria in it, had to be removed.

At a loss, Noguchi conferred with the pathologist Theobald Smith, who had helpful advice: "Why not add a bit of animal tissue to the serum mixture?" This worked well. The tissue remained alive for some time in the medium, absorbing the oxygen even as it provided food for the bacteria. At last Noguchi had his setup. He filled an extra-long test tube with the diluted serum, added a bit of organic tissue, confirmed that the medium was uncontaminated, and introduced the syphilis sample from a rabbit.

With these problems out of the way Noguchi was close to success. Still he sought to speed up the process, setting up hundreds of samples at a time where ordinary researchers worked with dozens. He packed his tubes in unglazed ceramic containers, covering them with paraffin paper to keep them airtight, and placed these inside incubators. Scientists came to call this technique, which kept oxygen exchange to a minimum in the heated samples, the "Noguchi method."

Each day Noguchi took out all his tubes and examined them one by one, looking for signs of new growth or contamination. This labor increased over time as he added new samples to the batch. But finally his labors paid off. In October 1910, and again in March 1911, he successfully isolated *Treponema pallidum*. More than a decade after leaving Japan he had achieved his victory. No longer was he reproducing other people's test results; this was a world first. The view of the pale spirochetes—and nothing else—in the microscope eyepiece made him giddy, sent him dancing about the laboratory shouting, "I've done it! I've done it at last!"

He announced his methods and findings to the medical community, which greeted the news with excitement. When interviewed, he explained the secret of his success in simple terms: "All you need is enough test tubes, sufficient money, dedication, and hard work . . . oh, and one more thing," he emphasized. "You've got to be able to put up with endless failures." In these comments, he echoed his earlier remark about genius: there was no such thing. There was only the question of willingness to work three, four, even five times as hard as the next man.

Noguchi now had a place alongside Schaudinn in the annals of syphilis research. A year earlier one of his countrymen, Sahachiro Hata, had also earned a spot in this group with his codevelopment with Paul Ehrlich of Salvarsan, an effective medicine in the treatment of the disease. In fact, this discovery, by a fellow Japanese and former member of the Kitasato Institute, had played a considerable role in spurring Noguchi on in his own quest for recognition in the field.

■ ■ ■

One happy event followed another for him. The year 1912 dawned and he told Araki that he would soon be leaving his flatmate behind, for he was going to be living with a wife! On April 10 Noguchi married Mary Dardis, whom he had met some years earlier, in a small, quiet church ceremony. Their decision to wed had been a sudden one made after they bumped into one another on the street one day and kindled a relationship that had gone nowhere in 1906, when they first met after his return from Denmark.

Noguchi called his wife Maisie, and she called him Hide. She was a tall, bright-eyed woman of Irish descent, slightly plump, the daughter of a mining engineer from Pennsylvania. The newlyweds began looking for an apartment, eventually finding one on the fifth floor of a building on Manhattan Avenue. Just one door over was another Japanese man, a painter named Ichiro Hori who became a companion for the scientist at home. Hori, a short, sturdy man with an observant look, had studied at an art school in Japan before coming to America to continue his work. Eventually he gained considerable fame as a photographer in the United States.

This was a happy time for Noguchi, but he was careful to keep his new marital status a secret at his workplace—the institute would have to make pension payments for a researcher's spouse, tied to the salary of the researcher, and he did not want to make any moves that would keep the organization from promoting him to a higher position with higher pay.

Nevertheless, he did settle down and become somewhat more of a homebody. There were still plenty of weeks when he went in to the institute even on Sunday, but Mary would call him at about one in the afternoon to ask him to come home for some of the weekend. On most weekdays he made it back to the apartment around seven, put down his things, and went immediately to find his wife.

His work, of course, followed him home. For example, he brought the film he had taken in the laboratory and developed it in the kitchen sink. Mary muttered about the mess on the floor, but Noguchi paid no attention, instead calling her over in an excited voice to take a look at a photo of some microorganism in his hand, eager to share his enthusiasm with her.

Some evenings he would pitch in and help with the cooking. This help was not always welcome. He would perhaps see Mary cooking a fine cut of beef, and crack eggs over it before she could stop him, calling it sukiyaki. Hori would come over sometimes and the two men would try to teach Mary this Japanese recipe, tossing into the pan an assortment of ingredients quite unfamiliar to any American while Noguchi proudly told his wife about this traditional dish.

Eventually it would be time to eat, and Mary went to put a cloth on the dining table. This was no simple chore. She had to move piles of manuscripts and microscopes to the sideboard to make room for the meal. The dining itself was over quickly: Noguchi wolfed down his food so he could get right back to work. He frequently failed to keep away from his research even during these brief meals, standing up to go and check on a specimen or sharpening a pencil and jotting notes into a notebook, cigar in mouth, with food still on his plate. If Mary spoke to him during this he might toss the pencil down, asking angrily how he was supposed to get any writing done with all these interruptions. Unfortunately Mary was not the kind of woman who could take—or even fake—an interest in her husband's research. This may have suited him, though, since little interest also meant fewer intrusive conversations about what he was up to.

He did, however, enjoy the sound of Mary's voice, and he passed many happy evenings peering into his microscopes while she read aloud from *Anna Karenina* or some other book. The fact that he worked nonstop didn't prevent him remembering most of what he heard. His love of literature lasted all his life.

On occasion Mary and Hideyo went out to the opera. She dressed her husband carefully on these nights. Left to his own devices he was little more than a child when it came to clothing, and she was constantly admonishing him not to wear his better suits to the lab where he would ruin them; not to fall for a salesman's pitch and buy shoes too large for his feet or hats too big for his head; not to mismatch his clothes. For her own part, Mary avoided flashy clothes and gaudy jewelry; despite being the wife of a celebrated scientist she had no ambition to attend parties and rub shoulders with New York society. Thus, after a night at the opera, they would just go straight home together, with Noguchi using his excellent memory to reenact parts of the drama they'd just watched. He loved to imitate other people: his coworkers at the institute were often targets of this, and he was a good mimic—the lab assistant who walked with a bit of a swagger, the studious researcher. . . Cane in hand, Noguchi would reproduce their mannerisms precisely. Mary couldn't help laughing at his playfulness.

Some evenings he was in no mood for work or energetic play, and would say "I'm tired. . . How about some wine?" Mary liked her drink, but her husband—surprisingly, given his family history and his own past—could no longer drink late into the night. He grew tipsy quickly, after which he would either start muttering complaints or tilt the other way, laughing and singing out loud. Perhaps he had finally taken to heart the warnings his mother had given him for years: "It's okay to drink a bit, but don't let yourself get out of control like your father."

■ ■ ■

The presence of Mary in his life meant that he had someone more willing than Araki to take up the slack at home while he poured his energy into his research. Continuing his work on pure cultures of *Treponema pallidum*, he branched out into the investigation of a possible vaccine for the disease. Salvarsan had proved to be an effective treatment for people who had syphilis, but to Noguchi's mind it was more important to prevent them from getting infected in the first place. He was in a good position to create such a vaccine, being the only person able to create pure cultures of the bacterium in question.

He first took a clue from the way in which patients with tuberculosis reacted to tuberculin skin tests, creating an extract of his cultures he called *luetin* that could be used in a similar fashion.* When applied to patients suffering from tertiary or congenital syphilis this substance produced a clear cutaneous reaction that indicated the presence of the disease. It did not, however, produce visible reactions in subjects with only primary or secondary syphilis.

His initial work on a vaccine for the disease went nowhere, though. Instead he began working on growing cultures of a variety of other germs. He sought to grow the agents of poliomyelitis, rabies, different forms of palsy, and *tabes dorsalis*, among others. At the time researchers in this field considered

* His report is at: http://www.jem.org/cgi/content/abstract/14/6/557

one-celled organisms to be in the same class as the smaller microbes they studied. They focused on these unfamiliar organisms by dividing them into a number of categories—bacteria, rickettsia, chlamydia, and filterable microbes, which are today known to be viruses. Noguchi was particularly happy about successfully growing a pure strain of the recurring fever spirochete, which he remembered almost fondly from his days at the Kaiyo Clinic. Some four decades had passed since Otto Obermeier had discovered this pathogen in 1868, and now the Japanese researcher had isolated it for the first time ever.

Some of these efforts proved to be beyond his abilities. This was through no fault of his own—the optical equipment of the day was simply not powerful enough to view the viruses that caused diseases like rabies and poliomyelitis. It wasn't until later in the century, with the invention of the electron microscope, that humans could view these agents of disease just nanometers in size. In the course of his own research on poliomyelitis, Simon Flexner confirmed that the microbe was small enough to pass through all the filtering mechanisms they had at their disposal. Noguchi, too, concerned himself with the problems of filtration and the ways it could separate certain kinds of microbes from others.

One of his most important successes during this period—and certainly one of the most dramatic discoveries he made—was his isolation of the spirochete causing a form of palsy thought to be related to syphilis. He had prepared two hundred slides of brain tissue taken from a deceased paralysis victim. Every evening, he went through vast numbers of these slides, looking for signs of the bacteria he was hunting. On one particular evening he brought his work home with him, and looked through the first hundred . . . then the next fifty . . . and finally the last few dozen. There was nothing to be found. He came to 190, then 195, and 199, and sighed as he slipped the last slide into place on the microscope, sure that this would be the same—another night's labor in vain.

But this last slide was different. It was almost dawn, and he was tense and tired, but the spirochetes he saw in that last slide's tissue sample jolted him awake. He had been searching for a different sort of pathogen in this tissue, but now that he had spotted the familiar spiral shape of T. pallidum he went back through the earlier slides and saw that this brain had been thoroughly infected. After a bit more examination he was on his feet, leaping around the room and shouting: "I've got them! There they are, I've got them!" Here was conclusive proof of the connection between syphilis, the brain under study, and this particular form of paralysis.

A bleary-eyed Mary came down the hall in her nightgown to see what the racket was about. It took some time for him to explain what he had discovered, but eventually she figured out what he was so thrilled about. Noguchi had to share his news with others. Clad only in a shirt he dashed out of the apartment, running next door to barge into Hori's room and tell him the news as well. In the dead of night, in the spring of 1913, Noguchi was truly living up to the image of the crazy scientist.

Wide awake now, he continued his investigation. By the end of the night he had found the familiar spirochete in brain tissue taken from twelve paralysis victims. Noguchi waited as long as he could, but excitement won out over decorum and early in the morning he was dashing through the quiet streets of New York to Flexner's home with a bundle of slides to show him. This was a great day for Noguchi, but it was only one discovery in many that he made during this extraordinarily fruitful period of his career. As a result, he was a star in the medical community, and even the general populace knew his name as one that appeared in the pages of newspapers with increasing frequency. Throughout North America and Europe Noguchi the researcher became a well-known figure.

■ ■ ■

People began mentioning his name along with two or three others as likely recipients of the recently created Nobel Prizes in medicine. Very few Japanese had made the list of people in the running for these awards—perhaps once every two or three years—and Noguchi joined a shortlist including a bacteriologist, a chemist, his friend Sahachiro Hata of the Kitasato Institute, a pathologist, and another medical researcher.

Noguchi did seem to be on the way to global recognition of this kind. He received a decoration from King Alfonso XIII of Spain, and much of his time in the laboratory now was spent with the French researcher Alexis Carrel, a fellow at the institute who had won the Nobel for medicine in 1912 for his development of techniques for suturing and transplanting blood vessels, and their collaboration brought the Japanese scientist further attention. In the midst of this growing acclaim for his accomplishments, though, there were some people—mainly in Europe—who publicly doubted his research results.

Anxious to prove the worth of his studies on the continent, Noguchi packed up some samples and sent them off to the German Paul Erich Hoffman, codiscoverer of *T. pallidum*, for confirmation of his findings.

Noguchi then received an invitation to attend the eighty-fifth meeting of the German Society of Natural Scientists and Physicians as a special guest. He was the first researcher active in America to receive this honor, and he immediately made preparations to go to Vienna for the conference. Leaving New York on September 2, he made his way first to Paris, where he met with members of the medical world for a few days before going to Strasbourg for a brief stop and then on to Vienna. Wherever he went he saw his own face staring out from newspaper pages, where it accompanied articles announcing his tour of Europe, introducing his research achievements, and in general describing him as someone who could save the world from syphilis. The welcome was especially warm in Germany, where the papers hailed his "triumphant arrival" in the country. An amazing crowd was on hand at the station when he got off, including not merely scientists but diplomats and political dignitaries. Dr. Kitasato himself had received no higher honor when he had visited Vienna in the past. It was lucky for Noguchi that he was able to make this trip when he did, considering that war would engulf the continent the following year.

Some four thousand scientists and doctors gathered at the German society's conference—top minds from fields ranging from physics and chemistry to biology and medicine. On the second day Noguchi was scheduled to make a presentation on his recent findings; this turned out to be such a popular offering that the audience filled the lecture hall and spilled out into the hallway, where calls of "Noguchi! Noguchi!" rang out. Noguchi had the help of another young Japanese man, Kaichiro Manabe, a researcher doing work in Germany who would go on to a professorship at Tokyo Imperial University. Manabe became Noguchi's secretary during his time in Vienna, helping to put him in touch with key scientists who wanted to speak to him and helping people spot the diminutive Japanese visitor in the crowds that surrounded him. The celebrated Wilhelm His Jr. took one look at Noguchi and announced, "Ah, now that I see him I can tell that he's a great man." When asked how he could tell this, he pointed to Noguchi's head, with its unAsian-looking tuft of hair: "You see how his hair curls up and sticks out from the top of his head? That's how I know his greatness!"

It was time for the presentation, and Noguchi walked to the front of the hall to loud applause. To the surprise of everyone, though, he didn't stand at the lectern but seated himself off to one side of the stage. His German reading and writing skills were good, but he had no delusions about his speaking abilities. With his thick Aizu accent layered over the challenging inflections of the language, he couldn't hope to make a good impression on this audience in his own voice, and he had arranged for a German doctor to read his paper to the crowd. The hall went silent as the listeners strained to hear the explanation of Noguchi's research techniques and what he had discovered through them.

Doctors and scientists pressed around him after the talk, following him out of the room and down the hall. It was difficult for him to turn down all the requests he got asking him to give lectures at gatherings elsewhere in Europe. Noguchi had hoped to see Friedrich von Mueller attend his presentation, but unfortunately some other pressing affair had kept the president of the German Society of Natural Scientists and Physicians from hearing the speech. Soon, however, this man was on the phone to Manabe, calling Noguchi's room at the Hotel Imperial to ask whether he could call on him.

"What?" responded Noguchi in shock. "Herr Mueller come to call on me? That's hardly likely. Ask again and make sure you're hearing this right."

Mueller was a giant in the world of science, preeminent in a country considered the Mecca of medical and scientific studies in that era. This was not the kind of man who came to call at the hotel of a foreign visitor to Germany. Manabe had actually earned increased respect from Noguchi simply by revealing that he had once studied under this figure.

Manabe got on the phone again to confirm the message. Yes, Mueller was to visit Noguchi, not the other way around. Right there in the hotel room, his shirt untucked and unbuttoned, Noguchi started capering about.

When eventually they met, Noguchi was the first to speak, saying what an honor it was to meet him.

"No, sir," replied Mueller, "it is I who am pleased to make the acquaintance of such a marvelous man of science." Mueller wasted no time in inviting Noguchi to Munich—an invitation that was of course accepted on the spot.

Some days later, Noguchi carried out a demonstration of his experimental techniques, and professors and doctors lined up to peer into the microscope as he described what he had found and how he had found it, pressing their calling cards into his hand—his right, of course—as they left the table. Most of them were respectful, with one notable exception: a young researcher from the Koch Institute who saw Noguchi's work as less than impressive, and let him know this with some hard-nosed questions. Never a particularly talkative man, Noguchi listened in silence to his queries and criticisms; this only seemed to egg the young man on, and soon he was openly rejecting Noguchi's findings, proclaiming the results obtained at his own laboratory to be superior.

Eventually the Japanese scientist had heard enough about the Koch Institute and the unlikelihood that a researcher working elsewhere could make any significant contribution. "You just hold it right there!" he roared at the German, before launching into a flat rejection of the man's claims, and going so far as to censure the Koch Institute itself—that "shining tower of knowledge" whose self-contented occupants congratulated themselves on their mastery of science without ever facing the realities of the scientific world outside its walls. And who among those proud men, Noguchi asked, could deny what he had discovered? Who would reject all his hard work? "You? Just how long have you been a bacteriologist, may I ask?"

Finishing this tirade, he slowly and deliberately removed the man's calling card from the stack in his hand, held it up before his eyes, and ripped it to shreds. Noguchi was in a room full of Germans, with the insulted party ready to fly at him. But several of the onlookers stepped in to separate the two and prevent matters from getting further out of hand. The day ended for Noguchi with a sense of satisfaction—it had felt good to let off steam like that—and a magnificent dinner hosted by the science society, at which a member of the German imperial family was present. Born into poverty in a Fukushima farmhouse, educated at an upper elementary school and a medical school whose lectures he had not properly attended, and flung into his overseas career alone, with barely a possession to his name, he had come a long way. But this was not his victory alone; he was quite conscious of the fact that it gave a boost to the international image of the Japanese people as a whole. In this accomplishment he was walking a similar road to that taken by Sahachiro Hata, who some six weeks earlier had presented his Salvarsan findings at an illustrious international medical conference in Washington, D.C. Hata, like Noguchi, had not come up the conventional ladder of organized medicine in Japan, but had forged his own way in the world of research.

Leaving Vienna, Noguchi next took a whirlwind tour of various other European cities, lecturing and meeting scientists and physicians wherever he went. He had the good fortune to stay at Friedrich von Mueller's home in Munich, before moving on to Frankfurt, then Copenhagen. It was his first time in this city in a decade, and he was delighted to be staying with his old friend Madsen once again. The Danish royal family honored him with the Order of Dannebrog there. Noguchi then went on to Christiania (Oslo) and Bergen in Norway, Stockholm, across the sea to London, and back to Berlin. In all he visited ten cities during the nearly seven weeks he spent in Europe in late 1913, making a total of eleven presentations. He had banquets scheduled for almost every single night—an incredible thirty-eight feasts in all. He had two royal audiences. In an age before television, he managed to make the name Noguchi known to people across the continent.

■ ■ ■

In November he made his way back across the Atlantic to find that things had changed in his absence. His friends looked at him with newfound respect; people on the street looked at him and wondered aloud whether it was Noguchi. Before the end of the year Mount Sinai Hospital came to him with a proposal: would he like to head up a new research facility to be built in the hospital? This was an attractive offer; he was still just an associate member at the Rockefeller Institute, and the hospital was talking about an annual salary of some six thousand dollars—about twice what he was making then. As enticing as this was, he didn't leap at the chance to move on; instead he went to speak to Simon Flexner about his position.

Flexner was more than happy to do what he could to keep Noguchi on board. He raised his salary to five thousand a year and made him a full member of the institute—a lifetime position that carried considerable prestige. He was now earning as much as any minister of state back in his home country. But his new position pleased him for more reasons than the money: the Rockefeller Institute had access to considerable funds to support research efforts. He took up this new position officially in July 1914, standing alongside Simon Flexner and the other members at the top of the organization.

The honors kept rolling in. In January 1914 the Viennese congress of internists and pediatricians inducted him into its ranks. In February an American academy of medicine made him an honorary member. He received the Swedish Royal Order of the Northern Star, Third Class. In July he got word that Tokyo Imperial University had granted him a doctorate in science for his paper on spirochetes. Though gratified—he was the first person who had come up via the state licensing examination to earn this degree—it made no difference to his plans. In fact, Noguchi showed a lifelong disdain for the titles and certificates that meant so much in Japan, and he had wanted the degree mainly to show that even a researcher who had worked outside the system could achieve this goal. Finally, he was made a member of the Association of American Physicians, cementing his place among the top medical minds of the nation.

Decorated and degreed though he was, Noguchi lived his life in much the same way as he had before. He would go to Hori's place or another friend's for a game of chess or *shogi* (at which he showed slightly more skill), returning in one of two moods: happy at winning or furious at his losses. Mary had little difficulty telling which mood he was in; all she had to do was listen to his footsteps in the hallway as he approached. A trudging Noguchi meant a disappointed husband, one who would head out the next evening anxious for a rematch. These games went on quite late—he liked to play until he won, and this could take until the next morning. His record was forty-two games in a single night; if skill could not win him the games, he would wear his opponent down with sheer stamina.

When he won he would come home buoyantly, his feet tapping energetically against the floorboards as he returned to share his pleasure with his wife. In chess, as in life, Noguchi easily swung between emotional extremes— his victories bringing joy and his defeats piling up over his head like dark clouds. These days, though, his victories were far more numerous.

ONE MORE TRIP HOME

The year 1914 saw the onset of events that rocked the world. The June 28 murder of Archduke Franz Ferdinand touched off a war that engulfed all of Europe. Alexis Carrel, one of the brightest minds in the Rockefeller Institute, could not continue his peaceful research in neutral America and returned to his native France to take up a military post as chief surgeon of a hospital in Lyon. Noguchi's nation also involved itself in World War I, pledging its support for its ally Britain despite having all of Eurasia between itself and the fighting. By so doing, the country hoped to elevate its position on the global stage.

This decision affected Noguchi personally. The Nobel Foundation's core philosophy was antiwar, and researchers from nations taking sides in the ongoing battles were effectively removed from consideration for a prize. He had been on the shortlist for an award in medicine, but now any prospect of this had been wiped out.

Noguchi's life seemed to follow some great sinusoidal curve. He had enjoyed a heady period of success; now a series of small defeats began to pile up rapidly. He had grabbed a top spot in the institute, along with all the perks that came with full membership—a significant raise in pay, private laboratory space, a secretary, and three assistants. But problems remained. Firstly, he had always been a "lone wolf" in the laboratory, preferring to work alone and unhappy with the idea of sharing his achievements with other people. As a member of the institute, though, he was expected to publish his results in jointly authored papers. This galled him.

Secondly, there *were* few achievements in his research these days. The institute assigned him certain tasks—producing a large quantity of serum for use in poliomyelitis work, for instance—that he was unable to complete. This was partly due to his reluctance to perform these bureaucratically assigned jobs. Although he managed to make enough of the serum to satisfy the institute's requirement, he did just an adequate job and not the sort of work he was capable of. Things got worse: even when it came to work where he could give his talents free rein—his personal research—he found it hard to make much headway. A long time had passed since his last discovery. He branched out in his experiments, researching polio, rabies, and swine cholera, but made no progress in any of these areas. After experiencing the pinnacle of success in the previous year, this trough in his performance felt exceptionally low.

Nothing he did seemed to go right. Compared to the Noguchi of 1913 he lacked passion in his work; he could not concentrate on a task for long. After all his years of research to improve other people's health, Noguchi at last gave his own physical condition some thought. He had left a serious case of piles untreated for years. Perhaps this was a factor in his inability to focus on his research. He was also a married man now, with a wife to think of. Maybe it was time to see a doctor himself, to buy some life insurance. Noguchi made an appointment and got the checkup required for purchasing a policy. This doctor had bad news, though:

"I'm sorry, we can't offer you coverage."

"Why not?"

"Your heart is considerably enlarged," came the alarming reply. "There's damage to your cardiac valves."

So it had come to this. Noguchi's heart was in such poor shape he couldn't even insure his own life. If he continued living and working as hard as he had been, he might last only three more years. He had never listened to his coworkers who told him to take it easy, and now he was paying the price. This physician's warning was a heavy blow to his ego and a wake-up call. Could he call himself a competent doctor if he couldn't even keep himself healthy?

He was not, however, particularly surprised by this news. Noguchi wrote to a friend that he knew what he'd been doing to his body with his brutal schedule, and that he now intended to do what was necessary to overcome this setback. He and Mary left their apartment building with no elevator for a more modern building near Central Park that would be easier on his heart. The doctor's instructions were not easy ones for Noguchi to follow, though. His ability to work superhuman hours was a source of pride, and he hated missing out on potential discoveries by not staying in the lab for that extra time.

■ ■ ■

His own health was not his only cause for concern at this time: he was worried about his mother. Shika had written a letter to him around three years earlier, the only memento of her that he kept. It was clumsily composed and scrawled in her own untutored hand, but it was a moving indication of her character.

> Your success. Everyone's amazed by it. I'm happy too. I go to the Nakada Kannon. Each year I go, I stay one night. I pray there.
>
> There's always more to learn. Always more to pay. People asking for money. If you come, I could make them wait. In the spring, everyone will leave. Off to Hokkaido. I'm afraid to be alone. Please somehow find a way to come.
>
> I got the money from you. Didn't tell anyone. If I talk about money, it disappears. They drink it away. Please come soon, please come soon, please come soon, please come soon. I beg you. Only this in my life. I pray for it. I face east and pray, I face west and pray. I face north and south and I pray. On the first of the month I do the *shiodachi*, the fasting. I eat no salty food. I do this at the Eishoin temple. The first of each month. I have the priest say prayers. Whatever else I forget, this I remember.
>
> I look at your photo. I have it here. Please come son. Tell me when you can come. I wait for your reply. Write soon. I can't sleep, waiting for you.

Noguchi knew what his mother was facing back home. Another letter from his old teacher Kobayashi had let him know the truth—the Noguchi family was close to total collapse, its members ready to leave Okinajima and scatter. Two thousand yen in debt, Shika was under pressure to come up with seven hundred by the end of the year. Her letter was a call for help.

Noguchi had received this call when he was deep in his spirochete research, and he was reluctant to let a trip back to Japan take him away from it. He sent as much money as he could spare with instructions to ask Shika's creditors to accept installments rather than a lump sum. He also promised to return home in a couple of years' time, which was a comfort to his mother. So she resigned herself to waiting, though the waiting dragged on, with her son living his own busy life, getting married, and giving his presentations in Europe.

That intensive period was now over, and Noguchi's thoughts went back to the letter from his mother. It was time to return to Fukushima. His brother, Seizo, had gone to Hokkaido to find work, and his father was preparing to do the same. The house Noguchi had been born in was literally falling apart. Luckily a neighboring family moved out of the village, leaving their sturdier home empty. Kobayashi spent three hundred yen to buy this for the Noguchis. Having a solid roof over her head did not save Shika from her creditors, however, and soon she had lost the title to the fields she worked. Far off in New York, her tearful son cursed his inability to look after his aging mother properly. "I became what I am today thanks only to my mother's hard work. All this glory, all this fame . . . it's nothing compared to the love she gave me."

The following year brought a spot of bright news. In April 1915 Noguchi learned he had been honored with the Imperial Prize, the highest award a scientist could receive in Japan. Noguchi's work had never sparked much interest in his own country, and there are several likely reasons why he received this recognition out of the blue. For one thing, his name had been mentioned as a potential Nobel prizewinner. If the Imperial Academy were to wait until after he had won this most exalted of awards to confer its own top honor on him, it would reflect poorly on this organization's ability to acknowledge the achievements of Japan's own researchers. World War I was another reason. With the nations of Europe at each other's throats, countries like Germany were no longer destinations for Japanese students heading abroad. More of these young researchers were going to America to get their degrees, and Noguchi, by far the biggest name in the Japanese scientific community in the United States, was someone to cultivate good relations with. Lastly, there were the tireless efforts of men like Chiwaki and Baron Ishiguro, who had been doing their best to bring news of Noguchi's discoveries to a Japanese audience.

In his late thirties now, and at the height of his research career, Noguchi chose not to return to Japan to receive the honor. Indeed, after the news from the insurance firm's doctor, he felt he had less time to work than ever, and did not want to give up any of it. So he sent Chiwaki in his stead to collect the prize. This was the first time for any recipient to skip an award ceremony for any reason other than illness, but Noguchi seemed to think little of his decision to miss it. The thousand yen that accompanied the prize was another matter, and he saw it as a way to put his mother back on her feet. Even if he had wanted to head back at this time, though, he personally didn't have the money for a boat ticket.

Saburo Ishizuka, who remembered Noguchi from his days at the Takayama college, mailed him a letter enclosing a picture of his mother. Ishizuka was now a dental surgeon in the city of Nagaoka to the northwest of Tokyo. He also dabbled in politics and was an avid photographer. His photography club had taken a trip to the shores of Lake Inawashiro, where he had met Noguchi's mother and been shocked by her run-down condition. The pattern on her kimono was faded beyond recognition, her *monpe* trousers seemed to be more patches than original cloth, and the deep lines on her face were topped by a disheveled mop of gray hair. There had been rain showers throughout the day, so Ishizuka took her portrait in a combination of evening light and light from a lamp held up by Hideyo's sister Inu. Along with the photo he sent Noguchi a warning: "Your mother isn't long for this world, I'm afraid. You'd better do whatever it takes to get yourself back to Japan as soon as possible. If you don't do this, you're likely to regret it for the rest of your life."

The message was a tough one to get, but Noguchi took what Ishizuka was saying to heart and respected him for the straightforward way he was saying it. In fact this letter helped later to cement a lasting friendship between the two men. Now, though, it brought him only pain. His mother was old, and far feebler than he had thought. He stared at the photo for ages. He had ignored the reality of his mother's situation for too long. It was now time to drop everything and go back to be with her.

Not having the necessary funds at that time, he dashed off a telegram to his friend Hajime Hoshi, who had left New York and gone back to Tokyo to establish the company Hoshi Pharmaceuticals. Hoshi had stayed in touch with Noguchi, offering him advice on various matters and, on occasions like this, financial support. He now wired him the impressive sum of seven thousand yen. With this Noguchi could travel to Japan in considerable style— in fact, he bought himself a new tuxedo to wear to the dinners he expected to attend.

Should he go alone, or with his wife? He thought hard about this. Taking Mary to the village he'd grown up in would lead to all sorts of gossip about "that white woman" accompanying him, and he was less than thrilled at the prospect of showing the grinding poverty of his youth to the person who shared his large Manhattan apartment. In the end, the problem proved an easy one to solve. When he asked Mary whether she wanted to go along, she told him frankly that she preferred not to intrude on this reunion. So that was that. Noguchi packed his bags and left. It was his first return to his home country in almost sixteen years.

■ ■ ■

On September 5 the *Yokohama Maru* sailed into Yokohama harbor. Noguchi gazed at the approaching land, and finally at the figures waiting on the jetty for the ship to come in. He was coming home! It felt like an age since 1900, when he had left this country; it was an emotional moment.

Chiwaki and Kobayashi had come to greet him. They were worried about the crowd that had come with the same idea—their old charge had been gone so long he might have forgotten how to behave properly in a Japanese setting, and the two men wanted to refresh his memory about it. They had planned to meet Noguchi before he got to the crowds, but this plan was hopeless now that the ship was at the wharf.

They had nothing to worry about. Noguchi was dressed for the occasion in formal attire, a morning coat and silk top hat. He cut a bold figure in this Western dress, and he greeted his welcoming party politely and confidently. Years of international experience, hard work, and success had changed the man.

The crowd on the dock included reporters as well as Noguchi's old friends and teachers. He gave a brief press conference, modestly describing his experiences in the West, and then climbed into a two-horse carriage provided by a friend from his old village. It was past eight in the evening when his party arrived at Tokyo Station, but there was another crowd of well-wishers on the platform here, too—friends of his, senior members of the medical community, and a group of students from Chiwaki's Tokyo School of Dental Medicine. After exchanging pleasantries with this crowd Noguchi took a car with Chiwaki and Kobayashi to the Imperial Hotel. The little wooden houses outside the car windows told him he was finally back in Japan. At the hotel, at last he was alone with the men who had done so much for him. He presented them with gold watches.

The next day was a busy one. Noguchi made the rounds of the capital, calling on a string of important men to report that he had returned and tell them of his time abroad. He visited several government ministers, major medical scientists, the mayor of Tokyo, and a number of his seniors from his days at school and work in Japan. With these duties completed, he and Kobayashi headed to Chiwaki's house. Mrs. Chiwaki joined the small group, and the four of them spoke together for several hours; there was plenty of news to share—Noguchi's speeches in Europe and other tales from overseas, the death of the Chiwakis' daughter, and so on.

Kobayashi said warmly: "Well, it's amazing that you went out into the world on your own and accomplished this much. But no matter how big a scientist you've become, a quiet guy like you must have had an awful time speaking in public, surely?"

"Not really, sir," came the reply. "I was talking about research I'd done myself. I found that my pride in what I'd discovered gave me the courage to speak about it. When a great man like Mueller in Germany came up to me and reached out to shake my hand, I tell you, it was like I'd become the greatest scholar in the world. With a feeling like that, it was easy to speak to the crowds."

"I'm proud of you, son. It's that drive you've had since you were a boy that lets you do things like make those presentations."

One topic that came up in conversation troubled even the phlegmatic Chiwaki. This was the American doctor's prognosis that Noguchi only had three years or so to live. Pale in the face, Chiwaki excused himself and went to another room, where he worked out Noguchi's horoscope. It seems odd that this dentist, a man of science, should turn to an ancient tool of superstition like this, but its prediction was heartening: Noguchi would live for at least another decade. (Oddly enough, this forecast would prove accurate— he had thirteen more years to live.)

September 7 was another day for meetings. People called on Noguchi at his hotel from early in the morning. Many of these visitors were politicians and journalists, but among them were also eminent men like Baron Ishiguro and Tanemichi Aoyama, dean of the Tokyo Imperial University medical school. Aoyama had not wanted to meet Noguchi. He had opposed the Imperial Academy's decision to confer its highest honor on the young researcher, and he wasn't about to go and call on him "just because he's moved up a little in the world." Kiichiro Manabe, now a professor at the university, talked him into going, though. It was a triumphant moment for Noguchi—the head of the school that stood for what he opposed in his work and his very background coming to call on him. In the evening, a happy day was capped by a visit from his old boss, Dr. Kitasato. Noguchi had truly come home in glory.

■ ■ ■

The next day he headed north to Aizu. Shika had decided not to come to Tokyo. She was waiting at home for her son, having sent instructions with Kobayashi on the proper way for Noguchi to behave on his return to the village. To a mother, even a world-famous scientist needs pointers on how to acquit himself. With her instructions in mind, Noguchi was now looking out the window of a northbound train. Those had often been difficult times when he made the trip between Tokyo and Aizu in the past, but now he looked back on them fondly. Memories flooded back as the familiar scenery rolled by.

Not all the memories were pleasant, though. He had left the village in considerable debt to his friend Yasuhei Yago, among others. Would they be glad to see him, or would they come asking for their money back? He also thought again of those who had made fun of his "pestle hand." Their mocking voices came back to him now: "How's a cripple like Seisaku going to be a doctor?" No, his return home might be less than triumphant after all.

Suddenly these thoughts were interrupted by a cry from outside the local train at Koriyama Station. "This is the one. He's in here," Yago shouted as he peered in at Noguchi. A group of villagers, the mayor at their head, had come down to the station to ride the last few stops with him. As the group piled onto the train, their familiar faces and accents brought Noguchi close to tears. This welcome was the best one yet.

The homecoming party was only just beginning, though. Preparations had been underway for days in Okinajima. As the train pulled into Okinajima Station fireworks lit up the evening sky. Over four hundred people jostled for space on the platform—county councilmen, village council members, employees from the town office, chiefs of community groups and so on—all hoping to see the returning hero. And there he was! As he stepped off the train the crowd erupted into shouts of *"Banzai!"* In his best formal attire, his moustache neatly trimmed, Noguchi smiled and bowed to the assembled throng.

The villagers had erected a large arch in front of the station, topping it with a placard reading WELCOME. Flags of countless nations fluttered in the breeze above Noguchi's head as he made his way down the main village lane. Orderly rows of schoolchildren stood beneath the bunting, waving paper flags. Men and women, young and old, everyone who could be there found a place at the side of the lane to get a glimpse of him. The homes along the main road had been spruced up for the occasion, flying the Rising Sun to welcome him back.

A rickshaw was waiting to carry him to the hamlet of Sanjogata, but Noguchi preferred to walk the hilly road. Approaching the western edge of his birthplace, he found this area decorated as well. He did not go straight home. His mother had given him strict instructions, and he followed them to the letter. First he went to pray at the Hachiman shrine, giving thanks for his safe return to Japan. Here he formally greeted the crowd on hand, thanking them for their warm welcome. His friend Yago stepped out from their midst, to reply on their behalf. This was actually something Noguchi had asked him to do: mindful that he owed this man a lot, he wanted to give him a chance to shine in front of the others.

After Noguchi raised a cup of sake to the gods of the shrine and gave another speech to the villagers, the assembly broke up and everyone went home. Noguchi still had Shika's instructions to follow, though. Next he walked the streets of the hamlet, paying his respects at the homes of all thirty families in Sanjogata and thanking them for helping his mother over the years. Finally, he went to the temple of Choshoji to pray before the family grave.

At last he had done his mother's bidding and could now go home. Shika was waiting at the door along with Sayosuke, who had come back from Hokkaido. She watched her son intently as he came up through the village. Age had hunched her back somewhat, and poverty kept her in an unlined serge kimono, but she was a proud figure as she waited for her son. As Noguchi approached he noted with relief how healthy she looked. Bowing his head, he spoke to her for the first time in sixteen years: "I've come home, Mother. I'm glad to see you looking so well. . ." Then he broke down and couldn't speak.

"You've had a long, tiring journey to get here. Thanks for coming. I'm glad you're here . . . I'm so glad." Shika may have prepared some finer words for her greeting, knowing that other people would be listening in. In the end, though, this simple woman had only simple words to say, before she too was overcome. Holding her close to him, he walked into the house. There were few dry eyes among the onlookers that evening. Even Noguchi's father stood off to one side, watching mother and son go inside.

Once indoors, Noguchi sat down with his family and spoke to each of them in turn, thanking them for putting up with everything to keep the family going in his absence. He did not have much time alone with them, though; there were too many people who wanted his attention. At nine that evening he made his way to a shop in town where the villagers were to celebrate his return and listen to him speak. The people pressed in on all sides to have a word with Noguchi or ask him to write a message for them. "Honesty is the best policy," he wrote in English for one villager; for another, "La patience est amère, mais son fruit est doux"—patience is a bitter thing to bear, but its fruits are sweet. (These messages, along with the Chinese characters reading *nintai*—perseverance—were later inscribed on a stone erected at his birthplace.)

This was just the first of many parties in a very busy schedule. The Sanjo-gata gathering was followed by one for the whole village of Okinajima, one for the alumni of the Inawashiro Upper Elementary School, and one for a number of government officials and private citizens in the city of Wakamatsu. Noguchi gave speeches for the Okinajima youth association, his old primary school, the upper elementary alumni, the Yama County physicians' group, and the Fukushima Society of Medical Science.

Of these events the ones he enjoyed most were with his old schoolmates. He found himself taken back to his youth by the familiar voices telling him he hadn't changed a bit, or asking why he never wrote. Even the complaints he heard now and then seemed rooted more in friendship than enmity. He had treated these friends poorly at times in the past, but now they nodded with acceptance as he tried to explain why he'd acted that way, why he'd said the things he did. And as he listened to a drunken childhood friend sing a folk song about Mt. Bandai, he felt his heart being tugged toward the idea of staying here for good. He was almost past his thirties, the "golden age" for a researcher, and his work had been perilously unhealthy for him. Wasn't it time for a change? Wouldn't it be wonderful to settle down on the shores of Inawashiro, to live out his days here? But even as he whispered this to himself, he knew his true allegiance was to things he couldn't do here, and that he would have to go.

■ ■ ■

Noguchi next paid closer attention to his family situation. Shika's news painted a grim picture. As he lay in bed thinking about this problem, with the lonely sound of the crickets coming up through the bare floorboards, he wondered how he could make things easier for his mother in her old age. Some villagers had taken to muttering about the doctor who had made it big overseas but who did nothing for his family or his hometown. Many of these complaints, of course, were motivated by jealousy, but still, they had a point. One day, for example, he went to Yasuhei Yago's house to give him a token of his appreciation—a basket of fruit and a gold watch. Yago made to accept these gifts, but his mother wouldn't allow it and shoved them back at Noguchi as if to say "You aren't canceling your debts to us that easily." This was perhaps a narrow-minded view for her to take, since Noguchi was trying in his way to make amends, but he had nothing to say in his defense.

It was at this point, though, that he was able to draw on the monetary award that went with winning the Imperial Prize. He now gave some of this cash to his main benefactors and those who had helped him most as he was growing up. To stop tongues from wagging in the village he made small presents to all the elderly men and women. As news of the prize spread, old friends came to congratulate him, and Noguchi used the opportunity to give Daikichi from the old Matsushimaya store, now fallen on hard times and living elsewhere, a gift as well.

His old teacher Kobayashi had a wise suggestion for using some of the remaining prize money: "Why not celebrate by buying some farmland?" The Noguchi family fields had fallen into the hands of creditors long ago, and one of Shika's fondest dreams was to buy this land back. In sympathy with Noguchi's intentions, a well-to-do farmer agreed to sell him a decent-sized wet paddy plot and a dry field at about half the going rate. Noguchi proudly named them the "Imperial Prize fields" and made his mother a present of them, thus turning her into a proper farmer once again. "There's nothing so delicious as rice and vegetables you've grown on your own land!" was her cheerful comment later, when the first harvest was in.

Now that the future of the Noguchi household was more or less guaranteed, Hideyo turned to other familial tasks. He had with him a photograph of his wife, which he hadn't shown his parents and siblings yet. Kobayashi had told them of Noguchi's marriage to an American woman, but seeing her picture for the first time was still a bit of a jolt. All the same, they liked her face, and were soon laughing warmly about the couple: "She looks like just the kind of woman who'll have you carrying her around town on your back!" they told him.

One day Noguchi the doctor went to examine the father of an old friend of his, who had suffered a stroke. The son pulled him aside and told him about some gossip that was going around. "Folks are saying that you don't treat your father with nearly as much respect as your mother. They don't see this as a good thing at all." The father-son relationship between the teacher Kobayashi and Noguchi was well known, and for the most part Sayosuke was out of the picture where the Noguchi family was concerned. But he was, in his own way, doing what he could for his son's success. Once a month he went to a shrine to pray for Hideyo. He was a humble man, too, who was never heard boasting about his famous boy.

"Your father isn't the kind of guy who needs fancy food and drink," his friend went on. "He's a man of simple tastes, and easy to please. Would it be so hard for you to help him out a little too? I know that if you let him get his hands on as much sake as he wants he'll drink himself into the grave, but if he had just a little from you to go on with, in addition to what he makes at work, he should lead a long and happy life."

Noguchi took this advice to heart. He spoke to his father soon afterwards in the half-joking manner the family used: "Listen, Father, I'll be sending you a little something to buy yourself a drink from time to time. Soon you'll be able to just crawl right into the sake barrel and live in there!"

Shika remained as religious as ever. Each year since her son had left for America she had gone to the Nakada Kannon to offer her thanks for the year. A festival held on the ninth day of the seventh month, going by the old calendar, was the occasion she marked by staying overnight at the temple, praying straight through until morning. On the way back she generally stopped at a friend's house to rest for a while, then went on to the Kobayashis' house, where she left a melon as a gift for her son's teacher. Now she declared it was time to make this year's trip to the temple. "But a doctor like you," she said to Noguchi, "is too busy here to go along with me. I'll stay two nights in front of the Kannon and offer prayers for you as well."

But Noguchi insisted on going with his mother. He did this not just to please Shika; he told her he wanted to offer his own thanks there. "There are a lot of people in this world who aren't happy. No matter how good they are, how hard they work, they can't stop feeling miserable. Compared to them I'm lucky, and I should offer thanks for this."

Saburo Ishizuka happened to be in the village at the time, and he and Kobayashi joined Shika and Hideyo on their pilgrimage. The four of them traveled by rickshaw to the temple on the western edge of the Aizu plain, where they spent the night in prayer before the eleven-faced statue of Kannon.

■ ■ ■

In the end Noguchi spent ten days in Fukushima with his family. These were days with a lasting impact on his life, giving him a deeper understanding of the place that had created him—both its brighter aspects, like his friends and the love of his family, and its darker ones, such as the poverty he had escaped by leaving Okinajima far behind. He was glad he had come back. Now, though, his crowded schedule called him back to the capital. In just over eight weeks there he sat in on a number of research sessions, gave well over a dozen presentations—some at such distinguished venues as Tokyo Imperial University, which sent one of the few automobiles then in Japan for him— and attended more than sixty parties welcoming him back to Japan and celebrating his accomplishments. He even received an invitation to the mansion of the Matsudaira family, the former lords of the Aizu domain.

His years of life overseas had made him an effective public speaker. He tailored his presentations carefully to his audiences, focusing on complex scientific material when addressing crowds of doctors and researchers and branching out into more human concerns, such as his rise from poverty and the hard times he had faced abroad, when talking to students or the general public. Ordinarily Noguchi was a rather quiet man, but when speaking before a crowd he became animated. Audiences found him a thrilling speaker when, face flushed, he began firing ideas at them in rapid succession. The effect he had on some young people was inspiring enough to send them packing for their own trips overseas to test themselves against the world.

An outbreak of Weil's disease in the Higata region of Chiba Prefecture led him away from Tokyo for a short while to keep track of the illness. There Noguchi met up with Ryutaro Miyahara, his old flatmate from New York, and the two of them happened to go to a local theater to catch a traditional

Japanese music show. The theater was soon in an uproar, though. The audience's attention was firmly focused on Noguchi, whose face had been in all the papers. Alarmed by the fame he had evidently gained in his home country, Noguchi left the theater before the show even began.

Not wanting to be in Tokyo on his own, Noguchi invited the Kobayashis and his mother to accompany him on a tour of the capital. (He extended the same invitation to Sayosuke, but his father didn't feel like coming along.) After some days there the party, now joined by Chiwaki, headed west to the Kansai region. Hideyo sat with his mother in the train and pointed out Mt. Fuji and other sights to her during the trip west. Shika was a rustic woman with no knowledge of the proper way to deal with people in the circles her son moved in, and had resisted the idea of coming along for this reason. But Hideyo had reassured her, saying "I'll be by your side the whole way, Mother."

The group got off the train in Nagoya, where Noguchi had a speech to give. From there it was a short side-trip to the grand shrine at Ise, a destination all Japanese of that era hoped to reach at some point during their lives. They took rooms at the Futamikan, an inn near the shrine, and headed for the hotel where Noguchi was to speak that evening. On arrival, Noguchi was greeted with a telegram bringing wonderful news: he had been awarded an imperial decoration, the Fourth Class Order of the Rising Sun—one of the highest honors available for an ordinary citizen, particularly a scholar with no military rank.

The next day the party went on to Osaka. There, entertained by the dean of the Osaka Higher School of Medicine, they dined at one of the finest restaurants in the city, a place called Kotoya in the Minoo district out west of the city. Noguchi and the others were on the second floor of the restaurant, looking down over the autumn foliage in the garden outside and listening to the bubbling creek that ran below the brilliant leaves. Noguchi was determined that his mother should have a good time here. As each of the exquisite dishes arrived at the table, he described them for her in detail and urged her to eat up. "Mother, do you see this? It's bonito sashimi. Try some of it!" He would then turn to Mrs. Kobayashi: "You like broiled fish, right? Have some of this!" Then it was back to his mother: "Here, this is a broth made from *matsutake* mushrooms—a real treat. Look, the lid turns into a bowl for the soup." It was hard to tell that he was actually the guest of honor at the banquet.

Also in attendance at this meal was Yachiyo, a celebrated geisha accustomed to being the center of attention at such gatherings. But Yachiyo apparently was moved to tears by the sight of Noguchi taking his mother's hand in his as he talked and laughed with her about this once-in-a-lifetime meal—an episode that later made its way into the Osaka edition of the *Mainichi Shimbun*: "Famous Doctor Makes Geisha Weep." The proprietress of Kotoya never forgot this night and, years later, after she learned of Noguchi's death, she commissioned a bronze bust of him to be displayed in the restaurant.

In all Noguchi spent nearly two weeks in western Japan. After a last flurry of activity—including a speech at Kyoto Imperial University at which he collapsed with severe stomach pains but managed to finish his talk—he knew he would soon have to leave for America. Before going, however, he paid Okinajima a final visit.

■ ■ ■

As a parting gift Kobayashi gave his old student a small Kannon statue. He also made him a present of a suit of armor that had been in his samurai family for generations. With these things packed and ready to go, there were a few last tasks for Noguchi to take care of before leaving. He spoke to his mother one more time about her work as a midwife, urging her to consider giving up for her health's sake a difficult, tiring job that took her out of the house at all hours of the day and night. Reluctantly, since she wanted to go on helping her community, she agreed. Shika's teeth were also in terrible shape, and she had trouble chewing meat, so Noguchi went with Mrs. Kobayashi to speak to Ishizuka about getting a set of dentures made.

With this, he had done what he could to make his mother's life as comfortable as possible. She had her fields to farm, she had no more midnight trips through the dark to help women give birth, and she had a new set of teeth. His research was waiting, and it was time to leave her behind again. As his departure drew near she grew increasingly concerned about him: "Don't worry about me. Kannon will be watching over me. You're the one who needs to be careful. Don't you go working so hard you wreck your health."

"You too, Mother. You're getting old, you know, no matter how strong you might feel."

"Me? I've got nothing to worry about. You've done more for me than I could have dreamed of. I can die happy now that I've seen you one last time."

Noguchi didn't want to hear this talk of "one last time" and told her, "You stop saying things like that, okay? I'll be back again in three years or so." But this would, in fact, be the last time he would see her.

Before leaving Japan Noguchi had one final meeting in Wakamatsu, which Ishizuka had arranged. In the course of the party, Ishizuka came up with some story to drag Noguchi away, and showed him to a room nearby. In it was Yoneko Yamauchi, the girl Noguchi had once so admired. There he left them alone.

Yoneko was now a widow. Her husband had left her with children to raise. She had been a passionate woman in her youth—although Noguchi had never been the object of that passion—but this had given way to a deep disappointment in the situation she now found herself in. She remained as ambitious as ever, though: "Listen," she told him, "I'm worried about my children's prospects. I know it's a lot to ask, but is there any chance you could take one of them back to America with you?"

Yoneko was still an attractive woman, and she knew it. Noguchi couldn't help being affected. Her request filled his mind for a moment . . . but he managed to come back to earth. He was nearly forty, and he had a wife and a demanding career to think about. As much as he would have liked to help this woman, he had to disappoint her. "I'm sorry, Yone. . . It would be easy enough to take your child as far as New York, but I'm just too busy to do anything beyond that. It wouldn't work out." Their reunion ended in tears.

This was Noguchi's final meeting in Fukushima. After this he accompanied Ishizuka on a trip to his home in Niigata Prefecture. During the train ride there he had one last pang of regret, and asked Ishizuka to send a telegram asking Yoneko to meet him at another station on the way across Honshu. This message did not reach her in time. They did not meet again.

Back in the capital, he gave an interview to various newspapers in which he spoke with wonder about the progress Japan had made in the fifteen years he had spent overseas. Tokyo had become a major metropolis. Medical research seemed to be thriving: Kyushu University and the Chiba Medical College were doing groundbreaking work on Weil's disease, and in Niigata research into scrub typhus was also something to be justifiably proud of. But Japan remained a remote and relatively backward country, and its scientists had little chance to share their discoveries with the rest of the world. Noguchi told the papers he would try to open new channels for them when he was back in America.

He had criticism as well as praise for his country's medical establishment. A researcher who moved up in rank tended to become a political animal, focusing more on status than on the pursuit of science. Noguchi expressed regret that so many of Japan's brightest minds had set their real work aside in favor of petty political games. He was different; he intended to devote his entire life to his work and to ignore these other concerns. And he stayed true to this promise. Japan, unfortunately, is to this day home to too many people who let themselves get caught up in administrative maneuvering, to the detriment of science.

On November 3, the day before he sailed, Noguchi went to the Waseda mansion of Shigenobu Okuma, the prime minister. Walking past the hulking statues of fierce Buddhist gods that flanked the entrance, he was shown into the reception hall where a smiling Okuma waited for him. The politician welcomed the scientist like a teacher greeting a favorite student. They spoke as equals, though, with their conversation touching on a range of topics. After asking about his microbiological research, the older man mentioned a personal theory of his, that under the right circumstances human beings could live to be a hundred and twenty-five years old, and he wanted Noguchi's medical perspective on this. Noguchi replied with his thoughts on the unity of the mind and body and his hope that Okuma would prove his theory of longevity correct.

Noguchi then questioned the prime minister about what he saw as a recent decline in morality in Japanese society. This was indeed a problem, agreed Okuma, arising from the increasingly acrimonious struggle for survival in the modern world and a growing emphasis on material possessions. Society needed to provide its members with more spiritual sustenance, via more enlightened forms of education.

As their time together grew to a close, the two men went out into the garden to have a commemorative photograph taken. There Okuma asked Noguchi where he came from. "Aizu, sir," came the reply, and the prime minister nodded knowingly. That was a land of strong-willed men. He gripped the doctor firmly by the hand. This elderly gentleman was in fact from the old Saga domain, one of those who had sided with the reform forces and battled against Aizu in the dying days of the Tokugawa era. But these men weren't enemies now. They hailed from two vigorous territories in one single nation, and today they were united in a desire to work for that nation and its people.

This was as fine a send-off as Noguchi could have hoped for.

■ ■ ■

On November 4 the deck of the *Sado Maru* overflowed with the crowds come to see Noguchi off to America. Bouquets soon piled up around him as he said his farewells, before everyone filed down the gangplanks and the ship set sail. When he had first headed for America in 1900 he had only gazed ahead; now he stood astern, soaking up every last glimpse of Japan he could—the mountains, the food stalls on the wharves. His trip home had recharged him, but it had also filled him with a new affection for his country that made it painful to leave it behind.

After landing in Seattle on November 22 and making his way back across the continent, he was walking the streets of New York City to get back home when a passing American muttered something about "that Jap." This stopped Noguchi in his tracks. He called out to the man and told him that he wasn't "a Jap," he was Noguchi from the Rockefeller Institute. This got him an apology, but he wasn't satisfied. "No, sir, you shouldn't avoid that word because I'm well known. You shouldn't say it about *any* Japanese." This was a more confident, prouder Noguchi who now walked the streets of New York. It was his chosen home, and he had a part to play in changing it for the better.

At last he made it to his apartment and his waiting wife. Mary immediately sat down to listen to everything he had to tell about his trip back home. She laughed with pleasure at the little gifts he'd brought her, going to show them to friends. Her husband had come home.

He did not stay home for long. After a single day of rest it was back to the institute for him. Before leaving for Japan he had been making little progress in his work. Now he was back in form, his batteries recharged. New obstacles cropped up, though. His new fame in Japan had brought him new obligations—people were now counting on him as a valuable connection in America. In early 1916 Hajime Hoshi sent him a young cousin, Seinai Akatsu, to work as an assistant, and in his wake came a string of researchers dispatched by Japan's Ministry of Education, beginning with Dr. Shotaro Yamakawa, a professor at the Tohoku College of Medicine. Having no interest in training them, Noguchi found their presence annoying, and he assigned them some work just to keep them out of the way while he tackled his research on his own.

The two sicknesses he now focused on were Rocky Mountain spotted fever and Weil's disease. The former afflicted a considerable number of people living in the American West, causing a rash to erupt all over the body. Doctors considered ticks to be the primary vector for the disease; in this respect, it was much like the scrub typhus common back in Japan. He had in fact selected the Rocky Mountain disease because of its similarity to the illness affecting so many people in his own country. The agent of spotted fever remained unidentified, but Dr. S. Burt Wolbach of Harvard had done some valuable research on it. Noguchi followed up this work with a number of experiments, meeting with Wolbach to discuss the disease with him. A friendly rivalry developed between the two as they pressed forward with their work.

Weil's disease, meanwhile, was also a threat in Japan, where it affected farming and mining populations. Transmitted by rats, its early symptoms were fever, chills, and headaches, making it easy to mistake for the common cold. As the disease progressed it caused nausea, diarrhea, conjunctival hyperemia, and jaundice. Once patients began bleeding from the skin and mucous membranes the fatality rate shot up to very high levels.

In 1915 two professors at Kyushu University had published a paper identifying the disease agent as a spirochete. Once Noguchi learned that he was dealing with a familiar bacterium, he went to work to discover whether it was present in rats in the United States as well. But his efforts to extract the spirochete from rats and infect guinea pigs with it were frustratingly difficult. As his frustration mounted he took it out on poor Akatsu and the others. A number of Japanese assistants made their way through Noguchi's lab during this period, and while they had praise for the researcher, they also told stories showing the more negative side of the man. The fact that he had this side should not have come as a surprise, though. Any person who works as hard and accomplishes as much as Noguchi did is likely to have odd quirks of character, and the complex research tasks he turned to only amplified these quirks. Inevitably, he lost his inner balance—and his outer calm—from time to time.

On Sundays, however, his Japanese assistants found him a different man altogether. Jovial and open, he chatted freely with them in their own language, which he did not allow in his laboratory during the workweek. Noguchi would invite Akatsu out for a meal and they would head for one of the two Japanese restaurants in town, Miyako or Kawazoe, where Noguchi would cheerfully order sake ten bottles at a time. These meals often turned into parties, an outlet for the pressure that had built up during the week. He would summon the lady running the restaurant for a long evening of conversation or go off to one of New York's social clubs frequented by Japanese, where he accosted anyone who came near him to see if they were on for a game of *shogi*.

His return to Japan and his present lifestyle had done wonders for him. He had put on weight, and he shocked the insurance company's doctor by showing up for another physical and getting a clean bill of health. At ease in his job and letting his curiosity wander, he headed back to the Marine Biological Laboratory in Woods Hole to study parasites living on shellfish. Back in New York he watched with pleasure as his work on Weil's disease moved steadily forward. He discovered a new variant of the disease agent, an even tighter spiral in the bacterium's body, and named a new genus, *Leptospira*.

■ ■ ■

Just as things were going smoothly, disaster struck. Noguchi was working with bacterial samples when an assistant asked him some question at the worst possible moment. Distracted, the doctor sucked too forcefully on the pipette clenched between his teeth, getting a mouthful of bacterial solution. He spat this out instantly and washed his mouth out with alcohol, smiling ruefully as he commented: "Not too likely that I got all those millions of germs before one of them got me."

His fears proved justified two weeks later when his head and spine began to ache. The Rockefeller researcher knew these symptoms better than anyone. "Does my face look yellow to you?" he asked his coworkers, afraid that the jaundice was already apparent. He ignored orders to rest, though, running his fingers through his unruly hair as he continued to scribble away at a report. The fever soon caught up with him, his eyes lost their focus, and he started singing softly to himself, mouthing nonsense lyrics, as he wrote aimlessly in his notebooks. Mary dragged him off to bed.

Despite being a doctor himself Noguchi seemed almost afraid of medical treatment of any kind, much less hospitalization. He insisted that the first week of this disease was the worst—that if he only got over the hump he would be okay. Noguchi was anything but okay by this point. The fever would not break, and his headaches and dizziness only got more severe. Before long Mary had him in an ambulance on the way to Mount Sinai Hospital. There the chief surgeon examined him. Dr. Emanuel Libman was famed for his diagnostic skills, but he seemed stumped by this case, and Noguchi was no help in his delirium. Weakened by illness he felt more and more like a foreigner in a strange land, bewildered by his surroundings and increasingly incapable of communicating with those around him. The hospital doctor, unable to make any headway on this disease, turned to the visiting Yamakawa, asking him to look into the case. The Japanese physician's examination resulted in a different diagnosis from the expected Weil's disease—Noguchi had typhoid. To build up his strength the researcher had recently taken to eating raw oysters. Another worker at the institute had recommended the shellfish to him for this purpose, and he had wolfed down some four dozen of them over the course of a few days, with this potentially deadly result.

There were many who looked beyond this recent eating habit and pointed to the way he had lived for years—pushing himself over the edge in his work, sleeping little—as a reason for him finally falling seriously ill. The Japanese in the institute spoke of the traditional belief that a man's forty-second year, counted in the old Japanese manner, was a particularly hazardous one for him. These views, of course, were rejected by their fellow scientists; it was a bacterium that had laid Noguchi low, not some Oriental curse.

The disease worked its way through Noguchi's system. His doctors feared that his enlarged heart made him particularly susceptible to the effects of the high fever. Complications set in: holes opened up in the walls of his intestinal tract, eventually developing into full-blown peritonitis. Now his life was truly in danger. The doctors debated whether to do an operation to shut off these holes, but reached no decision. Libman was against the idea, and the patient himself was not keen to go under the knife.

Toward the end of May 1917, on an appropriately stormy day, Noguchi's health took a turn for the worse. His friends and coworkers feared the worst. Mary was beside herself. She spent long hours at the hospital before eventually going home, only to put on her hat and head straight out to go back to her husband's side. He was haggard, wide-eyed, and hardly able to talk through the thick mucus coating his mouth. "How can you think of leaving me?" she asked the bedridden man. "What's happened to the happy, healthy Hide I know?"

Simon Flexner came to Mount Sinai to urge Libman to do everything he could for his star researcher. Noguchi was coherent at times, making gloomy comments to his visitors—his research was getting so neglected it might be better if others took over the work. It might be better if he died. He stopped making clear statements soon after this. In his mind, images of his wife spun faster and faster, mixing with those of Shika back in Japan.

The newspapers had picked up the story of his illness and began running articles listing his research achievements, illustrating them with pictures of him. Telegrams flashed across the Pacific to tell people in Tokyo and Fukushima of Noguchi's condition; similar reports made their way around Europe. Norio Araki rushed to the hospital as soon as he heard that his former flat-mate was sick. Receptionists turned him away: Noguchi was not receiving visitors. But Araki claimed he was a relative, forcing his way into the sick-room. "Sir! Sir, it's me, Araki!" he cried as he came near the unconscious man, but there was no response.

Everyone agreed that Noguchi's death was only a matter of time now. Halfway across the globe, the Okinajima villagers were gathering in the Hachiman shrine to pray for him. Many of them remained there for days and nights on end. Shika made the long walk to the Nakada Kannon, where she prayed before the statue for several nights in a row. She spoke softly but urgently to the wavering light of the candles: "If someone must die, let it be me. Come for me instead of my son." Her shoulders shook with fatigue; her mouth was parched. But surely the gods still had some work for her son to do—so she prayed. It was all she could do.

Deep in the night of June 13, some three weeks after Noguchi entered the hospital, her prayers were answered by a telegram noting that his condition had taken a positive turn. Shika appeared before the other villagers, bowing in thanks as they cheered the news.

Back in New York, Dr. Libman was equally delighted with this development. He spoke to Noguchi softly, asking how he felt. Four years older than the Japanese doctor, this man—single, and as dedicated to his work as Noguchi was to his research—would be a fast friend to him for years to come. The emaciated patient smiled weakly and said, "Not bad, thanks to you."

Noguchi was not out of the woods yet. Although exhausted, he had great difficulty in getting to sleep. In a waking dream he watched thousands of guinea pigs march in an orderly line before his eyes. He complained about them to the nurses, and about the bedclothes, which he found hot and oppressive, but the staff took these as welcome signs of recovery.

The great French actress Sarah Bernhardt happened to be in Mount Sinai at the same time as Noguchi. She had met him once before, and on learning that he was hospitalized in serious condition, she insisted that he have her room, one of the larger private ones in the hospital. The two got along splendidly. Noguchi took Bernhardt's photo one day, and his portrait became a favorite of hers—one of the nicest pictures ever taken of her, she said. She spoke with warmth about him, saying—with one hand held low in front of her—"What a wonderful man Noguchi is! He is only this small. . ." And then, with both hands spread wide to indicate a large and intelligent head: "But he is this big as well!"

Noguchi slowly returned to full health. He was pleased to receive from a friend a package of Japanese books containing pulp novels about the famous swordsmen Miyamoto Musashi and Iwami Jutaro. Unlike the highbrow foreign literature he had immersed himself in to date, they struck him as wonderfully fresh. Noguchi next asked for other tales of adventure like the *Saiyuki* (The Record of a Journey to the West), with its hero Son Goku the monkey. These books enthralled him as he lay in bed recovering.

In early August 1917 Noguchi was at last well enough to go home. The hospital bill was staggeringly high, but a quick telegram to Hajime Hoshi secured him another five thousand yen to cover his needs. He paid the hospital and had plenty left over to buy fancy gifts for all the doctors and nurses who had looked after him over almost three months as he had battled typhoid.

■ ■ ■

At last he was back in his own apartment with Mary by his side. He was drastically weakened. His weight had fallen from fifty-nine to forty-four kilograms, and he had lost much of his hair. He was so debilitated it was all he could do to sit up in bed for any length of time. The sweltering summer of New York beat down on him. Enticed by a newspaper ad, he and Mary decided to escape to the coolness of the hills for the first time since he had come to the city. The two had different ideas of where to go—Mary looked forward to spending some time by the sea, while Noguchi wanted to be somewhere mountainous that reminded him of Fukushima. In the end they went with his plan. Four hours north of New York by train, in the Catskill Mountains, was a small town called Shandaken, a popular refuge for New Yorkers seeking to escape the summer heat.

The night before the couple departed Noguchi received a package from Ichiro Hori, their old neighbor. The painter had sent a box of oil paints and all the brushes and canvas Noguchi would need to do some landscapes. The doctor had long been interested in painting, and this period of recuperation would be a good time to learn. Shandaken lay at an altitude of some eight hundred meters, and the sights would remind him of the Bandai foothills, Hori thought, inspiring him to put them on canvas. A shallow, noisy creek ran through the area, and a fisherman could catch small sweetfish and trout similar to those caught in rural Japan. There was even a lake to put him in mind of Inawashiro. Just a hundred people or so lived in this sleepy village; it would be a perfect place for the doctor to regain his strength. He and Mary took a room in a mountain lodge.

Noguchi had worked far too hard for too long, and his labors had caught up with his aging body. This was the first real vacation he had allowed himself since the days he'd played truant from school as a boy. It was a natural point in his life for him to look back at how he had lived it so far, and Shandaken gave him a quiet time in which to do so. He busied himself with writing thank-you notes to the people who had come to visit him in the hospital and taking walks outside when he felt up to it. Deep green trees, cobalt sky, and pleasant breezes greeted him, urging him to forget his research for a time and lose himself in his surroundings. He brought out the paint set from Hori and put up an easel in a lane. His pictures of the views began timidly but quickly grew bolder as his eyes opened to the world around him.

He acquired a love of painting on this trip. Even after the summer heat had subsided and he returned to New York he continued painting, producing a considerable number of canvases over time. Landscapes and still-life studies came from his brushes. He created portraits of Mary and Hori's sister, as well as a self-portrait; from memory he painted people like his mother and Kobayashi. A professional painter who saw Noguchi's works later had high praise for his vivid sense of color. Noguchi's powers of concentration allowed him to focus on the core of his subjects, capturing them in perceptive and original ways; for an amateur he painted at a very high level indeed. Had art been his course in life rather than medicine he might have been similarly successful.

In time he grew tired of living in the lodge, though. The two of them decided to build a small vacation home of their own. This became a simple structure with a generator for electricity and an electric pump to bring water up to the cabin. It was the first property they owned.

While they were making these plans, less than a month into their time in the mountains, Noguchi's fever shot up again. The disease wasn't an easy one to shake, it seemed; September became another month of worry for him and his wife. At times he thought that there really was something to the old Japanese superstition about a man's forty-second year. They returned to the city at once and Noguchi entered the hospital attached to the Rockefeller Institute. His condition was not as serious as the first bout of typhoid had been, but it was still severe enough to keep him in bed for another six weeks.

One of his assistants, a young man named Steve, came to visit frequently during these weeks, reporting on the progress being made in Noguchi's laboratory. He usually came with a pocketful of test tubes, being careful not to let Flexner and the other senior researchers know that he was helping Noguchi get back to work from his sickbed. After making sure nobody else was around Steve took out the samples and showed them to him. In this way Noguchi was kept abreast of developments regarding Rocky Mountain spotted fever, for example, which remained a deadly disease, killing about half of the people who caught it. The American researcher Howard T. Ricketts had done valuable work on this illness, giving his name to the microorganisms that caused it. These Rickettsia were smaller than most bacteria, but not as small as viruses, and therefore still visible with the aid of optical microscopes. Scrub typhus was another Rickettsial disease. Little was known, however, about Rocky Mountain spotted fever, which had taken Ricketts' life in 1910.

It was not until the end of October 1917 that Noguchi was out of the hospital for good. He went back to the apartment to rest some more, as painful as it was for him to be away from his research still longer. To pass the time he decided to learn Spanish. His solo studies and linguistic talents had already given him considerable ability in English, German, and French, not to mention the Chinese he picked up during his time in Niuzhuang. His interest in languages served him well at the institute on more than one occasion. One of his assistants, Ohira, came to him once with a three-page report in Italian that he needed to read. Noguchi did not know the language, but he took this report from the associate professor, asking him whether he had any Italian textbooks. "Yes," replied Ohira, "but it's only a primer I bought at a night market just before coming to America. It's just a little booklet."

"That'll do," replied his boss. "Bring me the thing and I'll see what I can do with this report of yours. It shouldn't be too tough to read."

Ohira thought this an impossible idea, but Noguchi hated being told anything was an impossibility. He sat down with the cheap Italian text and got to work on the report. Ohira was shocked a day or two later when he came back to him and told him exactly what the Italian paper was about. With this kind of application, Spanish wasn't likely to pose a serious challenge to him. Indeed he gained a decent level of fluency in the language, which served him well in later years when he went to Spanish-speaking countries for his work.

■ ■ ■

Noguchi was well once again and back in the swing of things at the laboratory, but his misfortunes were not over this year. Mary was the next to fall seriously ill, with appendicitis. Her husband rushed her to Roosevelt Hospital. There she was operated on immediately, and she settled down in the hospital for a three-week stay. Whatever gods of misfortune were watching over Noguchi this year were not done with him, though. No sooner had Mary recovered than he was struck down—by chance, also with appendicitis—and it was back to Mount Sinai with him. Dr. Libman insisted on operating this time. A half-year of illness had taken its toll: Noguchi was weak and the surgery was risky. Pulmonary edema set in and Noguchi's life was again in danger. The year 1917 drew to a close with Noguchi in miserable shape.

The following year was a different matter altogether. Noguchi surprised his doctors, coworkers, and wife with the ferocity of his recovery. Day by day he gained fresh energy, bouncing around and playing the fool to amuse Mary. Mimicking Charlie Chaplin, he would hang his cane from his breast pocket and make as if to stroll off jauntily only to start walking backwards. He did in fact look something like the actor, a similarity especially apparent in his self-portrait.

The year got off to a good start, but it was not without tragedy. Noguchi's assistant Steve fell ill with the disease he was working on at the time. It was a danger that all bacteriologists of the day faced. This flea-borne disease, murine typhus, is treatable today, but there was no vaccine or serum for it in 1918, and after battling it for some days Steve succumbed, leaving behind a wife and a young child. This death shook Noguchi. At his assistant's funeral he wept louder than anyone. People said it was as though he'd lost his own child. When he returned to work a new rule was laid down in his laboratory: from now on he would be the only one allowed to handle pathogens. The impact of Steve's death remained with him, however; he could not bring himself to carry on the work on murine typhus.

In his post-illness phase Noguchi was beginning to set a new course for his life's work, rededicating himself to doing battle with his invisible enemies in the test tubes. Yet the dedication with which he went about this brought him into serious conflict with those around him—particularly his fellow Japanese scientists. He had literally no time for them, and his treatment of travelers and students from his home country who had come to New York was similarly brusque. As word of this spread in Japan, his reputation took a nosedive. Dr. Noguchi was a great success, people muttered, but at what cost? He did nothing for his countrymen who went to visit him. He was filled with his own importance and dismissive of other people's achievements. He had no sense of patriotism!

Many who came to New York with a letter of introduction in hand found it got them nowhere. Noguchi rejected almost all requests for meetings, particularly those from students in the elite imperial universities in Tokyo and Kyoto and from exchange students on government scholarships. Even full professors from Japanese schools were usually turned away by his receptionist. Those lucky few who did get in to see the researcher saw him frown and grimace at them if their appointments dragged on. Sometimes Japanese tourists would come to speak with the famous doctor, but he responded to these unwanted guests in English no matter how badly they spoke it. One visiting bigwig was shocked when Noguchi refused even to look up from his microscope during the entire (very one-sided) conversation.

As his fame increased, however, the number of visitors only rose as well. He responded to this by curtailing his social activities even further, both his public duties and in his private life. He would still be dragged off to meetings and conferences with great regularity, but he developed a defense mechanism, frequently prefacing his comments with phrases like "I'd love to attend, but . . ." Despite living in one of the most gregarious cities of the modern world he started to live the life of a recluse, shunning the attention of people who wanted some of his time.

Easier to avoid were the floods of letters that arrived at the Rockefeller Institute. He generally dealt with these by giving a cursory glance at the sender's name, leaving the envelopes unopened in all but a few cases. Once an avid reader, he now ignored most newspapers and magazines. He made time only for research and report-writing in his life; nothing else was worth his while any more, except for sleeping, eating, and spending time with Mary. Cutting himself off from the world in this way did not seem to inconvenience Noguchi, though. "My only worry," he said, "is that I may miss hearing about some misfortune that's occurred to someone dear to me, or fail to pay my proper respects to someone I care about."

In this ruthless approach he took, he did have one ally: Tsuneo Matsudaira, who had first met Noguchi while serving at the Japanese embassy in London and was now the ambassador to the United States. Noguchi had gone to Washington D.C. several times to attend to something at the embassy, but as soon as he wrapped up his brief business there he went on his way. As another Fukushima man Matsudaira wanted to spend time with the researcher—to have dinner together and reminisce about their hometowns—but his efforts to do so were unsuccessful. He didn't hold this against him, though; indeed, the ambassador sympathized with his antisocial behavior. "The doctor is a human dynamo, as his nickname suggests. He can't be expected to follow the same social conventions that others have time for, and he can't possibly be expected to spend his days guiding visitors around while his work sits undone. I say the people who criticize the doctor are the ones in the wrong, not him."

It was not only his desire to get his work done that made Noguchi act the way he did. His refusals also stemmed from a disdain for the conventional Japanese approach to scientific work. He simply could not bring himself to help out the sort of students who came to study in America as a means of adding a little prestige to their personal record, not to really learn something of value. Many of them had only chosen the United States because they could not go to their first choice, Germany, in the midst of a world war. Noguchi was tired of dealing with Japanese who came to the Rockefeller Institute because it was the most famous research facility in America, and he had no interest in helping them to further their own careers.

The researcher was not the kind of man to hide his feelings in order to build good relations with people who might be of use to him later. In a way this rough, honest attitude was quite appropriate in a man of science. Even as some blasted him for his unfriendliness toward those who sought his help, others praised his dedication to his work.

■ ■ ■

But it was in the laboratory, not the institute's reception room, that Noguchi's personality—his impatience with social niceties, his single-minded focus on achieving results—was most evident. His eyes shone as he shouted out the name of some assistant, calling over the poor man to rebuke him for some blunder. The assistants had learned to step lively when their boss demanded their attention, but this seldom saved them: "You fool! You clumsy idiot!" Noguchi would shout. "I'll kill you!" He was short-tempered and impatient, and he saw no further than the task he was working on at the moment. Many who only observed him when he was in a mood like this came away with a very negative image indeed.

He did have his nicer side, of course. He was especially kind to Evelyn Tilden, helping her to move beyond her stenographer's position and build a career as a researcher herself. She had come to the Rockefeller Institute after studying English literature at Brown University. Her secretarial duties included typing up the papers by foreign researchers at the institute, cleaning up the grammar and phrasing errors that crept in when the author was writing in a second or third language. Not all the Rockefeller scientists welcomed her services, though. What could a young woman like her know about science? They often refused to let her touch their reports.

Noguchi was different. He appreciated the work she did on his papers, and before long she was working under him alone, a member of his research group. He produced more reports than anyone else in the organization, and predictably he had little time to polish the prose in them. He found her services invaluable. Before long he had her doing more than rewriting his papers. She was alongside him in the laboratory, performing experiments with the other assistants and learning enough in the course of this work to earn the title of technician. Tilden also went to Columbia University's graduate school for night classes, and Noguchi wrote her a letter of permission to do a summer's research at Woods Hole. Making rapid progress as a microbiologist, she was soon coauthoring papers with her supervisor. It was doubtless her own drive that took her to a Ph.D. from Columbia and eventually a college professorship toward the end of her career, but certainly Noguchi had some part to play in helping her along the way with his guidance and the influence he was willing to wield for her.

Two very different sides of the researcher's personality became increasingly clear during this phase of his life, but these were both rooted in a purity of personality—whether shown in work or in personal relations—that appears to be a hallmark of genius in many historical figures. As a scientist he was focused and driven, with little time to waste on the concerns of society at large. As a friend, though, he was warm and helpful to the extent of his abilities. He showed this, not only with his secretary, but when Toyosuke Tashiro, a friend who had worked with him at the Kitasato Institute, stopped off in New York on the way home from a period of study in Germany. Noguchi dropped his work for some days to entertain this old friend. One day the two of them met with another Japanese, a well-known academic who asked for a commemorative photograph to be taken with Noguchi alone— after all, who was this Tashiro fellow, and why should he be in a picture with men as celebrated as these? But Noguchi's response was swift and clear. Turning to Tashiro, he offered to take the photo with him instead. A person with more concern for social position or manners might have tried to work out some compromise, suggesting a photo of the three men together or two separate shots to be taken with each of them in turn, but when given a choice between social concerns and personal ties Noguchi placed importance on the latter every time. One has only to think back to the time he ignored one of the most popular geisha in Japan to look after his mother to confirm this.

One exception to Noguchi's prejudice against Tokyo Imperial University was Kiichiro Manabe, a graduate of the school with whom he had been close since his tour of Europe. When he visited America he was welcomed as family. Noguchi did not often invite Japanese people to his home, knowing that Mary couldn't speak the language and would be at a loss as a hostess. But Manabe came for breakfast. He struggled along in English at first, but eventually turned to Noguchi's wife and asked permission to speak in Japanese, seeing as his English was so poor. She of course gave it. Noguchi then told his friend, "It's easy to tell that you've spent time overseas and have a more international outlook on things. Most Japanese who come to see me speak nothing but their own language from the word go. Thank you for being different from them and thinking of my wife."

The night before Manabe was to depart for Japan Noguchi took him to a

Japanese restaurant in town. His order was simple but magnificent: "Bring us every Japanese dish you make in this place." Manabe made a short speech to thank his host for interrupting his work schedule for so many days. He began with a common Japanese phrase apologizing for the lengthy disturbance. Noguchi angrily cut in without waiting for the full comment that would, in polite, long-winded Japanese, explain who had suffered this disturbance: "Hey! Just how have I disturbed your travel plans? Yes, you've been here for a while instead of heading straight back, but that's only because I've tried to give you the warmest welcome possible during your time here!"

He was childlike in his misunderstanding of Japanese social niceties. He wrote penetrating essays and reports in several languages, but he never seemed to get the hang of the self-deprecating phrases that fill the polite language of his own country. On another occasion he received a gift from a friend who explained in common Japanese terms: "This is a mere nothing. . ." In that case, Noguchi asked aloud, why he should thank him for getting it? The question has amused generations of more knowledgeable Japanese who since then have heard this anecdote about a man whose mastery in other fields more than made up for his ignorance of how to get along smoothly in Japanese society.

■ ■ ■

As dismissive as he was of the Japanese academic world, he could be equally frank in his opinions of American schools, too. Once Ohira asked for Noguchi's advice on which school he should attend. When Harvard came up as an option the doctor scoffed: "Hah, that second-rate place?" About another reputable college: "No, that one's even worse." He refused to soften his comments just because a place had a good reputation. This earned him his own reputation over time—as an arrogant person with arbitrary opinions.

The flip side of this attitude, though, made him unstinting in his praise of anything he found worthy of respect. Another time Ohira came to him with a booklet his teacher had written on research into parasitic life forms. Noguchi flipped through its pages for a few moments, then said, "Hey, this is good. This is really something." Ohira offered him the text, saying his teacher would be delighted to know Dr. Noguchi rated it so highly. It was now the recipient's turn to be delighted. "Really? I can have this?" His pleasure in it was something that most people would have seen as an excessive response to this small gift, but it was clearly sincere.

The directness of his emotions, positive and negative, was equally clear in his treatment of the people in his life. One of his acquaintances was Kamon Hata, a young man from Mie Prefecture who was in America to study medicine. Noguchi had met him on the ship from Japan back to the United States, and they could hardly be called close friends, but when the doctor learned that Hata had come down with a serious case of influenza and had nobody to look after him he went all-out to help him.

Noguchi first called up another Japanese doctor, asking him to go and take a look at the patient. When this man came back with news that Hata's fever had shot up during the night, Noguchi went straight to the astonished young man's bedside. He may have refused to open his doors to many of the great medical men of Japan and thrown away letters from important figures without reading them, but he made time to help nurse Hata, a sick man in a strange country, back to health. With a pocketwatch balanced in his claw hand Noguchi took Hata's pulse, saying: "This doesn't look too good. Let's get you to a hospital."

"But the money . . . "

"I'm by no means a rich man, but I do have enough to pay your hospital bill. I trust you won't be offended by my offering to do so."

A HUNTER OF PATHOGENS

D uring his visit to Japan Noguchi had flirted with the idea of returning to his home country to live and work. "If they build a research
institute, I'll go home." This was his constant inner refrain, and there
was a good chance of its becoming a reality.

The head of the Furukawa family, the wealthy owner of the Ashio Copper
Mine, was intent on establishing a medical research facility in Japan. Much
like the New York institute had been for the Rockefellers, this was a calculated
move to improve the family's image. In the late nineteenth century the mine
had released vast quantities of pollutants into surrounding waterways, poisoning thousands of farm people downstream, and an institute staffed by
Japan's brightest medical star would be just the thing to restore the Furukawa
name. The proposals only grew grander: the facility would help Japan close
the gap with Western nations not just in medicine but in all the sciences, and
there would be offices in both New York and Tokyo, helping to increase the
flow of ideas across the Pacific.

This talk excited Noguchi at first, but it never led to any concrete developments. The head of the Furukawa family changed his mind again and again,
and Noguchi's illness posed a serious impediment to his participation in any
new undertaking. He regretfully abandoned the idea of returning to work
on his home ground, and the course of his life headed in new directions.

World War I was in full swing, and America had at last joined in the fighting. The Rockefeller Institute, the Stars and Stripes fluttering from its roof,
was on a war footing now. The military took control of the institute's activities, and Simon Flexner became a lieutenant colonel. Noguchi had to register
for service as a civilian resident in America, but his illness kept him from

direct involvement in the war. He was, however, given new orders. He was to take up his own weapons, the equipment in his laboratory, against a new enemy: yellow fever.

■ ■ ■

Yellow fever was a frightening disease. Its symptoms were similar to those of Weil's disease, making the two illnesses difficult to tell apart clinically. For three to six days after infection no symptoms were present; following this incubation period it manifested itself in headaches, dizziness, and a rapid rise in temperature. Patients were susceptible to alternating bouts of hyperemia and resting stages. During the former, the fever would abate for three or four days as nausea and severe pain set in and the face and eyes swelled with blood, sometimes actively bleeding. In the resting stages the fever would actively return, bringing with it a slowing of the pulse, an almost complete cessation of urination, and jaundice. As the disease wore on the patient would experience subcutaneous bleeding, and blood would be found in the stool and in coughed-up mucus, giving the illness its other name—the black vomit. White blood cell levels plummeted, reaching their lowest levels during the worst phase of the disease, five to six days after symptoms first appeared. Many cases resulted in death after a week or so.

Yellow fever had broken out in several places across Europe and North America in the late nineteenth century. It had also soon moved to equatorial zones, afflicting populations in Mexico, South America, and Africa. Any ship coming into a tropical harbor was likely to take this disease with it. The U.S. authorities had tried for some years to battle yellow fever and keep it from American shores. In 1900 a Yellow Fever Commission went to Cuba to find the answers to the key questions: what caused the illness, how did it propagate, and how could it be prevented?

Numerous military and private doctors headed to the region to help in these investigations. Yellow fever had been thought for some time to be transmitted by mosquitoes. As evidence for this theory, researchers pointed to the fact that sites high up in the Andes, where there was no insect presence, did not see outbreaks of the disease. They also noted that a person who had caught and survived the disease once was immune to it for the rest of his life. The mortality rate was far lower during childhood; adults died at a higher rate than young patients. Also interesting to the researchers was the fact that people from the mountainous areas where the disease was unknown seemed to lack some resistance to the disease, and when these people descended to lower regions for military service and caught yellow fever it was especially deadly to them, killing half of those it infected.

The first order of business for the American team was confirming the vector for the disease. Yellow fever was feared no less than plague or cholera. It had broken out twenty times over the past half-century in Philadelphia alone, and had killed more soldiers in the 1898 Spanish-American War than the enemy had. Walter Reed, who headed the commission, was a military man himself, and he and his team took drastic steps. The Americans infected volunteers with the disease—soldiers, civilians, and medical staff, twenty-two young men in all—to study the effects of the fever on them.

The first step was to observe the subject to see whether the disease appeared within a few days of his being bitten by a certain type of mosquito. In other cases the blood of infected patients was injected into healthy volunteers. James Carroll and Jesse Lazear, two members of the research team, offered themselves as subjects for these experiments. They both fell ill; only Carroll survived. The team did make some valuable discoveries through this shocking research. The disease didn't spread through contact with the clothing or excreta of patients. The most likely vector was indeed the striped mosquito common to tropical regions. The female mosquito, immune to the disease, spread it from victim to victim in the course of its feeding. The best way to prevent the disease, therefore, was to eradicate this insect population.

In 1903 the United States began work on the Panama Canal. Yellow fever posed a huge threat to the workers sent to the isthmus, and defeating the disease became an even more urgent task. Walter Reed was succeeded by William Gorgas, newly promoted to U.S. Surgeon General. The Rockefeller Foundation took part as well, establishing an International Health Division to tackle the yellow fever problem.

Despite all these efforts, the pathogen remained unidentified. Without a known enemy to fight against, people were powerless to stop the disease. This was the task that Gorgas took on. Dr. Arthur Kendall, a key figure in the world of microbiology and a friend of Gorgas, offered his counsel, and then his service. In 1918 he was tapped to head another commission on the disease, focusing on Ecuador, the site of the worst outbreak yet, and Kendall knew the name of one man he wanted with him on this mission—Hideyo Noguchi.

This seemed like a poor choice at first. Noguchi had no immunity to the disease, never having had it, and he was just coming off a long convalescence. If he caught yellow fever in this condition, while suffering in the equatorial heat, there would be little chance of his surviving. After hearing of the invitation Noguchi asked for some days to consider it. In the end, though, he decided to go. His work at the Rockefeller Institute was at a standstill, and this trip could be a way to break through to new paths of investigation. What's more, the diseases he had been working on—Weil's disease and murine typhus—were far from major research themes when compared with yellow fever, and conquering this sickness would be a real contribution to humanity. Yellow fever also had some similarities with the diseases he had been studying, so his experience could come in handy. Noguchi grew confident: he had a chance of discovering the yellow fever pathogen.

■ ■ ■

The team that headed south in July 1918, doctors, nurses, and scientists, was about twenty strong. After making it as far as Panama they transferred to the *Ucayali*, a steamer headed for Ecuador. Noguchi cut a rather stylish figure in his white summer suit, a Panama hat, and spats. With his seventeen crates of equipment stacked behind him as he waited to disembark at the port of Guayaquil he looked like a big-game hunter—though his game was infinitely smaller.

The hours he had spent brushing up his language skills during his convalescence came in handy, and he greeted the assembled medical officials courteously in Spanish, much to their delight. Not everything went smoothly, however. One Ecuadorian politician on hand to greet the team objected to Noguchi's spats, saying that the country was no tropical backwater where one had to wear expedition attire to remain safe from infection. His attitude wasn't helped by the news that a famous singer scheduled to come to Ecuador on the same ship had stayed in Panama after hearing of the yellow fever outbreak. The crowd's disappointment was audible.

Kendall defused the situation by stepping up to make a speech in which he had praise for the cleanliness of Ecuador's cities and censure for the wild rumors flying around about the epidemic. This calmed the politicians and pleased the crowd, and the next day's papers proclaimed the nation's hope that the deadly disease would be eradicated by this foreign team.

Noguchi got right to work. The day after their arrival he went to a yellow fever hospital that had been offered to the visitors for use in their research. The clinic's entrance and its research laboratories were encased in wire netting to keep out mosquitoes, and the discipline of keeping doors shut was drilled into everyone working there. Still, this was a dangerous place for Noguchi: the hallways between the netted laboratories were undefended; the mosquitoes were silent in flight, unlike the buzzing ones he was used to in Japan; and he had no immunity to yellow fever.

Some of the team's gear had yet to arrive, so Noguchi set about purchasing the coolers, incubators, and sterilizing equipment they needed. The locals were eager to help, and he soon found himself with a staff of doctors, assistants, and even the head of the hospital at his disposal—an offer of assistance he characteristically preferred to do without. This left the Ecuadorians at a loss—such a friendly man, so hard to cooperate with.

Drawing extensively on his previous experience, Noguchi plotted out a way to identify the pathogen. This fever was different from Weil's disease, and he took the discrepancies into account as he began his experiments. Samples obtained from yellow fever patients went into the incubator. As he cultivated these he injected them into guinea pigs, observing the symptoms that resulted: jaundice, fever, and liver damage.

In a remarkably short time he had results to show Kendall. "Come and have a look at this. I think this is what we're dealing with," he said as he directed the team leader to peer through the microscope at the tiny organism on the slide. It seemed to be a form of spirochete, similar to that causing Weil's disease, but tapering at both ends and showing kinks toward the tips of its protuberances. Noguchi named the organism *Leptospira icteroides*. Only nine days had passed since his arrival; the speed of his discovery struck most people as suspicious, given the long years this disease had confounded those who studied it. One man in particular—Dr. Mario Lebredo, a Cuban on the commission—felt that Noguchi was wrong in his supposition. There may have been some bad blood between these two researchers, but whatever the original cause, Lebredo's opposition to Noguchi's hypothesis was gradually to take root in much of the scientific community.

In early September the rest of the team went back to America, but Noguchi remained behind to work on isolating a pure strain of his *L. icteroides* and preparing a vaccine and serum from it. With this medicine in hand he organized a vaccination program for a thousand highland soldiers. This worked well. At the height of the mosquito season the incidence of yellow fever remained low among this test group, and the death rate was slashed to just sixteen percent. The Ecuadorians cheered this news when they heard it. The government asked him if he would consider staying in the country. There were plans afoot to establish a national medical research facility, and he would be welcome to serve as its highly paid director. Grateful for the offer, Noguchi nonetheless turned it down; he still had work to do at the Rockefeller Institute in New York.

If the Ecuadorians could not have Noguchi there with them, they could at least send him off with a hero's banquet. A theater in Guayaquil housed the feast, which was attended by leading figures from all walks of life: the commanders of the army and police, the chief justice of the country's supreme court, the dean of the national university, and the director of the nation's health agency. Even the governor came from Quito to send him off. With the Ecuadorian flag at center stage, flanked by the Japanese and American flags on either side, the hall was filled with people and decorated with laurel branches.

Then came the speeches. One dignitary after another mounted the stage to thank Noguchi with flowery tributes: Dr. Noguchi, your discovery has given our land a new future. . . You have the gratitude of every single Ecuadorian. . . You have our utmost respect, and your name will go down in Ecuador's history for all time. . . On and on went these comments, lauding the Japanese doctor and celebrating the bright future that Ecuador now faced thanks to him.

The orchestra launched at last into *Kimigayo*, the Japanese national anthem. To great applause, Noguchi stepped up to receive his decorations and gifts. He was made a surgeon of the army of the Republic of Ecuador and given an honorary colonelcy as well, along with the ceremonial saber that went with this rank. The universities in Quito and Guayaquil named him professor emeritus. People stepped forward to hang gold medallions around his neck and pin bronze insignia upon his chest. The army christened one of its dirigibles *Noguchi*, and his name was given to a boulevard in Guayaquil. The city honored him with a bust standing in front of the capitol building. Even the American Medical Association had sent along an award to present to Noguchi at this gathering. His time in Ecuador drew to a close in triumph.

■ ■ ■

As was so often the case in his life, a time of elation was followed closely by tragedy. As he set out on the sea voyage back to New York his mother Shika fell ill in Okinajima. She had rarely been sick in her life, but Spanish influenza was raging in Japan at the time, and she seemed to have caught it. Noguchi could have no way of knowing this, but he recalled later that during a stopover in Panama, during a presentation on yellow fever to a group of doctors there, he looked up from his microscope to see a vision of his mother's face. She appeared tired and lonely, and looked as though she had something to tell him.

Shika had promised her son that she would retire from the tough work of a midwife, but she had not been able to do so. Too many villagers still relied on her services. She had kept up this labor until she felt a cold coming on; even then, she remained confident in her constitution, drinking hot water with grated ginger and bitter orange rind in it. "Bah, I'll be as fine as always," she told people. This was no common cold, though, and no joking matter: she was already well into her sixties, and November is a cold month in the mountains of Fukushima. Her fever would not come down; she grew weaker. Soon she was bedridden, and pneumonia set in.

Eventually she called for a doctor, a distant relative. Kobayashi and the village's Dr. Rokkaku also came to care for her, and word went to Noguchi's friend Miyabara in Tokyo, who had promised him he would do what he could for the old woman. But the men gathered at her bedside could do little but make her more comfortable. She spoke with Kobayashi, who told her of her son's success in Ecuador. Her face immobile, but her eyes alive with pride, she said: "It looks like the doctor's done better than we'd hoped back when he was still a little 'un. He's done well . . . done so well." She spoke of her promise to Kannon, made when Hideyo had been desperately ill in New York: take my life if it means my son can go on living. This prayer had been answered, and now Hideyo had been of assistance to all those other people. She had accomplished what needed to be done.

When Miyabara arrived from the capital Shika was beyond speech. She drifted in and out of consciousness, her lips a pale blue color. The Tokyo doctor examined her but found only signs of an imminent end. Her husband made it back from Hokkaido to see her before she went. On November 10, with her family by her side, Shika came to the end of a hard life.

It was two weeks later that Noguchi landed in New York. Mary greeted him on the pier with the sad news. He only nodded a little. The shock of news like this can rob people of their speech; it wasn't until much later that he found his voice and repeated something he'd said in Japan: "All this glory, all this fame . . . it's nothing compared to the love she gave me."

It is not inaccurate to say that she had been his only parent. He took after his father physically, and to some extent in his personality, but throughout his life it was Shika who remained always in his mind. From time to time he would send his father some of his old clothes and shoes, as a man might lend things to a friend—the two of them were roughly the same size, and Sayosuke loved wearing the foreign clothes when they arrived. But it was only to his mother that he sent his deepest respect. She had been the one to warn him against bad behavior; she had been the only one he ever feared. And she had done all she could to help him overcome his childhood injury and become the doctor he was.

Some time later he received a letter from Miyabara and Kobayashi detailing his mother's last days. This letter went unanswered, although he carried it with him everywhere he went. Being confronted with the inevitable fact of her death seemed to free him from the everyday concerns around him. He later spoke of the broader world—the strange freedom—that news of Shika's death had opened up to him. "This world around us, our very lives and deaths, are all just temporary things. I really believe that there's no boundary between life and death for us."

■ ■ ■

A year later, toward the end of 1919, a yellow fever epidemic broke out in Mexico. Noguchi had continued working on this disease—he had already published eight papers on it—but he was not content to remain in an ivory tower, studying it from afar. Beginning with Mexico, he made several journeys to Central and South America, preferring whenever possible to be in the field. He was supported in these efforts by the deep pockets of the Rockefeller Foundation. Wherever he went he was accompanied by a veritable zoo of laboratory animals and crate after crate of equipment to produce vaccines and serums for the population in affected areas. This work was quite different from the quiet research he had done to isolate the syphilis spirochete.

In December 1919 Noguchi made his way to Merida, Yucatan, where Dr. Israel Kligler waited to assist him in his work there. On the way he stopped in Havana, where he met Lebredo again. The Cuban doctor had always opposed the theory that Noguchi's leptospire was the agent of yellow fever, and the two of them debated it again at this meeting. The discussion grew quite heated; the validity of Noguchi's theory was a matter that went to the heart of his career, and to reject one was to threaten the other. The two men did not reach any agreement; Lebredo would continue rejecting Noguchi's explanation, publishing papers that suggested other pathogens as the cause of the disease. This kind of active opposition to his work was something Noguchi had not experienced before in the academic world, and it inflamed him, making him determined to be as successful in his work in Mexico as he had been in Ecuador.

When he arrived in Merida the epidemic had almost run its course. It was not a good research environment: there were few remaining sufferers, and it was hard to assemble the materials he needed for his work in this city. Noguchi took over a room in the national hospital, collected blood samples from as many patients as possible, and began injecting them into guinea pigs. He worked long hours. Assistants brought in a dead pig one day, and he carried out an autopsy, discovering the same leptospire he had found in Ecuador. Yes, this was it! Noguchi was exhausted from days of nonstop work, but his spirits were still high enough at this discovery for him to stride outside into the courtyard and stand there gazing up at the night sky.

He then took samples and refined them to produce a serum. Once he had confirmed that it was effective against the strain of the disease seen in Merida his victory was complete. He remained in Mexico until February 1920, returning home with an honorary membership in the Mexican Academy of Sciences.

Two months later he was off to Peru, where he had a similar success. This trip had one dramatic moment when Dr. Kligler, who was there once again working at Noguchi's side, and a Peruvian army surgeon both began showing symptoms of yellow fever. Noguchi gave them injections of his serum, and their conditions improved in just three days. He capped this field trip with a journey to Lima, the capital, to give a speech in Spanish on the disease. His fame thus spread in yet another Latin American nation, and he was made an honorary professor of the University of Lima's school of medicine. The president of Peru was moved to make the same offer that the Ecuadorians had earlier: a new research facility, with Noguchi at its head. He offered an annual salary of twenty thousand dollars, with an additional promise of fifty thousand to be paid to Noguchi's family in case he died in the line of work. These were excellent terms, and the doctor was unable to turn down the offer right away. He asked for some time to consider his options.

While in Peru Noguchi came across two other diseases that intrigued him. These were Oroya fever and verruga peruana. The former was a particularly deadly disease seen in mountainous areas of Peru, Ecuador, and Colombia since Incan times. With a mortality rate of some forty percent, this fever had killed seven thousand the last time it struck. Verruga peruana, meanwhile, caused bloody pustules to form on the face and limbs, remaining from a month to as long as a year. The mortality rate was not as serious as that from Oroya fever, just five percent, but it also attracted Noguchi's attention as a fever-related disease.

Verruga peruana was only seen in the same mountainous regions as the more deadly sickness, and it often appeared in patients recovering from Oroya fever. For this reason some proposed that both illnesses were caused by the same pathogen, with different symptoms showing up at different stages of infection. But nothing concrete had been established. In 1885 a Peruvian medical scholar named Daniel Carrión had performed a risky experiment on himself: he extracted liquid from a verruga peruana pustule and injected it into his own arm. When he developed a full-blown case of Oroya fever it seemed he had established the link between the two, but unfortunately he died of the disease without writing a detailed description of his experiment and the symptoms he showed, so the matter was far from settled. Now a research team from Harvard was in Peru to try to solve the mystery of these diseases once and for all. After repeated experiments this American team reached the conclusion that they were unrelated illnesses—a different hypothesis from the one commonly accepted in Peru.

A while later, when Noguchi had basically finished his work on yellow fever and was looking for a new topic to research, these Andean diseases again caught his imagination. Beginning in 1925 he set to work to produce a pure culture of the disease agent. He used not guinea pigs but rhesus monkeys for this task, which continued for some years. In the end he succeeded in proving that the pathogen was indeed one and the same for Oroya fever and verruga peruana. In particularly virulent cases an infection would develop into the fever; but when the infected person had a stronger immune system or was otherwise less susceptible to the germ it led only to the pustules. Noguchi was able to prove his hypothesis by cultivating pure cultures from each of the two illnesses—something that had not been possible before—and showing them to be the same.

This result turned the Harvard team's results on their head and resurrected the unfortunate Carrión's reputation. More than anything, though, it backed up Noguchi's own reputation as a masterful scientist with advanced technical skills. He was hailed as one of the foremost microbiologists of the day. The British government placed a formal request with the Rockefeller Institute asking him to come to England to help with ongoing research into foot-and-mouth disease, which afflicted cattle, goats, and pigs, among other animals. This high-level exchange program was a flattering proposal, but Noguchi turned it down, as he did the offer from the Peruvian government. Instead he went back to Yucatan, where he kept himself busy helping to prevent further outbreaks of yellow fever.

This work earned him an honorary professorship from the medical school in Yucatan, too. Next he was recognized by the city of Philadelphia, the first city he lived in after arriving in America, with the John Scott Medal. He took a thousand yen from the prize money accompanying this award and sent it to Kobayashi with instructions to put it toward a pet project of his, the reestablishment of the Nisshinkan, Inawashiro's top school during the feudal period. Finally, in the following year both Brown and Yale universities conferred on him the title of doctor of science. This was a great honor to him, as he received it at the same time as Marie Curie did for her discovery of radium.

■ ■ ■

None of these successes would have been possible without the help he had received time and again from Morinosuke Chiwaki. Noguchi knew this better than anyone, and he was determined to thank his benefactor properly. In 1921, at Noguchi's invitation, the dentist traveled to London and then made his way to New York, examining Western dental facilities and treatments as he went, in order to bring back advanced techniques and equipment to Tokyo, where he was planning to construct new facilities for his school.

Noguchi was also thinking of traveling to London at around that time, having been invited to give a lecture to the national health board there, but chose to remain in America to greet Chiwaki when he arrived. He reserved a room for his old friend in one of the finest hotels in the city and went to the harbor to meet his ship. It was a joyful reunion, the first in seven years for the two men. Chiwaki noted right away, though, that the hotel Noguchi had selected was too grand and expensive, and he insisted on finding cheaper lodgings for his time in New York.

Each morning, Noguchi headed to the institute at 6:00 A.M., where he left detailed instructions for his laboratory assistants. At around eight he would then go to meet Chiwaki at his hotel and guide him around the city all day. After this went on for some days in a row, Chiwaki worried aloud that Noguchi was falling behind in his work, telling him not to bother about showing him around everywhere. But the younger man pressed ahead with a full schedule of events to welcome his benefactor to the United States in style. There were visits to dental clinics, tours of medical facilities, meetings with famous people, and dinners every night. Flexner shook his head and laughed as he warned Noguchi: "Don't you go killing your friend with all that kindness."

Noguchi had built up a considerable network by this time, and he made full use of it now, introducing Chiwaki to everyone he could. The two men went to Washington, where the top medical staff of both the army and navy turned out in full force to greet them. When Chiwaki gave a lecture to the army dental school Noguchi was right by his side, interpreting for him. While in Washington they even paid a call to President Warren G. Harding, as well as his secretary of state, Charles Evans Hughes. Hughes spoke to Chiwaki of his old charge: "Dr. Noguchi is the pride of America." With high-level connections like these, it isn't surprising that Chiwaki felt bowled over with the attention he was getting.

The pair went on to visit the University of Pennsylvania, then Boston and finally Chicago. For thirty-eight days in all the two men were together. Noguchi reserved seats on all the trains they took and kept in touch with his laboratory by telegraph. His work must have suffered a bit during these weeks, but it didn't seem to bother him at all—he was happy to be able to show his gratitude to Chiwaki in this way now that he had made a success of himself. Both men were alike in their excessive generosity.

As the highlight of Chiwaki's trip Noguchi hosted a grand banquet in New York. This took place at the Nippon Club, but the guests were not all Japanese. The section chiefs from the Rockefeller Institute were all in attendance, as were some of the top dentists in New York. Simon Flexner gave the keynote address, praising Noguchi but adding for good measure: "There is another man who stands behind Noguchi. We must not forget that without his presence, Noguchi would not be who he is today. I salute Morinosuke Chiwaki, the spiritual father of our Hideyo!"

Chiwaki could do little more than press a handkerchief to his eyes as Noguchi translated Flexner's remarks for him. The doctor closed out the evening by presenting Chiwaki with a Panama hat as a memento of his own work overseas and a gold watch for his wife. This was no ordinary hat—it was one that the president of Ecuador had given him.

At last it was time for Chiwaki to leave for home. Noguchi traveled with him part of the way across the continent, and the two men spent some of their final hours together on the shores of Lake Michigan. Here the dentist let his old charge know the depth of his gratitude for all Noguchi had done for him during his time in America. "When you were younger, I helped you out quite a bit. But now that I've been here and imposed on you to this extent, for so many days, I can truly say that all the debts between us have been settled. Thank you for all you've done, Noguchi-san."

Noguchi was taken aback by this. He gazed at Chiwaki for some moments before speaking. "First of all, sir," he began, "please don't add 'san' to my name. . . I certainly haven't done anything to earn this sort of respect from you. It's been more than twenty years since I left home, but I haven't forgotten what it means to be Japanese. I won't let you cancel all my debts like this. I want to pay you back."

Chiwaki insisted that this was no longer necessary, but his protests were mostly for the sake of form at this point. More than anything else he was happy to see the younger man's determination to do the right thing.

■ ■ ■

Before the memory of these happy times had a chance to fade, a shadow again fell over Noguchi's life: a letter from Japan informed him that his father's health was now failing fast. Sayosuke had always been a sturdy individual, but years of drinking had done serious damage to his liver. His condition had gone rapidly downhill after Shika's death, which had been a hard blow to him. A local physician did what he could for this elderly patient, but the cirrhosis of a lifelong alcoholic was not treatable in those days, and he could do little but watch as Sayosuke developed enteritis. Dr. Rokkaku and even Dr. Watanabe from Aizu Wakamatsu came to see whether they could help, but the prognosis was grim.

Noguchi's reply to this letter was short and sad. "It pains me to write this, but I'm afraid he won't last long in that state. Please do what you can to make him comfortable in his last days. Thank you for your care."

Noguchi must have felt powerless as he wrote this to the doctors looking after his father thousands of miles away. As a doctor himself, he probably felt ashamed of not being there by Sayosuke's bedside. There had been little contact between father and son through the years, but the two of them were quite alike in many ways—likable, unpretentious, and energetic when it came to the activities they enjoyed. In the father's case this had been drinking, unfortunately, taking him out of the family picture and leaving Shika to take charge of the children. He died in July 1923, at the age of seventy-three.

On September 1 that year the Great Kanto Earthquake rocked Tokyo. The papers in New York mentioned the temblor in passing, but carried no detailed coverage. Noguchi grew frantic in his search for more information about the disaster, which—in an age without international telephone calls or television—was hard to come by in a timely manner. On the third he mailed a letter to Kobayashi, asking him to send what details he could, and specifically whether certain people were all right—the Chiwaki family, his benefactor and friend Hajime Hoshi, and Miyabara—all people who had helped him in some way. To his intense relief, and despite the enormous destruction, he learned eventually that they were all alive and uninjured.

In November 1923 Noguchi's attention was again drawn to his own country when the Imperial Academy named him a full member. This was a considerable achievement for a man who was just turning forty-seven that month. The honor came at an awkward time, though. His work had been getting a mixed reception. He had recently been to Kingston, Jamaica, where he delivered two presentations at a conference on tropical diseases—one on flagellate organisms, the other on yellow fever in Brazil. With this second paper the old debate erupted once again: was his hypothesis correct, or did something other than his leptospire cause the disease? Aristides Agramonte, a researcher with long experience in Cuba and a friend of Mario Lebredo, rose to reject this theory before the assembled crowd. "Dr. Noguchi today has explained to us his ideas on the pathogen that causes yellow fever, but I cannot accept his explanation. The *L. icteroides* that the doctor has discovered bears too many convenient similarities to the agent of Weil's disease, another sickness he studied for many years."

Agramonte had more than just words to offer; he backed up his point with various examples gleaned from his own research. This was no personal vendetta, but rather a respectable attempt by a man of science to get closer to the truth. And Noguchi treated this attack on his theory as nothing more. In his youth his reaction would have been more impetuous, but he was a seasoned scientist now, with a worldwide reputation, and he calmly listened to the counterevidence. He was, as he had told himself before, less certain about this *L. icteroides* theory than he had been about his discovery regarding syphilis. This lack of confidence showed in his rebuttal to Agramonte's criticism at the conference. He tried to defend his ideas, but he could say little more than that the Cuban researchers had mainly observed secondary infections in their work. He could not attack the core of their argument.

Other scientists, however, came to his defense. Henry Rose Carter expounded on the virtues of Noguchi's vaccine, whose efficacy was clear to see in the data on army recruits exposed to the mosquito-ridden areas of Ecuador after living in the Andean highlands. Soldiers receiving full doses of the vaccine proved especially resistant to the disease, while those getting smaller doses fell ill with far more frequency. As welcome as this news was, though, it was not in and of itself a refutation of the Cuban argument that Noguchi had misidentified the yellow fever's real pathogen.

At this point Henry J. Nichols, a U.S. Army doctor, stated categorically "that the U.S. Army Medical School recognizes *L. icteroides* as the agent of yellow fever." This was a powerful endorsement, and a number of people in the audience were swayed by it, but his confident assertion did not carry the day, and doubts remained about Noguchi's theory.

After the meeting Noguchi invited Agramonte to see some of his laboratory samples. The animals showed classic signs of the disease, and Noguchi provided evidence of the presence of his leptospire and the effectiveness of his medicine. This brought the Cuban closer to his point of view. "When I return home," remarked Agramonte, "I'd like to try to produce similar reactions in some human subjects."

"There's no need to put people through that, though," Noguchi pointed out. "With today's science it's enough to confirm that this works in animals.

You can produce these results any number of times in the laboratory if you like."

These were the words of a confident man. Noguchi seemed untroubled by the idea that he might be mistaken, and indeed most of the medical establishment was on his side at this stage. Simon Flexner was trumpeting his discovery in numerous speeches to eminent groups, and the U.S. government was moving to use the Noguchi vaccine to inoculate soldiers and overseas travelers. Further animal experimentation only bolstered his claims, defusing the allegation that his newly discovered bacterium was similar to the one that caused Weil's disease by showing how the two pathogens reacted differently to various forms of treatment.

The main thrust of the criticism of Noguchi's hypothesis was that his leptospire was actually the same as that causing the North American disease, or at least a closely related strain. Others wondered why he had not used primates in his experiments in place of guinea pigs, which were known to be especially susceptible to Weil's disease. Noguchi also had shallow clinical experience in treating the tropical sickness; could this have led him to diagnose cases of Weil's disease as yellow fever? But no, argued his supporters—the former disease was unknown in Ecuador, where he had made his discovery.

With the matter still unsettled, Noguchi again headed south in November 1924. Yellow fever had broken out again, this time in Brazil. This was Noguchi's fifth expedition to Central and South America. After arriving in Rio de Janeiro he traveled north to Bahia.

This trip would not be as simple as the earlier ones. Brazil was a hotbed of opposition to his theory about *L. icteroides* and yellow fever. Lebredo's arguments had taken root here, and a scientist named Guiteras followed them up with articles attacking the Noguchi hypothesis, all of which Noguchi took seriously. Part of his reason for undertaking the journey was to prove to these people on their own soil that his ideas were correct—to show them his proofs first-hand.

The Brazilians greeted him courteously. Local newspapers sent reporters to interview the visiting doctor, giving his arrival prominent treatment in their pages. He found this attention reassuring, but was dismayed by the research conditions he confronted. Much of the work would have to be done with his own two hands. Here he lacked the equipment and personnel he had at his disposal back in New York. Some of the gear he'd brought with him had gone missing, and the local facilities were not up to par; moreover, there were few infected patients in the area from whom to take the samples he needed. There was not a single dark-field microscope—a relatively new device that employed a special lighting apparatus to make minute particles more visible—for him to use.

"What do they mean, keeping even this equipment away from me?" he protested. "Without this microscope I can't hope to spot the spirochetes. Strange people, to criticize me while preventing me from showing them the truth." He promptly took apart three ordinary microscopes, using pieces of them to cobble together a dark-field instrument for his makeshift laboratory.

Determined to prove his theory correct, Noguchi worked with few breaks, although he did allow himself time away from the laboratory to play chess occasionally, inviting a friend to his room for a series of games. These tended to be marathon sessions: the players would suddenly realize that nobody else was awake in the building and, outside the window, dawn was breaking.

The passion he brought to his experiments (as to his chess) impressed the Brazilian women who assisted on him in his work. Eremita, a pretty young woman, would bring him pots of tea to help him through the long evenings, hovering nearby, ready to fetch anything he might need. Another medical student, a young woman from one of the local tribes, grew so fond of this foreign physician she was also constantly by his side, laughing at the jokes he told (in rudimentary Portuguese).

In due course Noguchi was ready to show the medical professors at the local university and the region's doctors what he could. He invited them to his laboratory to observe certain experiments, explaining to them what he was doing and what it told him about the disease. He had collected blood samples from nine yellow fever patients in Bahia; using these, he displayed the organisms present, and compared them to the *L. icteroides* samples he had collected in Ecuador, Peru, and Mexico. He also showed them the Weil's disease pathogen, stressing the ways it diverged from his leptospire. The observers had to agree that the two looked quite different. It was also apparent that the yellow fever pathogens collected throughout Latin America were one and the same. Again and again they peered into the microscopes, allying themselves with his cause as they did so. Noguchi then telegraphed New York and began packing for the journey home . . . much to the dismay of Eremita and his other fans.

■ ■ ■

After returning to America it was time for a vacation. He and Mary headed to Shandaken with a full carload of magazines, a stereoscopic camera, fishing gear, and oil paints. Even the cat came along for the ride. Mary's brother Tom drove the couple up to the mountains. Noguchi had at one time been a reckless man behind the wheel, once screeching to a halt so suddenly that the passengers in the front seat were nearly flung over the hood and another time almost sending the entire car over the edge of a cliff—only Mary's foot on the brakes had saved them that time. (It was little different when he was on foot; he was a fast walker who paid little attention to where he was going.)

Noguchi was in his late forties, and the repeated journeys to southern countries had taken their toll on him. Even his tuft of black hair was starting to show signs of white here and there. This trip to upstate New York was a good one for him. After arriving at the cabin he made his way onto the veranda, where he stood quietly gazing at the mountains and smoking a cigar. The slower pace of life away from the laboratory sank into him, and his fatigue seemed to slough away.

In his youth he had told himself that the key work in a man's life must be done by the time he turns forty. This he had revised, giving himself another ten years—he still had work he wanted to complete on yellow fever, on trachoma, and on Oroya fever, for example—but he no longer felt quite the same urgency about it. Now, for a month or so, he gave himself over to oil painting, or evening fishing in the creek behind the cabin. When he grew tired of these pursuits he had his books: he was learning Dutch.

Even after he returned to New York, people noted that he was not as fiercely devoted to his experiments as he once had been. Often enough, he could be found leaving the institute for the apartment of his friend Ichiro Hori, where he rang the bell, poked his head in the door, and asked about a game of *shogi*. Hori's sister Tokuko would bring the men some Japanese tea, announcing the hour as she did so: "It's already eleven, you two." Noguchi loved this tea. He also loved the chestnuts and sweet potatoes she brought them—treats that any Japanese with a taste for home cooking would enjoy. At times like these—sipping some fish soup and chatting energetically to Hori—it was clear that Noguchi enjoyed being Japanese. He never tried to acquire American citizenship during his time in the country.

Noguchi came alive during these visits with Hori and his sister. He told stories that engrossed his listeners, his eyes flashing at the memory of some old humiliation he'd suffered, while he muttered about a farmer's background not being anything to feel ashamed of. "It's your own strength," he maintained, brandishing his fist, "that gets things done." Yet, despite his talk of a humble upbringing, he enjoyed dressing up in fancy clothes, and on some days a knock at the Horis' door would be followed by his appearance in some new double-breasted suit, which he would ask Tokuko to judge. "It's a bit flashy, isn't it?" she would comment coolly. "You look sort of like a circus clown. In fact you must be mad, wearing something like that." Noguchi winced, but didn't seem to mind.

■ ■ ■

By this time Noguchi had spent some seven years studying yellow fever. He had been decorated with the French Légion d'Honneur (one of only three awarded to people working in America), and had produced thirty-four papers on the disease. Among the other challenges he took up now was trachoma, which he had investigated to some extent before, but hadn't dealt with for some years. This eye disease was not limited to one region, but was spread around the world in widely separated circumstances, making it difficult to concentrate research efforts. More than thirty researchers had pitted themselves against the disease without success.

In 1926 Dr. Francis Proctor came to Noguchi, asking him to help with work on the disease. Proctor had gone to New Mexico to study trachoma in the Native American population there, and had found a wealth of cases for his research. Fully ten percent of the three hundred thousand Native Americans in the state suffered from it. The doctor had operated on several hundred of them, but the results had not been promising. Conquering this disease would require tackling the root cause, not treating the symptoms, and Noguchi was the man for this job, thought Proctor.

"The only way to save these people's eyesight is to identify the pathogen causing trachoma," Proctor told him.

The opportunity intrigued Noguchi. "Are there really so many people there suffering from the disease?"

"Yes indeed," came the reply. "I can show you thousands of cases if you like."

"Then let's be on our way! The sooner the better."

The two wasted no time in heading to New Mexico to begin the work. Noguchi saw a steady stream of patients, examining their symptoms and taking samples for his experiments. He then set about cultivating cultures of the bacteria taken from the diseased tissues, and observed the resulting microorganisms closely, discovering several that were unfamiliar to him. These he injected into the eyes of rhesus monkeys and orangutans. The symptoms that appeared seemed to differ little from human trachoma, and he injected samples from these eyes into a series of other animals to refine the infections.

Soon he had successfully isolated a likely candidate for the trachoma pathogen. However, it was not until October 1927, the following year, that he presented his findings to the American Medical Association at a conference in Washington, and even there he shied away from definite statements—this was the most probable cause of the eye disease, but he could not say so with any real certainty, and he left the final confirmation to the researchers who were following up his work. This was a humbler Noguchi than before, but his cautious scientific approach met with wide approval from his designated audience.

■ ■ ■

After completing his trachoma research, Noguchi had been thinking of taking some time off and going back to Japan to visit his parents' graves. Before he made any concrete plans to take this trip, though, he got word from Kobayashi that his wife had died. Noguchi regretted that he hadn't gone in time to see his own "second mother" one last time, and sat down to write to his teacher:

> My eyes fill with tears as my thoughts go back to the past. One day soon I hope to be back in Inawashiro, to see your kind face again, and to sit with you and share a meal together—perhaps that fish soup whose taste I can't forget—as we talk about times gone by. . . So many of us live out our lives like cogs in clockwork machinery. So few of us can take the time to spend slow days in touch with our surroundings. Behind us, pushing at our backs, are all those things we feel we ought to do before it is too late. . .

THE FINAL JOURNEY

Some time before, a Dr. White had visited the institute and suggested that Noguchi consider going to Africa. "What of African yellow fever? Surely the only way of checking whether it's different from the disease in Brazil is to go there yourself."

"When the time comes, I'll be on my way," replied Noguchi confidently.

"If you do go, though, you may find you *are* wrong... Is that a possibility you're willing to face?" White had accompanied Noguchi to Brazil to confirm the identity of the yellow fever pathogen, and he had to ask Noguchi this question, both out of purely scholarly interest and out of friendship.

Noguchi hung his head and said, "Yes, I'm willing."

Adverse criticism of his theory would not go away; indeed, it was gaining support. He maintained confidence in the methods he had used in his research, but a steady stream of counterevidence was appearing. The medical community was now focusing its attention across the Atlantic, on the shores of Africa. Yellow fever had broken out in Senegal in 1924, and the following year the Rockefeller Foundation's International Health Division established a Second Yellow Fever Commission to research the disease. Headquartered in Lagos, Nigeria, the commission had set up a field station in Accra, Ghana. Basing its work on Noguchi's theory, the commission compared African yellow fever with the strain of the disease found in South America, attempting to identify the pathogen and clarify the routes of infection.

Accra was in British territory, and the colonial authorities there operated a medical research institute headed by Dr. William Young. Young reported that Noguchi's vaccine was ineffective and that the laboratory had failed to find *Leptospira icteroides* in any patient with African yellow fever. Other British and French researchers—and even some members of the commission—reported the same findings. That these people had a record of involvement with Noguchi's own laboratory made the situation all the more troubling. Furthermore, as the pathogen was able to pass through a filter, the theory that yellow fever was caused not by a bacterium but by a virus began to gain ground. Noguchi was already using the term "filterable pathogen," positing that the disease might be caused by a microorganism invisible to optical microscopes. But his problems were not confined to Africa. A research team from Harvard University expressed doubts as to whether Noguchi's theory held water even in the case of the yellow fever found in northern Brazil. Again it was suggested that he had confused yellow fever with Weil's disease.

Noguchi had been contemplating a trip to Africa ever since his time in Shandaken. The Rockefeller Foundation had funded his research on yellow fever to the tune of $3,760,000—a hefty amount—and he had spent almost ten years of his academic life studying the subject. From his early departure from Shandaken to his impassioned speeches in Hori's apartment, however, he had lived all along with the anxiety that he might be wrong.

Staring into space, he gave lengthy thought to the problem. How could South American and African yellow fever be different? The germs could easily be transported from Africa to northern Brazil by ship, he reasoned. Or perhaps the commission members sent to Africa were too inexperienced to find *L. icteroides*. "They must be mistaking it for some other disease," he said to Flexner. After all, another Harvard team had made glaring errors in its work on Oroya fever.

But what if White was right, and it was he who was mistaken? He recalled the time when Professor Inada had come over from Japan to examine *L. icteroides* under his microscope. Inada had discovered the Weil's disease pathogen, and Noguchi pressed him to affirm that *L. icteroides* was a different organism. He remembered the awkward look that appeared on Inada's face. Then there was Agramonte's criticism. Sitting in the dark, Noguchi wanted just to cover his eyes and shut out the world.

He suffered two further blows when he learned that Nichols, one of those who supported his theory, had died of appendicitis, and not long afterwards that a British scholar in Africa had died from yellow fever. Dr. Stokes had been there conducting experiments on monkeys at Noguchi's behest; almost as soon as his report on this work reached Noguchi, this doctor became the latest victim of the disease he was studying. On hearing the news of Stokes's death, Noguchi made up his mind. He had to go to Africa himself.

■ ■ ■

In those days Africa was a distinctly unhealthy place, much more so than South America. Yellow fever there was virulent, with a high mortality rate. The region he was heading for was a baking equatorial zone, moreover, which was of no small concern for a man over fifty years old with an enlarged heart and mild diabetes. When he mentioned his planned trip to close friends, every one of them implored him to reconsider. Dr. Flexner, his other friends at the institute, acquaintances at the Nippon Club, even Ambassador Matsudaira—everyone was against the idea.

His colleague and friend David Kaliski spoke to him with some urgency: "I understand why you want to go, but you're a senior researcher at the institute. There's no need for you to make this trip."

"It takes several weeks for blood sent here from Africa to arrive," Noguchi argued. "By that time it's not fresh enough to use for anything. I have to go."

His friend replied frankly, "People are dying of yellow fever left, right, and center. Even Stokes is dead. You're not in the best of health. It'll be like a death sentence if you go."

Noguchi affected a smile, but his temper was aroused. "Thanks for the advice, but I'm not afraid. I've been put into this world to do something, and I want to finish it. When my time comes, I'll take my leave—I'm enough of a fatalist to know that."

"That may be fine with you," cried his friend, "but you're irreplaceable! So what if you've made a mistake with yellow fever? You should look at the big picture and take better care of yourself."

"I know this disease—and I know I'm coming back."

It wasn't until three weeks before he was due to leave that he first spoke of his imminent voyage to Mary. She had never tried to stop him from doing anything before, but this time she was adamant in her opposition.

"It's in British territory. Why can't you let the British do the research?"

"I'll only stay a little while. Let me bring this thing to a conclusion."

"No! I won't have you going to such a dangerous place!"

"Please, be strong about this. . . Keep me in good spirits, and promise you'll pray for my success." She didn't answer.

Noguchi sent what would turn out to be his last letter to Kobayashi at around this time. In it he described his outlook on life and made statements that now seem strangely prophetic:

> There is no boundary between the life and death of living creatures, just as in life there is no dividing line between happiness and sadness. The rich man is not necessarily content, and the sick man may find enjoyment that others can't comprehend. When I look at the world, it strikes me that everything in the end attains an equal state of self-effacement. I am sometimes doubtful as to what the purpose of life really is. The bright moon that the ancients gazed upon four thousand years ago is the same moon that I saw in my hometown and that I look up at from this place. Time, though it appears infinitely long, is in fact short; though it appears short, it feels immeasurably long. . .

This letter, written by a man in firm control of his thoughts, could have been the work of a philosopher or priest, and suggested a state of detachment that might explain his recklessness in going to Africa.

One of Noguchi's colleagues at the institute suggested that he sit for a bust before leaving. Although he was busy getting ready for his trip and had no time to spare for distractions like this, he sometimes found it hard to ignore this sort of request. The sculptor was a Russian named Sergei Konenkov, and the resulting work survives to this day. At his sittings Noguchi spoke cheerfully with Konenkov, who found his subject charming yet somewhat intimidating behind the charm. The bust gives a clear impression of Noguchi's fatigue and his advancing age. But the artist also managed to convey an equally clear image of a strong-willed man bearing up against adversity.

■ ■ ■

On the evening of October 19, Noguchi was invited to a party by one of his Japanese friends. Looking pale, he sat in silence throughout the gathering. After a while, he stood up and left the room. His friend ran after him and asked after his health, but with a brief smile Noguchi waved his right hand dismissively, saying he was used to working alone and still had a mountain of things to take care of. He went from the party to the institute and didn't get home until four o'clock in the morning.

After sleeping in a chair for about an hour, he then left for the institute again, not returning until the evening of October 20. He was determined to file his report on trachoma before his departure. Returning home briefly on the morning of the twenty-first, he smiled at Mary and remarked that he'd come back only because he was afraid she would worry. He went to work once again and gave his report to the staff late in the afternoon. He still had some matters to attend to, though, and wasn't home finally until the middle of the night.

He was exhausted, and his face had become even paler. He looked as if he couldn't carry on much longer.

"Get me a little wine, would you? Let's not go to bed tonight," he said, collapsing into a rocking chair.

"But you haven't slept for two nights," replied his wife with a worried look. "And you have to be on the ship tomorrow."

"Okay, if you insist, let's go to sleep."

Mary's heart sank as she looked at the color of his face. "Going on such a long journey when you're so tired out . . ." She took his left hand and gently stroked it. He soon fell asleep with his crippled hand still held by his wife, who was unable to sleep herself.

Before leaving the next morning, Noguchi took out of a drawer a rice-paper scroll on which there was a tracing of the inscription on his mother's tomb. Mary begged him not to take this sort of thing with him. Then, when he was outside, he realized he had forgotten to bring his lucky charm from the Nakada Kannon temple in Aizu. This bothered him, but he quickly dismissed it from his mind. On October 22, 1927, he set sail for Africa aboard the *Scythia*.

He slept well on the ship and managed to send a wireless message to Mary on the second day out of port. He also received a message from the president of the Rockefeller Foundation, George Vincent, wishing him a healthy and successful trip. This relieved Noguchi: he could devote himself to his work safe in the knowledge that the foundation had confidence in him. In his spare time he continued to learn Russian. He had improved considerably since practicing the language with Konenkov as he sat for the bust. The ship called at Liverpool, where Noguchi began liaising with those whose assistance he would need to conduct his research. He contacted the Rockefeller Institute's branch in Lagos by telegram but was disappointed to receive a reply from the director, Henry Beeuwkes, informing him that there had been no further cases of yellow fever since Stokes's death. While at sea, he heard that there was an outbreak of yellow fever in Dakar, in French territory, so he wired the medical services there asking them to send him some blood samples. He also asked Beeuwkes to provide some refrigerated blood samples, but Beeuwkes replied that they didn't have any available from Stokes's research. Noguchi knew, though, that the institute in New York already had twenty samples of blood resulting from Stokes's work—the material did exist.

Although the Lagos branch had modern research facilities and was staffed by twenty Western researchers, Noguchi chose to work in Accra. Some researchers in Lagos had published findings that contradicted his theory, and he wanted to avoid this kind of complication and do his work from scratch on his own. Beeuwkes's deception regarding the samples was the first indication of the politics surrounding his visit. Beeuwkes traveled to meet Noguchi for the final leg of his journey, bringing with him a clinician named Alan Walcott, who was to stay with Noguchi in Accra. This improved Noguchi's mood, but the presence of Walcott was in fact another maneuver on Beeuwkes's part, who had instructed Walcott to keep tabs on the Japanese doctor. No politician, Noguchi was ill equipped to deal with such intrigue, which probably accounted for many of the problems he encountered in Africa.

■ ■ ■

Accra was a major city of the Gold Coast, with a population of around eighty thousand, some of whom lived in slums concentrated near the port facilities. The Rockefeller Foundation had prepared a range of facilities for Noguchi and had also sent him a laboratory assistant. After coming ashore, he greeted the people he met modestly, telling them: "Gentlemen, I shall do my best. I can't promise any results, though—there's no certain prediction to be made here."

The Mahaffys, a recently married couple with whom Noguchi had been friends since his days in Brazil, were to take care of his day-to-day needs, and he was to stay in a small wing of their house. Dr. William Young, the director of the British medical institute in Accra, which was located three miles away, let Noguchi use part of his space as a laboratory. Young was a pathologist ten years Noguchi's junior. As Noguchi proceeded with his research, Young came to greatly admire him. One day he asked Noguchi to allow him to lend a hand, and from that time onward the two men worked together.

Noguchi required a large number of monkeys for his experiments. Beeuwkes, who had control over the acquisition of these animals, telegraphed Noguchi to say that he couldn't get hold of any. But Noguchi, unwilling to waste time on what was only a short visit, approached a local animal dealer, who told him he could deliver several hundred monkeys if he wished. Noguchi wired Beeuwkes to inform him that from now on he would order his animals himself. He also placed an order on behalf of the Lagos branch, assuming that it, too, must have been short of animals. This forced Beeuwkes to write to thank him for his consideration. Beeuwkes could not publicly criticize a renowned scholar like Noguchi, but these independent actions infuriated him.

The other researchers were amazed at Noguchi's intensive approach to his work. As he was living alone, without his wife to keep him in line, he lost all track of day and night. Not wanting to return to the Mahaffys' house late at night, and with the Rockefeller field station too far away, he found a bungalow near the laboratory and hired a driver and a laboratory aide to work night shifts. Sometimes when the assistants arrived in the morning they would find Noguchi asleep at his desk in a corner of the room. His extraordinary dedication to his work became legendary. Even today the local people speak admiringly of the time when the Japanese doctor worked among them.

The facility was a large one and required a lot of people to keep it running smoothly. The animal shed alone was fully eighty meters long and housed nine hundred laboratory animals, which consumed about three tons of food every day. Noguchi used about fifty locals for his work and was generous in handing out gratuities. But though he didn't look down on them as the white men did, they tended to work at a leisurely pace and were by no means reliable, and Noguchi sometimes let his impatience get the better of him.

On Christmas Eve, just over a month into his stay, Noguchi wrote his first letter to Mary since arriving in Africa. "Don't worry about me. Read a good book or go see a movie or a show to take your mind off the loneliness," he advised her. As it turned out, though, he should have been more concerned about his own condition. The day after writing this, he failed to appear at the laboratory. Two employees there called at his bungalow, found him sick, and took him immediately to a hospital.

The identity of his illness was unclear—perhaps mild yellow fever, perhaps amoebic dysentery. He was not an easy patient and scared most of the nurses away with his scowl. He disliked the food, and his brusque manner led one of the nurses to describe him as "a bossy child."

"If I could only finish my work, then dying wouldn't bother me so much," he remarked to a nurse one day.

"Don't take dying so lightly. I don't want to hear talk like that."

"You're a mean woman," he told her jokingly.

■ ■ ■

Noguchi had vaccinated himself before leaving for Africa. Thanks, perhaps, to the vaccine, his symptoms were mild, and he was soon on the road to recovery. News arrived from Dakar that his vaccine had been effective there, too, which also helped to raise his spirits. To confirm his own diagnosis, he had taken some of his own blood and injected it into a monkey. Twelve days later, when the animal died, he dissected it to confirm that it was yellow fever. In a letter to Flexner he wrote: "Vomiting blood, signs of jaundice—one could not imagine a more typical case. It amazes me to think that even after observing these symptoms the doctors and the members of the commission still don't know the true identity of my illness."

Noguchi couldn't bear to stay any longer in the hospital, so on the next day, January 7, he slipped out unnoticed and went straight back to work. As he was still feeling nauseous, however, the Mahaffys decided he should stay with them again for the time being. His research soon began to show signs of progress, and by late January he had discovered five strains of yellow fever. Earlier, before Christmas, on hearing of an outbreak of the disease inland, he had gone to investigate for himself. Blood samples taken from three patients there yielded two strains. The samples he had ordered from Dakar arrived, bringing a further two strains. And as he himself had been infected, he had obtained one strain from his own blood.

Each of the pathogens passed through a filter, and all of the animals that came into contact with them died. Dissections revealed abnormalities in their livers and kidneys and black hematemesis in their stomachs. All five strains displayed the same properties and differed from the South American yellow fever pathogen. Judging that this microorganism must be the yellow fever pathogen, he focused all his energy on confirming it beyond doubt, though he refrained from making any categorical claims. Walcott had been sent by Beeuwkes to snoop around, and Noguchi had taken Walcott with him when he went to investigate the inland outbreak of yellow fever. Although he had kept the crucial elements of his discovery hidden, Noguchi could not hide his excitement, and Walcott knew that he had made a breakthrough. Although Noguchi eventually sent Walcott back to Lagos in March, he should have done so sooner. On the night of March 19, Noguchi dissected an animal and became convinced that the microorganism he had discovered was the pathogen responsible for yellow fever. He woke Young to have him confirm his findings.

Noguchi had been considering returning to New York since late February. Flush with optimism that his research would prove successful, he began to cable Mary much more frequently and to long for her replies. He even wrote a letter, dated March 27, in which he passionately declared his love for her. This was most unusual behavior; he had done no such thing during his previous extended absence in South America:

> I spend every moment of every day waiting for a telegram from you. When I am dispirited or tired, you are the one thing that raises my spirits. I am always thinking of you. It is rare that I dream, but when I do it is always of you.

In another of his March letters to her he apologized for keeping her waiting so long and, promising to be home in May, appealed to her to let him complete his research. This was more than idle talk. He had already begun making preparations for his return. He had decided to undertake the rest of his research in America, where the facilities were superior, and had even reserved a cabin on the boat home. Indeed, in a telegram to Dr. Flexner, he announced that he would leave Accra on May 19.

Before leaving, though, he wanted to visit the Lagos branch, but by this time he was thoroughly exhausted—indeed, he was so tired that he didn't even attempt to conceal his left hand when a photograph was taken to commemorate his time in Ghana. He boarded a ship on May 9 and arrived in Lagos the following day. Despite his exhaustion, he showed the staff at the facility the records of his experiments and discussed his work with them. But two days later he started to feel ill. His eyes took on a haggard look and his cheeks grew gaunt. He was due to return to Accra on the morning of the twelfth, but before boarding the boat he began to suffer from chills.

The chills ran down his spine and soon spread to the rest of his body. He was dressed in white and wearing a hat to keep off the brutal equatorial sun. Even though he could feel the heat baking up from the ground, he was still shivering. He thought he might be suffering from malaria, which was rampant in tropical regions.

Noguchi went to a laboratory and hurriedly took a sample of his own blood, but when he examined it under a microscope he could find no trace of the microorganisms he had hoped to see. Dark clouds gathered in his mind. He was glad to be returning to Accra. On board, the other passengers took good care of him, and his chills subsided.

Night was drawing in as the ship approached Accra, and his shivering started again. As Accra had no deep-water harbor facilities, disembarking passengers had to be ferried to the shore by surfboat. No sooner had the boat left the ship than the wind picked up. With its tarpaulin cover flapping, it was making little headway. Someone stood up and ripped off the cover, but soon it began to pour with rain, which beat down onto the head of the sick doctor. The Mahaffys met the launch when it finally landed and took him back to their house. Shocked at how sick their friend appeared, Mrs. Mahaffy took his hand, saying worriedly: "Your face is so pale. Whatever is the matter with you?"

"I thought it was malaria, but . . . it seems I was wrong. I'm sorry, but I'd like to go to bed straight away." Noguchi fell into a deep sleep as soon as he lay down. He was feverish, but his face appeared calm as he slept. Outside the wind was still blowing, swaying the palm trees.

The next day Dr. O'Brien came to examine the sick man. Finding that he had a raging fever and a high protein count in his urine, O'Brien admitted him to the Ridge Hospital. Ever resilient, Noguchi remained cheerful, and he was able to walk quite steadily. But his illness was more serious than last time, and the nurses treated him with great care. Soon he began to complain of a headache and aching muscles, and he vomited three times in one day. The doctors gave him an antipyretic and Ringer's solution and kept a close eye on his progress.

There were no signs of improvement, however. Noguchi was hardly urinating at all, and his strength was ebbing away. He is said to have realized the identity of his illness on the fourteenth. He suspected it might be yellow fever, but that only raised all kinds of questions—he had already suffered a mild bout of the disease, so there should have been no danger of contracting it a second time. As he had written to Flexner, "Having become immune to African yellow fever, I can safely continue my experiments." Besides, he reasoned, he had inoculated himself with his own vaccine, so it was inconceivable that he should contract the disease twice. There were only two explanations: either his previous illness had been something other than yellow fever, or his present affliction was not yellow fever after all. Yet last time he had confirmed that it was yellow fever by transfusing his own blood into a monkey. He had been dealing with the disease for more than ten years. He knew the symptoms inside out, and he had described his first sickness as a classic case. It had been quite unlike amoebic dysentery, so he found it hard to believe that he had been mistaken.

■ ■ ■

When news that Dr. Noguchi was ill reached New York, Simon Flexner cabled the hospital to ask that the doctors take good care of his colleague and inquired after his condition every day without fail. People took comfort in the knowledge that this was his second bout of yellow fever and that he had overcome the disease before. All they could do was monitor his progress and hope he survived. (Even today there is no cure for yellow fever; all that can be done is to inject a preventive vaccine.) Mrs. Mahaffy nursed him untiringly, and the doctors treated him as best they could. How he had become infected remained a mystery, however. He is said to have had no recollection of being bitten by a mosquito. Another possible explanation was that the disease had been transmitted to him while he was dissecting an infected monkey—and indeed, it was because of this very risk that he did not allow others to perform his dissections.

On the morning of May 14 his condition deteriorated. He needed complete rest, so all visitors were turned away. By the evening his fever had subsided somewhat, bringing some welcome relief. His condition continued to improve on the fifteenth and sixteenth—to such an extent that he even complained of feeling hungry. The Mahaffys took heart from his improvement. This temporary improvement is typical of the latter stages of yellow fever, though; the sixth and seventh days are the most critical, and patients who survive the seventh day rarely die.

The fifth day passed slowly. He was frail and simply lay on the bed, almost motionless. He was fully conscious, however, and couldn't take his mind off his research. He had not announced his discovery of the pathogen publicly, a stance that Flexner had endorsed. Making the announcement without due care carried the risk that someone else might steal it. Besides, he was planning to do some further verification work after returning to New York. The discovery, therefore, remained hidden inside his head, where the ability to complete the work was also to be found. To be sure, there were test tubes and research notes around, but they were fragmentary and did not provide a coherent explanation of his work. Having come this far, he thought, he couldn't die now.

But in his weakened state, the mounting hostility to his work from Harvard, Lagos, and elsewhere began to dominate his thoughts. He was overcome with worry. What if this discovery, too, were mistaken? He would not be able to face his friends, his colleagues, the people at the Rockefeller Institute. His mind and body were both exhausted from researching yellow fever. He wondered whether it wouldn't be preferable to die now in peace rather than to live on in mistrust.

As his strength slipped away and he found himself between sleep and waking, his mind drifted from the present back to the distant past. He spoke of his mother and of Japan, and as he spoke he seemed somehow at ease. The British researcher Stokes had died of this same disease. In the hope of saving Noguchi from this same fate, the doctors injected him with a heart stimulant and a tranquilizer and maintained his drip.

His condition ebbed and flowed, but on May 18 he appeared to have taken another turn for the better. He even regained enough energy to ask about the laboratory. It was already the seventh day of the illness, and his apparent progress gave those around him hope. Perhaps he was over the worst. His uncommon fortitude had, after all, enabled him to survive a similar crisis ten years earlier, when he had contracted typhoid.

On the next morning, however, he suffered an epileptiform seizure. The sight of his convulsing body shocked everyone. The seizure subsided after about three minutes, but left him drowsy and noticeably weaker. Despite this, Noguchi fought off sleep, fearing that if he closed his eyes he might never open them again. He remained conscious and even talked to the hospital staff, who would marvel at his will to survive..

That afternoon, Young came to visit him. Young had been Noguchi's right-hand man throughout his African research, and Noguchi had told him of his secret discovery. As he saw his colleague approaching, Noguchi smiled and inquired in a faint voice, "Are you in good health?" Whenever a rhesus monkey had died of yellow fever, Noguchi had dissected the animal himself, never allowing Young to perform the task.

"I am," replied Young.

"Really? As long as you're well . . ." There was a pause. "I don't understand." What was it that he didn't understand? The route of infection? Or the fact that he had contracted yellow fever despite having been infected before? Whichever it was, these last words showed that he remained, right up to the end, a man with an inquiring mind.

That night he slipped into a coma. Working in shifts, the doctors monitored him around the clock. Even the unconscious stage of the disease took much longer for Noguchi than it did with other people. Just once he clutched at a nurse's hand. This was no convulsion; rather, it was as if he was trying to cling onto something, like a frightened child reaching out for his mother.

At noon the next day, May 21, 1928, Dr. Hideyo Noguchi passed away. He was fifty-one years old.

■ ■ ■

"Dead men cannot speak to defend themselves," goes the proverb. Noguchi died in the middle of his research, never seeing the subsequent studies that established beyond doubt the viral nature of yellow fever. His theory that it was caused by *Leptospira icteroides* was erroneous; the general opinion is that he confused yellow fever with Weil's disease. Since viruses are only visible under an electron microscope—a device that was not invented until 1931, four years after Noguchi went to Africa—he is viewed as having been thwarted by the limits of 1920s technology. But is this interpretation really fair?

First of all, Noguchi had recognized that the African yellow fever pathogen was qualitatively different from its South American equivalent. What is more, in a letter to Evelyn Tilden he had written of a "filterable microorganism," a point that merits particular attention. Viruses are filterable, and he realized that one of these smaller microorganisms was the true enemy. Indeed, he had inoculated monkeys with five strains of such an organism and determined that each caused the same lesions. Clearly, he was convinced that this was the yellow fever pathogen.

Seen from the perspective of his South American research, therefore, it is clear that he had made substantive progress, although this progress is often overlooked in the blanket description of his conclusions as erroneous. The existence of viruses had been confirmed in 1892 with the discovery of the tobacco mosaic disease virus, and Noguchi was aware of these tiny pathogens; it is unfair, therefore, to state that he would never have identified an organism that he had not seen for himself under a microscope as the agent of yellow fever. He was about to return to New York to put the finishing touches to his research, and there he might have made the necessary connections if he had lived to do so.

There was one final coda to this tragedy. When Young learned of Noguchi's death he was deeply shaken. Still stunned, he and Beeuwkes set about the task of tidying up Noguchi's laboratory. On hearing about Noguchi, Mrs. Young cabled her husband to check up on his health. Young replied on the twenty-sixth, assuring her that he was quite all right. But on the twenty-seventh he did not feel well, and he thought that he had perhaps caught malaria. He became feverish, however, indicating yellow fever, and was admitted to the hospital. His condition worsened during the twenty-eighth and twenty-ninth, and on the night of May 29 he followed Noguchi into darkness. He was only thirty-nine.

Its two principals now gone, the Accra laboratory lay empty as the tropical moonlight flooded through its windows.

GRIEF AND LASTING HOPE

After his astounding rise from grinding poverty to glory in the medical world, Noguchi was gone, his brilliant career cut short. The death of a hero is far more poignant on the level of that person himself, and those around him, than when viewed as the end of a historic figure.

The disease that had killed him was a dangerous one, and severe precautions were necessary now. The brutal African heat made his autopsy an urgent matter, and the authorities carried it out on the day he died. His organs were then removed and his body cavity filled with embalming oil. No simple coffin was allowed if his body was to be sent back to America: the corpse was encased in two hundred pounds of lead, and his laboratory assistants set about making a casket to carry this.

The laboratory itself was disinfected right away. The staff packed up the samples and equipment, preparing to ship them back to New York. Mrs. Mahaffy collected Noguchi's personal effects, along with the souvenirs he had bought for Mary and Simon Flexner. In the end the only sign that remained to show that he had been there was the Japanese flag fluttering over the roof.

The Africans who had worked with Noguchi and benefited from his medical care threw themselves on his coffin, weeping, before it was loaded onto a small launch and rowed out to the waiting steamer. Mrs. Mahaffy came out to the *West Kebar*, where she paid her last respects, then headed back to shore. Before long the ship carrying Noguchi back to America had disappeared over the horizon.

On June 13 the *West Kebar* made port in New York. The homecoming was made even more painful for Noguchi's wife and friends when the port authorities refused to allow his body on shore, claiming the yellow fever that had felled him was a threat to the city. John D. Rockefeller himself stepped in to press for the reversal of this decision, and eventually Noguchi was able to return to American soil.

A memorial service was held on June 15 at the Rockefeller Institute, where he had spent almost a quarter century—half his life. To salute their departed colleague the staff flew a Rising Sun flag at half-mast from the roof of the facility; the American flag in front of the institute was also lowered in mourning. Mary Noguchi was there, a black veil over her features. This had been a difficult year for her: her younger brother had died in March, and, without children, she felt desolately alone now.

John D. Rockefeller gave a eulogy, then Simon Flexner stood to address the crowd. He had been instrumental in helping Noguchi become a world-renowned scientist, inspiring him to come to America during his 1899 visit to Japan and offering his friendship and support ever since Noguchi turned up uninvited on Flexner's doorstep in 1900. Their relationship had been like that between teacher and disciple, or even parent and child, and Noguchi's death had hit Flexner especially hard. Now sixty-five, the white-haired scientist stood before the assembly and spoke of Hideyo's career and achievements. His voice broke as he told of the late doctor's endurance in the laboratory, his unparalleled devotion to his science. "This is a great loss. Noguchi's death has robbed us of an irreplaceable man. He lives on, though, through us as we carry forward his work."

The casket went onto the hearse. Covered with flowers and flanked by American and Japanese mourners, Noguchi made his final journey to Woodlawn Cemetery in the Bronx. Quarantine law forbade opening his casket, so Mary and his friends had no last look at him before he went into the ground.

Heading to the right from the main gate of the cemetery, one comes to an area called the Tulip lot. Here, at the end of a small clearing among tall trees, rests Hideyo Noguchi. His is a large, rough-hewn granite memorial flanked by a rose bush that Mary planted. On the front of his grave marker is this inscription:

HIDEYO NOGUCHI
BORN IN INAWASHIRO JAPAN NOVEMBER 24 1876
DIED ON THE GOLD COAST AFRICA MAY 21 1928
MEMBER OF THE

ROCKEFELLER INSTITUTE FOR MEDICAL RESEARCH
THROUGH DEVOTION TO SCIENCE
HE LIVED AND DIED FOR HUMANITY

News of his death flashed around the globe. Obituaries appeared in newspapers and magazines in numerous countries, describing his lifetime accomplishments and his death in tropical Africa. Their evaluation of his work made it clear that his end had not been a loss for just one country, or just one branch of science, but for humanity. In death he received the highest honor yet, in the form of this praise.

The Japanese government on May 21 posthumously awarded him the Order of the Rising Sun, Gold and Silver Star. The French government, too, presented him with a medal for distinguished service in the fight against disease. And around the world people gathered to salute what Noguchi had done during his career. Members of the Japanese Club of America met to mourn the doctor's death; the government of Ecuador cabled a message of condolence to the Japanese foreign minister. Numerous events took place in Japan to mark his passing: his friends, members of the Imperial Academy, the medical department at Tokyo Imperial University, and Shibazaburo Kitasato's epidemiological institute all combined to organize a grand memorial service, held on June 29 in Tokyo's Marunouchi district. Back in Fukushima, meanwhile, a quieter service took place at Choshoji, the temple at which Shika had prayed so fervently during her life. A lock of Noguchi's hair made its way to his home village, where it was later enshrined in a grave for Noguchi and his wife. He had rarely slept enough in life, and the villagers did what they could to prepare a restful place for him in death.

His widow, Mary, was inconsolable. A glimpse of his watch was enough to reduce her to tears for months to come. With no child to pass this keepsake on to, she mailed it off to her husband's teacher, Kobayashi. She also maintained a connection with his family by sending Inu, Hideyo's sister, twelve dollars a month out of the bereavement allowance she received from the Rockefeller Institute. Mary lived on for almost another twenty years, dying on the last day of 1947, at the age of sixty-five. She now rests beside him in Woodlawn Cemetery.

■ ■ ■

Many who shine in life see their fortunes fade after they are gone; people forget their deeds soon after they die, or reconsider their achievements and find them somehow wanting in the end. Even a man who is mourned deeply when he passes away may see his legend fade as the decades pile up. In Africa, though, Noguchi enjoyed a particularly long-lasting renown after his death through the many children whose parents named them after the great doctor. This would no doubt have pleased him far more than the decorations his own government granted him.

In May 1937, to mark the tenth year after the death of Noguchi and William Young, the British government commissioned a memorial to the two researchers, erecting it at the laboratory in Accra. This was just one of many statues and plaques put up around the world to honor the Japanese scientist: they can be found at the Rockefeller Institute, in Ecuador, and in Ghana, and in dozens of locations around Japan including a number of schools, the castle at Inawashiro, the city of Aizu Wakamatsu, the National Science Museum in Tokyo, and Minoo Park in Osaka.

Noguchi's memory is also kept alive in museums dedicated to him: more than a million people a year visit the Hideyo Noguchi Memorial Halls in his village in Fukushima and in Shinjuku, Tokyo. Prizes for medical research and scholarships are given in his name, as are lectures on medical topics. In 1976 the hundredth anniversary of his birth was marked by celebrations in Japan and Ecuador. In Ghana, where Noguchi is hailed alongside Albert Schweitzer as a healer and humanitarian, the Noguchi Research Institute continues to work on finding cures for diseases.

The ripples from this extraordinary life make themselves felt to this day.

（英文版）正伝 野口英世
Dr. Noguchi's Journey

2005年 4 月25日　第 1 刷発行

著　者　北　篤
訳　者　ピーター・ダーフィー
発行者　畑野文夫
発行所　講談社インターナショナル株式会社
　　　　〒112-8652　東京都文京区音羽 1-17-14
　　　　電話　03-3944-6493（編集部）
　　　　　　　03-3944-6492（営業部・業務部）
　　　　ホームページ　www.kodansha-intl.com
印刷・製本所　大日本印刷株式会社